PHARMACOGNOSY OF TRADITIONAL DRUGS - I

S. B. GOKHALE
M. Pharm., A. I. C.
Former Co-ordinator
R.C. Patel Institute of Pharmaceutical Education and Research
Shirpur – 425405 (M. S.)

Dr. C. K. KOKATE
M. Pharm., Ph. D., F.G.A.E.S. (Germany)
President,
Indian Society of Pharmacognosy and
Vice-chancellor,
KLE University, JNMC Campus, Nehru Nagar,
Belgaum - 590010. (Karnataka)

Dr. ALPANA GOKHALE
B.A.M.S.
Consulting Physician, Swargate
Pune 411 037 (M. S.)

M. G. KALASKAR
M. Pharm.
Asstt. Professor
R.C. Patel Institute of Pharmaceutical Education and Research
Shirpur – 425405 (M. S.)

PHARMACOGNOSY OF TRADITIONAL DRUGS - I

ISBN 978-93-5164-205-3

Second Edition : July 2015
© : Authors

The text of this publication, or any part thereof, should not be reproduced or transmitted in any form or stored in any computer storage system or device for distribution including photocopy, recording, taping or information retrieval system or reproduced on any disc, tape, perforated media or other information storage device etc., without the written permission of Authors with whom the rights are reserved. Breach of this condition is liable for legal action.

Every effort has been made to avoid errors or omissions in this publication. In spite of this, errors may have crept in. Any mistake, error or discrepancy so noted and shall be brought to our notice shall be taken care of in the next edition. It is notified that neither the publisher nor the authors or seller shall be responsible for any damage or loss of action to any one, of any kind, in any manner, therefrom.

Published By :
NIRALI PRAKASHAN
Abhyudaya Pragati, 1312, Shivaji Nagar,
Off J.M. Road, PUNE – 411005
Tel - (020) 25512336/37/39, Fax - (020) 25511379
Email : niralipune@pragationline.com

Printed By :
Repro Knowledgecast Limited,
Thane

☞ DISTRIBUTION CENTRES

PUNE
Nirali Prakashan : 119, Budhwar Peth, Jogeshwari Mandir Lane, Pune 411002, Maharashtra
Tel : (020) 2445 2044, 66022708, Fax : (020) 2445 1538
Email : bookorder@pragationline.com, niralilocal@pragationline.com

Nirali Prakashan : S. No. 28/27, Dhyari, Near Pari Company, Pune 411041
Tel : (020) 24690204 Fax : (020) 24690316
Email : dhyari@pragationline.com, bookorder@pragationline.com

MUMBAI
Nirali Prakashan : 385, S.V.P. Road, Rasdhara Co-op. Hsg. Society Ltd.,
Girgaum, Mumbai 400004, Maharashtra
Tel : (022) 2385 6339 / 2386 9976, Fax : (022) 2386 9976
Email : niralimumbai@pragationline.com

☞ DISTRIBUTION BRANCHES

JALGAON
Nirali Prakashan : 34, V. V. Golani Market, Navi Peth, Jalgaon 425001,
Maharashtra, Tel : (0257) 222 0395, Mob : 94234 91860

KOLHAPUR
Nirali Prakashan : New Mahadvar Road, Kedar Plaza, 1st Floor Opp. IDBI Bank
Kolhapur 416 012, Maharashtra. Mob : 9850046155

NAGPUR
Pratibha Book Distributors : Above Maratha Mandir, Shop No. 3, First Floor,
Rani Jhanshi Square, Sitabuldi, Nagpur 440012, Maharashtra
Tel : (0712) 254 7129

DELHI
Nirali Prakashan : 4593/21, Basement, Aggarwal Lane 15, Ansari Road, Daryaganj
Near Times of India Building, New Delhi 110002
Mob : 08505972553

BENGALURU
Pragati Book House : House No. 1, Sanjeevappa Lane, Avenue Road Cross,
Opp. Rice Church, Bengaluru – 560002.
Tel : (080) 64513344, 64513355,Mob : 9880582331, 9845021552
Email:bharatsavla@yahoo.com

CHENNAI
Pragati Books : 9/1, Montieth Road, Behind Taas Mahal, Egmore,
Chennai 600008 Tamil Nadu, Tel : (044) 6518 3535,
Mob : 94440 01782 / 98450 21552 / 98805 82331,
Email : bharatsavla@yahoo.com

niralipune@pragationline.com | www.pragationline.com
Also find us on f www.facebook.com/niralibooks

PREFACE TO THE SECOND EDITION

In the revised Second Edition of "**Pharmacognosy of Traditional Drugs - I**", due care has been taken to provide "Standards of Quality" for most of Traditional drugs of natural origin from the sources where so ever they are available, such as standard reference books, Pharmacopoeias etc.

Synonyms in various Indian languages will benefit the students, pharmaceutical industries and researchers to identify these drugs as raw materials for their research work.

Conventional abbreviations such as LOD (Loss on drying), FOM (Foreign Organic Matter), WSE (Water Soluble Extractives), ASE (Alcohol Soluble Extractives) have been used freely, where so ever they are applicable.

July 2015   **AUTHORS**

PREFACE TO THE FIRST EDITION

Since a decade "Pharmacognosy of Traditional Drugs - I" is being taught as 'Independent subject' for Degree course in pharmacy in several universities of various states of India and has acquired real importance in pharmacy profession.

The products made from *natural drugs* are being preferred by medical practitioners as compared to allopathic or synthetic drugs.

Comparatively 'Traditional Drugs' are safe and are available in the form in which they are preferred by patients.

Authors have made an attempt to mention the names of present **'market products'** of the respective natural drug alongwith conventional pharmacognostic description, as a *special feature* of the book.

One of the surveys organised by World Health Organization has revealed that 20% of world population is still using natural drugs for its treatment. Out of known 7000 natural drugs only 600 to 700 are in actual use.

Non-availability of books in the market, covering detail study of 'Traditional Drugs - I' has prompted us to write the book.

Criticism and suggestions received from the teachers and industry personnels to improve the quality of the book will be highly appreciated.

August 2014 **AUTHORS**

CONTENTS

	Introduction	01 – 03
1.	Significance of Pharmacopoeial Standards	1.1 – 1.10
2.	Chemical Nature of Traditional Drugs	2.1 – 2.12
3.	Glycosidal Drugs:	
	Apamarg, Babachi, Brahmi, Chakramadhu, Chirata, Dhamaso, Ginseng, Gokhru, Gudmar, Gulwel, Kalmegh, Kanher, Kutki, Lodhra, Mandukparni, Manjishta, Methi, Mulethi, Palash, Rasna, Garden rue, Shatawari, Indian senna, Talispatra.	3.1 – 3.54
4.	Alkaloidal Drugs:	
	Nux-vomica, Sarpagnadha, Daruhaldi, Opium, Belladonna, Hyoscyamus, Cinchona, Tea-herb, Ashwagandha, Kutja, Tylophora, Kantakari, Vasaka, Bhringraj, Kachnar, Punarnava, Shankhpushpi, Pipalamul, Bhui-amala.	4.1 – 4.50
5.	Drugs Containing Tannin:	
	Amla, Amra, Arjuna, Ashoka, Behra, Catecnu, Pale catechu, Haritaki, Pterocarpus, Shirish, Galls.	5.1 – 5.28
*	Bibliography	B1 – B1

APPENDICES

A.	Manufacturers of Phytochemicals and Phytopharmaceuticals in India	A.1 – A.8
B.	Glossary of Important Ayurvedic Terms	A.9 – A.10
C.	Synonyms in Various Indian Languages	A.11 – A.15

INDICES

1.	Biological Index	I.1 – I.2
2.	Synonym Index	I.3 – I.4
3.	Chemical Index	I.5 – I.7
4.	Subject Index	I.8 – I.8

INTRODUCTION

Several medicinal plants and animal products are being used in India since long, for the treatment of various diseases as a part of customs or beliefs of Indian culture. Highly potant modern antibiotics and even the synthetic drugs, have also not reduced their utility and they continue to provide the basic raw materials.

Such natural drugs being used traditionally are called "Traditional Drugs". Medical practitioners of many well developed countries like, USA, Germany, England, Japan, Russia and even India are using Traditional Drugs in their day-to-day medical practice.

The substances from plants and animal sources were being used as food since antiquity and later on, these substances were differentiated as food stuffs and therapeutic agents, as man tried to explore and utilize these natural products for treating the ailments. Thus, their utility to remove the disorders, earned them the title **Drug** (originally from French language).

Indian history of medicinal plants is dated back to 3500 B.C. The curative properties of plants have been mentioned in the Suktas of *Rigveda* and *Atharvaveda*. *Ayurveda* has also described good number of plants with their therapeutic properties. The ancient well known treatises in Ayurveda the Charak Samhita and Susruta Samhita are written by **Charak** and **Susruta** respectively.

Applying paste prepared by grating fresh ginger on the forehead, use of raw onion in the cap (turban) to keep away from sunstroke, chewing of roasted lemon and ginger together as a preventive measure for motion sickness are the specific examples of traditional drugs in day-to-day life.

As mentioned in *Papyrus Ebers*, an old document written in 1500 B.C., Egyptians were aware of medicinal uses of several plants and animals and also about human anatomy. The great Greek physician **Hippocrates** (460 – 360 B.C.) known as 'Father of Medicine', dealt with anatomy and physiology of human beings. **Aristotle**, the renowned philosopher (384 – 322 B.C.), is well known for his studies on animal kingdom and **Theophrastus** (370 – 287 B.C.) for plant kingdom.

Dioscorides, (040 - 080 A.D.) a Greek physician in 78 A.D. described several plants of medicinal importance in " De Materia Medica". It was **Pliny the Eider** (23 – 70 A.D.), who compiled 37 volumes of natural history. Greek Pharmacist **Galen** (131 - 200 A.D.) described various methods of preparation containing active constituents of crude drugs, and even at present the branch dealing with the extraction of plant and animal drugs is known as Galenical Pharmacy.

Gradually, all the natural products, utilized by physicians were compiled together to form the 'Materia Medica' giving their detailed information. The products from plants, animals and mineral origin are the three broad classes of naturally occurring drugs.

Fig. 1 : The Great Contributors

Definition :

While studying Sarsaparilla, it was **Seydler**, A German scientist, who coined the term Pharmacognosy in 1815 in his work entitled, "Analecta Pharmacognostica" from combination of two Greek words viz., *Pharmakon*, a drug and *gignosco*, to acquire the knowledge of. Further, **Tschirsh** made it more meaningful by restricting the term to the utilization of products from natural sources. Thus, pharmacognosy is the subject of crude drugs obtained from the plant, animal and mineral origins. It is the objective study of crude drugs of the natural sources processed scientifically. The word '**crude drug**' itself is self-explanatory and is used with the meaning of 'simple drug' and also as it exists in the natural form. The crude drugs are plant or animal drugs that have undergone no other processes than collection and drying.

Broadly, *Pharmacognosy is defined as "the scientific and systematic study of structural, physical, chemical and biological characters of crude drugs along with their history, method of cultivation, collection and preparation for the market".*

The synthetic drugs do not fall within the scope of Pharmacognosy. With the recent developments in science and technology, several chemicals, which were originally found in plants and animals are synthesized at present. The reasons for their synthesis are either the scarcity or non-availability of natural drugs in which they occur, apart from the lack of knowledge of chemical processes required to extract them.

Scope of Natural Drugs :

Most of the crude drugs are obtained from plants and only a small number comes from animal and mineral origins. Drugs obtained from plants consist of entire plants or their parts. Ephedra and datura are entire plants, while senna leaves and pods, nux-vomica seeds and cinchona bark are parts of plants. Honey, bees wax, cochineal are from animal origin. Crude drugs are also obtained by simple physical processes like drying (opium) or extracting with water (catechu, agar).

Several other useful substances affecting health of animals and human beings are also included alongwith crude drugs in the study of Pharmacognosy. These substances include allergens, antibiotics, flavouring agents, colours, pesticides, immunizing agents, vehicles and diagnostic aids.

The following are few examples of each class of crude drugs.

Table 1 : Different Sources of Drugs

Source	Examples
1. Vegetable	Cinnamon, digitalis, saffron, clove.
2. Animal	Bees wax, cantharides, cod-liver oil, gelatin.
3. Mineral	Chalk, bentonite, asbestos, talc, kaolin, fuller's earth.
4. Allergens	Pollen grains, mold spores, feathers, webs
5. Immunizing agents	Vaccines, sera, antitoxins.
6. Pesticides	Pyrethrin, rotenone, nicotine.

IMPORTANCE :

Even though, pharmacognosy is a branch of science dealing with crude drugs, it is very important to know all other indirectly related aspects of biomedicinals.

To understand crude drugs completely, various terms used to describe the vegetable drugs as covered in botany and animal drugs as covered in zoology must be known to a pharmacognosist. He should also possess knowledge of pharmacology in order to understand the actions of drugs in human body. Pharmacology, like pharmacognosy, is an outgrowth of Materia Medica. Pharmaceutical chemistry and Phytochemistry are also essential to understand the chemical composition of crude drugs. The art of preparing the galenicals and the use of pharmaceutical aids are covered under the subject, Pharmaceutics. Knowledge of several other subjects apart from those mentioned above is necessary for various reasons. The knowledge of the principles of genetics, plant breeding and plant pathology is essential to understand cultivation of medicinal plants. The basic knowledge of biochemistry, chemical engineering and storage technology helps us to know the principles of collection, preparation and preservation of crude drugs. Chemotaxonomy and Biosynthesis are the fields, which ought to be understood for inter-relationship of active constituents and their physiological importance to the plants and animals.

Pharmacognosy plays a very important role in the development of pure sciences, e.g. in descriptive botany, plant classification (taxonomy) and plant chemistry (phytochemistry).

Thus, pharmacognosy is an important liaison between pharmaceutical and all related subjects.

Chapter 1...

SIGNIFICANCE OF PHARMACOPOEIAL STANDARDS

For efficacy and evaluation pharmacopoeial standards are required to be finalised scientifically and also legally by competent authorities.

Standardisation of a drug means confirmation of its identity and determination of its quality and purity. If adulterated, it also includes the detection of the nature of adulteration in the crude drug.

Several methods are employed in detecting adulteration in genuine drugs. The form of drug provides a clue for the method of detection of adulteration to be followed. In ordinary course of study, the morphological characters may suffice the need of detection. But in case of powdered drugs, the microscopic characters, while in case of liquid drug chemical tests and one of the physical standards such as specific gravity, optical rotation, solubility etc., may be helpful in detection of adulteration.

Over the years, the nature and degree of evaluation of crude drugs has undergone a systematic change. Initially, the crude drugs were identified by comparison with standard description available. Due to advancement in chemical knowledge of crude drugs, at present, evaluation also includes the method of estimating the active constituent present in crude drug, in addition to its morphological and microscopic analysis.

Taking into consideration variation in source of crude drugs and their chemical nature, they are standardized by different techniques. Since methods of estimation of chief active principles of various crude drugs fall within the purview of pharmaceutical analysis, we shall only outline different methods of estimation. The crude drugs can be identified on the basis of their morphological, histological and chemical studies. The different techniques involved in standardization of crude drugs are as follows.

1. ORGANOLEPTIC STANDARDISATION

It refers to evaluation of drugs by colour, odour, taste, size, shape and special features, like touch, texture, sound etc. Aromatic odour of umbelliferous fruits and sweet taste of liquorice are the examples of this type of evaluation. The study of form of a crude drug is **Morphology**, while description of the form is **Morphography**.

However, it should be noted that colour, shape and size of crude drugs as described in official books should only be considered as guidelines and may vary depending upon several factors. For example, colour of the crude drug may fade if it gets exposed to sunlight for very long duration or if, the drug is not stored properly. Depending upon the condition under which the drug is growing or cultivated, i.e., availability of proper irrigation, fertilizers or even high temperature may influence the size of the drug. If it gets favourable conditions, leaf, seed and fruit drugs of maximum size may be available and the crude drugs if grown in adverse conditions, size may get reduced.

The adulteration of seed of Strychnous nux-vomica with the seed of Strychnous nux-blanda or Strychnous potatorum, caraway with Indian dill, Alexandrian senna with dog senna or palthe senna are identified by morphological technique.

In case of acellular products (unorganised drugs), form of the drug depends totally on the method of preparation of the drug. Thus, gum acacia is found in the form of ovoid tears, while tragacanth is marketed as vermiform ribbon with longitudinal striations.

2. MICROSCOPIC STANDARDISATION

This method allows more detailed examination of a drug and it can be used to identify organised drugs by their known histological characters.

Microscope, by virtue of its property to magnify, permits the minute structure under study to be enlarged and can be used to confirm the structural details of the drugs from plant origin. For the effective results, various reagents or stains can be used to distinguish the cellular structure. The microscopic evaluation also covers study of constituents by application of chemical tests to small quantities of drugs in powdered form or to histological sections of the drug (Microchemistry). Histological studies are made from very thin sections of the drugs. The characteristics of cell wall, cell contents, trichomes, fibres, vessels etc., can be studied in details, e.g. Signified trichomes in nux-vomica. The microscopic linear measurement and quantitative microscopy are also covered under this technique of evaluation.

The following few constants illustrate the importance of microscopic measurements.

(a) Stomatal Number : It is the average number of stomata present per square mm of the epidermis.

The actual number of stomata per sq. mm of leaf preparation may vary for leaves of the same plant grown in different environmental conditions. Stomatal number is relatively a constant for particular species of same age and hence, it is taken into consideration as a diagnostic character for identification of a leaf drug. The adulteration can also be detected by stomatal number. It can be further illustrated by following examples.

Table 1.1 : Stomatal Number of Few Leaf Drugs

Species	Stomatal number
1. *Datura stramonium*	087 (upper epidermis)
2. *Datura innoxia*	141 (upper epidermis)
3. *Hyoscyamus niger*	125 (upper epidermis)

(b) Stomatal Index : It is the percentage which the number of stomata form to the total number of epidermal cells, each stoma being counted as one cell. It can be calculated by a formula :

$$I = \frac{S \times 100}{(E + S)}$$

where   I - Stomatal index;

S - Number of stoma per unit area;

E - Epidermal cells in the same area.

Whilst, stomatal number varies considerably with the age of leaf and due to changes in climatic conditions, stomatal index is relatively constant and therefore, of diagnostic significance for a given species. It is useful in differentiation of closely related species and also for detection of adulterants (Table 1.2).

Table 1.2 : Stomatal Index of Few Leaf Drugs

Species	Stomatal index (lower surface)
1. Atropa belladonna	20.2 to 23.0
2. Atropa acuminata	16.2 to 18.3
3. Indian senna	17.0 to 20.0
4. Alexandrian senna	10.8 to 12.6

(c) Vein Islet Number : It is the number of vein islets per sq. mm of leaf surface.

It is a constant for a given species of the plant. It usually does not alter with the age of plant and is independent of the size of the leaf (Table 1.3).

Table 1.3 : Vein Islet Number of Few Leaf Drugs

Species	Vein islet number
Erythroxylon coca	08 -12
Erythroxylon truxillense	15 - 26
Digitalis purpurea	02 - 5.5
Digitalis thapsi	8.5 - 16
Cassia angustifolia	19 - 23
Cassia acutifolia	25 - 30

(d) Palisade Ratio : It is the average number of palisade cells, beneath one epidermal cell, using four continuous epidermal cells for the count.

Since the palisade cells in the mesophyll of the leaves bear a definite relation to the epidermal cell, the palisade ratio as defined above, is constant for a species of a genus (Table 1.4).

Table 1.4 : Palisade Ratio of Some Leaf Drugs

Species	Palisade ratio
1. Atropa belladonna	06 -10
2. Datura stramonium	04 - 07
3. Digitalis purpurea	3.7 - 4.2

(e) Quantitative Microscopy (Lycopodium Spore Method) : It is an important analytical technique for powdered drugs, especially when chemical and other methods of evaluation of crude drugs fail as accurate measures of quality. Lycopodium spores are very characteristic in shape and appearance and are exceptionally uniform in size (about 25 µm). On an average, 94000 spores per mg of powdered lycopodium are present.

A powdered drug is evaluated by this technique, if it contains :

(i) well defined particles which may be counted, e.g. starch grains or pollen grains,

(ii) single layered cells or tissues, the area of which may be traced under suitable magnification and actual area calculated or

(iii) the objects of uniform thickness, the length of which can be measured under suitable magnification and actual area calculated.

The percentage purity of an authentic powdered ginger is calculated using the following equation,

$$\text{Percentage purity} = \frac{N \times W \times 94000 \times 100}{S \times M \times P}$$

where, N - number of characteristic structures (e.g. starch grains) in 25 fields.

W - weight in mg of lycopodium taken.

S - number of lycopodium spores in the same 25 fields.

M - weight in mg of the sample, calculated on the basis of sample dried at 105°C.

P - 2,86,000 in case of ginger starch grains powder.

Lycopodium spore method can be used for evaluation of powdered clove, ginger, cardamom, nutmeg and umbelliferous fruits.

The study of microscopical or histological characteristics is useful in detection of adulterants in both entire and powdered forms of crude drugs. Apart from variations in cellular arrangement, many a times, the type of cuticle of epidermis and cell inclusion also help in detection of the adulterants. The common adulterant of *Digitalis purpurea* is *Verbascum thapsus*, containing candelabra trichomes, while digitalis contains either multicellular uniseriate trichomes or glandular trichomes. The powdered cloves contain neither prisms of calcium oxalate nor the sclereids, but in case of powdered clove stalks both are present. Starch is absent in clove, but is present in the powdered clove fruits. The leaves of *Digitalis purpurea* do not contain calcium oxalate crystals, while they are present in all other varieties of Digitalis. Surinam quassia does not contain calcium oxalate, but Jamaica quassia contains prismatic crystals of calcium oxalate.

The size of a starch grain is also important in detection of adulterants. In case of *Cinnamomum cassia*, the diameter of starch grains is usually more than 10 microns. The dimension of fibres also helps in detecting adulteration in case of cinnamon. The number of sclerenchymatous cells per square cm in cardamom is one of the criteria for detection of varieties of cardamom seed in powdered form.

3. PHYSICAL STANDARDISATION

Physical standards are to be determined for drugs, wherever possible. They may help in evaluation, specifically with reference to specific gravity, density, optical rotation, refractive index, melting point, viscosity and solubility in different solvents. A few of them are described below.

(i) Moisture Content : The percentage of active chemical constituents in crude drugs is mentioned on air-dried basis. Hence, the moisture content of a drug should be determined and also be controlled to make the solution of definite strength. The moisture content of a drug should be minimised in order to prevent decomposition of crude drug either due to chemical change or due to microbial contamination.

The moisture content is determined by heating a drug at 105°C in an oven to a constant weight (Table 1.5). For the drug containing volatile active constituents, the toluene distillation method is followed.

Table 1.5 : Crude Drugs with Limits of Moisture Content

Drugs	Moisture content (%) w/w (Not more than)
Aloes	10.0
Brahmi	12.0
Ergot	08.0
Acacia	15.0
Starch	15.0

(ii) Viscosity : Viscosity of a liquid is constant at a given temperature and is an index of its composition. Hence, it can be used as a means of standardising liquid drugs.

The following are the suitable examples :

1. **Liquid paraffin :** Kinematic viscosity not less than 64 centistokes.
2. **Pyroxylin :** Kinematic viscosity, 1100 - 2450 centistokes.

(iii) Melting point : It is one of the parameters to judge the purity of crude drugs. In case of pure chemicals or phytochemicals, melting points are very sharp and constant. Since crude drugs from animal or plant origin contain mixed chemicals, they are described with certain range of melting point. The purity of the following crude drugs can be ascertained by determining their melting points in the range shown against each of them (Table 1.6).

Table 1.6 : Melting Point Range For Few Crude Drugs

Drugs	Melting point (°C)
Colophony	75 - 85
Kokum butter	39 - 42
Cocoa butter	30 - 33
Bees wax	62 - 65
Anhydrous wool fat	34 - 40
Hard paraffin	50 - 57

(iv) Optical Rotation : Certain substances are found to have the property of rotating the plane of polarised light in pure state or in the solution. Thus, they are described to be optically active and this property is known as optical rotation. Plane of polarised light may be rotated towards right (dextrorotatory) or left (laevorotatory). Normally, the optical rotation is determined at 25°C using sodium lamp as the source of light.

Following is the list of few drugs of pharmacognostic origin with their optical rotation (Table 1.7).

Table 1.7 : Optical Rotation Values For Few Crude Drugs

Drugs	Angle of optical rotation
Caraway oil	+ 70° to + 80°
Castor oil	not less than + 3.5°
Clove oil	0° to − 1.5°
Honey	+ 3° to − 15°
Eucalyptus oil	− 5° to + 10°
Chinopodium oil	− 3° to − 8°

(v) Refractive Index : When a ray of light passes from one medium to another medium of different density, it is bent from original path. Thus, the ratio of the velocity of light in vacuum to its velocity in the substance is termed as refractive index of the second medium. Depending upon purity, it is a constant for a liquid and can be considered as one of the criteria for its standardisation. Refractive index of a compound varies with the wavelength of the incident light, temperature and pressure. Refractive indices of the following compounds are for sodium light and at a temperature of 25°C (Table 1.8).

Table 1.8 : Refractive Indices of Some Phytoconstituents

Drugs	Refractive index
Arachis oil	1.4678 to 1.4698
Caraway oil	1.4838 to 1.4858
Castor oil	1.4758 to 1.4798
Clove oil	1.5300 to 1.5310

As mentioned earlier, evaluation of drug basically needs its identification and can be done by morphological or microscopic characters. Many a times, the drug identified by its diagnostic characters, is of substandard quality due to either faulty collection or incorrect storage. Thus, to prove its acceptability as a drug, the following tests can be applied to it, wherever possible.

(a) Ash content

(b) Extractives

(c) Volatile oil content

(a) Ash Content : The residue remaining after incineration is the ash content of the drug, which simply represents the inorganic salts naturally occurring in drug or adhering to it or deliberately added to it as a form of adulteration. Therefore, it is a criterion to judge the identity or purity of crude drugs (Table 1.9). Total ash usually consists of carbonates, phosphates, silicates and silica.

Table 1.9 : Crude Drugs with Their Ash Contents

Drugs	Total Ash (% w/w)
Aloes	05.00
Ashoka	11.00
Bael	03.50
Black catechu	06.00
Mandukparni	24.00
Cardamom	06.00
Clove	07.00
Termeric	09.00
Ginger	06.00
Valerian	12.00

Acid insoluble ash, which is a part of total ash insoluble in dilute hydrochloric acid, is also recommended for certain drugs. Adhering dirt and sand may be determined by acid-insoluble ash content (Table 1.10).

Table 1.10 : Crude Drugs with Their Acid-insoluble Ash Contents

Drugs	Acid insoluble ash (% w/w) Not more than
Agar	1.0
Amla	2.0
Jatamansi	5.0
Cardamom	3.5
Clove	0.75

(b) Extractives : Many a times, the extracts obtained by exhausting crude drugs are indicative of approximate measures of certain chemical constituents they contain. Taking into consideration the diversity in chemical nature and properties of contents of the drugs, various solvents are used for the determination of extractives. The solvent used for extraction is in a position to dissolve appreciable quantities of substances desired.

The following are various methods used to find out the extractive values.

(i) Water Soluble Extractives : This method is applied to drugs which contain water soluble active constituents of crude drugs, such as tannins, sugars, plant acids, mucilage, glycosides etc. (Table 1.11).

Table 1.11 : Water Soluble Extractive Values of Some Crude Drugs

Drugs	Water soluble extractive (% w/w) Not less than
1. Aloes	25.0
2. Glycyrrhiza	20.0
3. Linseed	15.0
4. Senna leaves	30.0
5. Kalmegh	20.0
6. Ginger	10.0

(ii) Alcohol-Soluble Extractives : Alcohol is an ideal solvent for extraction of various chemicals like tannins, resins etc. Therefore, this method is frequently employed to determine the approximate resin content of drug. It is also an official method for assay in case of myrrh and asafoetida. Generally, 95% ethyl alcohol is used for determination of alcohol-soluble extractive. In some cases, diluted alcohol may also be used, depending upon solubility of constituents in a crude drug.

The limit for alcohol soluble extractive is applicable to following few drugs.

Table 1.12 : Alcohol Soluble Extractive Values of Some Crude Drugs

Drugs	Alcohol soluble extractives (% w/w)
1. Aloes	not more than 10.0
2. Benzoin	not less than 90.0 (Siam benzoin)
	not less than 75.0 (Sumatra benzoin);
3. Kutki	not less than 15.0
4. Asafoetida	not less than 50.0
5. Ginger	not less than 04.5
6. Methi	not less than 20.0
7. Shatavari	not less than 05.0

(iii) Alcohol Insoluble Extractives : Alcohol insoluble extractive values as applicable to some resinous drugs are given in Table 1.13.

Table 1.13 : Alcohol Insoluble Extractives of Some Crude Drugs

Drugs	Alcohol insoluble extractives (% w/w)
1. Myrrh	Not more than 70.0
2. Benzoin	Not more than 24.0

(iv) Ether-Soluble Extractives : Two types of ether-soluble extractive values determined for evaluation of crude drugs are volatile and non-volatile ether soluble fractions.

The **volatile ether-soluble extractive** represents volatile oil content of the drug, whilst **non-volatile ether-soluble extractives** represent resin, fixed oils or colouring matter present in drugs. The limit for these extractives is applicable to the following drugs (Table 1.14).

Table 1.14 : Non-volatile Ether-soluble Extractive Values of Some Drugs

Drugs	Limit for non-volatile ether soluble extractives (% w/w) (Not more than)
1. Capsicum	12.0
2. Male fern	01.5
3. Linseed	25.0
4. Myristica	25.0
5. Cocoa	22.0

(c) Volatile Oil Content : Efficacy of several crude drugs is due to their odorous principles (i.e. volatile oils). Such crude drugs are standardized on the basis of their volatile oil contents. A few examples are quoted here (Table 1.15).

Table 1.15 : Volatile Oil Contents of Some Crude Drugs

Drugs	Volatile oil content (% w/w) (Not less than)
Caraway	02.5
Fresh lemon peel	02.5
Clove	15.0
Fennel	01.4
Dill	02.4
Cardamom seed	04.0

Different chromatographic techniques such as, thin layer chromatography (TLC), high performance liquid chromatography (HPLC), gas chromatography, column chromatography, gel permeation chromatography, affinity chromatography, as well as techniques like IR; NMR; spectrophotometric method, radio-immunoassays are used very frequently for physical evaluation of crude drugs.

Foreign Organic Matter :

The parts of the organ or organs other than those named in the definition and description of the drug are defined as Foreign Organic Matter.

The maximum limit for the foreign organic matter is defined in the monograph of crude drugs. If it exceeds the limits, deterioration in quality of the drug takes place. The limit for foreign organic matter is specially mentioned for natural drugs of vegetable origin.

Few of them are as under:

Table 1.16: Foreign Organic Matter of Crude Drugs

Drugs	Limit of Foreign Organic Matter
Brahmi	≯ 2.0
Saffron	≯ 2.0
Chirata	≯ 2.0
Gulwel	≯ 2.0

4. CHEMICAL STANDARDISATION

It comprises of different chemical tests and chemical assays. The isolation, purification and identification of active constituents are chemical methods of evaluation. Quantitative chemical tests such as acid value, saponification value etc., are also covered under this technique. Some of these chemical tests are useful in evaluation of resins (acid value), balsams (acid saponification and ester values), volatile oils (acetyl and ester values); and gums (methoxy determination and volatile acidity).

The preliminary phytochemical screening is a qualitative chemical evaluation which indicates spectrum of chemical constituents present in a plant drug. The successive solvent extraction of a drug is carried out with petroleum ether, benzene, solvent ether, chloroform, ethanol and water in succession.

The conventional titrimetric estimations as applicable to estimation of alkaloids from crude drugs, ester and aldehydes contents of volatile oils, gravimetric methods etc., are the techniques of chemical assays.

The chemical tests also help in proper identification of varieties of the crude drugs. The solutions of lead acetate or lead sub-acetate are used specifically for chemical identity of gums. The alkaloid containing drugs such as rauwolfia, belladonna, ergot, ipecacuanha etc., and glycoside bearing drugs like senna, digitalis, squill, strophanthus etc., can be identified with the help of specific chemical tests. The different classes of natural products present as active constituents in crude drugs can be identified by performing several general and specific chemical tests. Halphen's test for cotton seed oil, Van Urk's reagent for ergot, Vitalis test for tropane, alkaloids Borntrager's test for anthraquinones, murexide test for purine bases are examples of such chemical tests.

The estimation of chief constituent or group of active constituents is an integral part of chemical evaluation e.g. total sennosides in senna, morphine in opium, citral in lemon-grass oil, eugenol in clove oil, eucalyptol in eucalyptus oil, water-soluble alkaloids in ergot, tropane alkaloids in belladonna, emetine in ipecac, reserpine and rescinnamine in rauwolfia, quinine in cinchona etc.

5. BIOLOGICAL STANDARDISATION

When the estimation of potency of crude drug or its preparation is done by means of its effect on living organisms like bacterial, fungal growth or animal tissue or entire animal, it is known as bioassay. This method is generally called for, when standardization is not adequately done by chemical or physical means. In other words, bioassay is the measure of sample being tested capable of producing the biological effect as that of the standard preparation. Such an activity is represented in units known as International Units (I.U.) The specific biological activity contained in each I.U. of few drugs is mentioned as follows :

- Digitalis - 1 IU is contained in 76 mg of standard preparation
- Vit. A - 1 IU is contained in 0.344 micrograms of standard preparation
- Vit. D - 1 IU is contained in 0.025 micrograms of standard preparation
- Heparin - 1 IU is contained in 7.7 micrograms of standard preparation

Biological assay methods are mainly of 3 types,
(i) toxic (ii) symptomatic and (iii) tissue methods.

In toxic and symptomatic techniques, the animals are used, whereas in tissue method, the effect of a drug is observed on isolated organ or tissue. Among the drugs that are subjected to bioassay are cardiac glycosides, vitamins, hormones, saponins anthracene glycosides and antibiotics (microbiological assay).

❖❖❖

Chapter 2...

CHEMICAL NATURE OF TRADITIONAL DRUGS

INTRODUCTION

Drugs and diseases are two sides of the same coin, and to know one without the other is meaningless. Man has been suffering from various diseases right from the beginning of civilization and the attempts to reduce the severity of diseases or to cure the disorders are being made since ancient times. Ours is the age of synthetic and natural drugs, antibiotics and radioactive substances which are largely used to treat ailments. It was possible only due to recent developments and achievements in chemical field. With rapid strides in the knowledge of natural sciences, the crude drugs have come to be studied more exhaustively at present than at any other time in past.

To realise the applied importance of crude drugs, one should have a closer-look at their phytochemical profiles, irrespective of origin of crude drugs.

Therapeutic importance of animal and vegetable drugs is due to chemical substances which they contain. Various chemicals are reported in plants or animals but, each of them is not responsible for pharmacological actions all the while. Hence, those effectively responsible for therapeutic effects are called active constituents of drugs and those which do not have definite mode of action are called inert constituents. Active constituents satisfy the twin actions - pharmacological and pharmaceutical.

The active constituents of crude-drugs are divided into two classes: pharmacologically active constituents and pharmaceutically active principles. Both of them are equally important to a pharmacognosist. Crude drugs owe their therapeutic effects to pharmacological constituents only. These constituents can be mixtures or single chemical substance. The examples of single chemical substances are alkaloids, glycosides, enzymes, proteins, sugars, hormones and vitamins. Fixed oils, fats, volatile oils, oleo-resins, oleo-gum-resins, balsams etc. are the mixed chemicals.

In this chapter, the importance of these chemicals shall be dealt with briefly.

A few of these constituents, their chemical properties and crude drugs containing them are covered in this chapter.

1. ALKALOIDS

Alkaloids occur in plant both in free form and as salts of organic ancient times, but it is in recent years that sufficient information about their physical, chemical and physiological properties has been obtained. **Sertuerner**, in 1806, laid the foundation of alkaloid chemistry, when he reported isolation of morphine from opium. Discovery of other important alkaloids, particularly by **Pelletier** and **Caventon**, rapidly followed : emetine (1817), strychnine (1817), caffeine (1819), quinine (1820), etc. The term *Alkaloid* or *Alkali* like was first suggested by **Meissner** in 1829, which he applied to the basic compounds.

The *alkaloids are the basic nitrogenous organic products of plant origin, having marked physiological actions when administered internally.* Alkaloids have complex molecular nature, wherein, generally nitrogen is in heterocyclic rings. Alkaloids are secondary, tertiary or quaternary amines. Being amines, they have basic properties.

Alkaloids occur in plant both in free form and as salts of organic acids such as muconic, quinic, maleic, citric or oxalic acid. They are reported to be present in different parts of the plant and can be isolated from seeds (nux-vomica, areca), fruits (black pepper), leaves (belladonna, vasaka, datura), rhizomes and roots (ipecac, aconite, rauwolfia), stems (ephedra), bark (kurchi, cinchona) and fungi (ergot).

(a) Identification of Alkaloids by Precipitation Method

1. **Mayer's reagent (potassium mercuric iodide solution)** : Cream or pale yellow precipitate.

2. **Dragendorff's reagent (potassium bismuth iodide solution)** : Brown or reddish-brown colour or precipitate.

3. **Wagner's reagent (iodine and potassium iodide solution)** : Brown or reddish-brown colour or precipitate.

4. **Hager's reagent (saturated solution of picric acid)** : Yellow precipitate. Phospho-tungstic acid and tannic acid are also used for detection of certain alkaloids by precipitation.

(b) Identification of Alkaloids by Colour Reagents:

Purine and xanthine group of alkaloids (e.g. caffeine) do not respond to these tests. Colour reagents like potassium chloride with caffeine, mineral acids for colchicine or p-dimethyl aminobenzaldehyde with indole alkaloids produce distinct colours.

Amongst the angiosperms, Leguminosae, Papaveraceae, Ranunculaceae, Solanaceae, Rubiaceae, Berberidaceae, Liliaceae and Amaryllidaceae are outstanding plant families for yielding alkaloids.

Alkaloids are colourless, crystalline, non-volatile and bitter solids. Most of them are optically active and are laevo-rotatory. They are insoluble or sparingly soluble in water and fully soluble in organic solvents like alcohols, ether, chloroform. There are exceptions to these general rules. Coniine, nicotine and hygrine are liquids. Berberine salts are coloured. Ephedrine, colchicine and mesocaline are non-heterocyclic alkaloids. Coniine is dextro-rotatory, while papaverine is optically inactive and ricinine is neutral. Erythromycin and chloramphenicol are antibiotic alkaloids. Alkaloids are also obtained from synthetic sources, e.g., heroin; homotropine etc.

Alkaloids are highly potent medicaments and possess curative properties, e.g. morphine (opium) has a narcotic action, reserpine (rauwolfia) is a tranquiliser, strychnine (nux-vomica) is a nervine stimulant, cocaine (coca leaf) is a local anaesthetic, and hyoscine (belladonna) is an antispasmodic. Alkaloids in higher doses are poisonous.

Alkaloids are biosynthesised due to participation of several amino acids and enzymatic systems. Tobacco alkaloids are derived from ornithine. In the biogenesis of solanaceous alkaloids, phenylalanine, ornithine and methionine are involved. The indole alkaloids of rauwolfia, vinca, nux-vomica etc. are derived from tryptophan. Phenylalanine is also the precursor for biogenesis of ephedra, opium and colchicum alkaloids.

The chemical tests with heavy metals are not solely limited to alkaloids. Proteins, coumarins and α- pyrone also give precipitates with these reagents. It may be also noted that some alkaloids do not give such tests, like caffeine which is highly water soluble. Hence, the tests with heavy metals are in some cases false positive reactions or false negative reactions. For this purpose, the specific tests for individual alkaloids are more important for qualitative evaluation of crude drugs. These tests are covered under individual drugs.

Functions of Alkaloids

(i) Protective agents and discourage animal or insect attacks.

(ii) Plant stimulants or regulators in physiological activities, such as growth, reproduction and metabolism.

(iii) Detoxicating agents.

(IV) Reservoirs of protein synthesis.

Role of Alkaloids in Plants

The alkaloids are poisonous in nature, but when used in small quantities, exert useful physiological effects on animals and human beings and hence they have secured significant place in medicine. Their exact role in nature and functions in the plants, if any, are still a topic of ambiguity. Only one aspect is clearly understood that they are synthesized by a particular, stereospecific, many a time complicated, and energy consuming pathways and further they are metabolized to other alkaloidal or non-alkaloidal substances.

Some of the predicted roles of alkaloids in the plants are discussed below.

1. They are the reserve substances with an ability to supply nitrogen.

2. They might be the defensive mechanisms for plants growing in dry regions to protect from grazing animals, herbivorous and insects.

3. It is also possible that they are end products of detoxification mechanism in plants, and by this way check formation of substances which may prove to be harmful to the plants.

4. They might have a possible role as growth regulatory factors in the plants.

5. They are present normally in conjugation with plant acids, like meconic acid, cinchotannic acid etc. Therefore, alkaloids could be acting as carriers within plants for transportation of such acids.

Occurrence and Distribution of Alkaloids

The number of alkaloids discovered from plants has been continuously increasing. It is noted that alkaloids are of taxonomic importance. Their distribution in nature appears to be restricted or specific. Hence, the pattern of distribution of these compounds and their biological variability is of chemotaxonomic interest.

In general, the major distribution of alkaloids occurs in the angiosperms. But their presence is also detected in microorganisms, marine organisms, insects, animals and some of the lower plants. Some of the alkaloids reported from animal kingdom are castoramine from Canadian beaver, muscopyridine from musk deer and saxitoxin from "red tide". *Gonyaulax catenella* which has neurotoxic activity and a sex hormone which is a pyrrole derivative called 2, 3-dihydro - 7 methyl-1 H - pyrrolizin -1- one which occurs in many insects. It has been reported that among the bacteria, about 47% species indicate the presence of alkaloids, e.g. pyocyanine from *Pseudomonas aeruginosa*. In the lower plants, although the alkaloids are found in less number, some important sources are ergot fungus giving peptide alkaloids, ergometrine, ergotamine etc., lycopodine from lycopodium - a club moss, and also gymnosperms like ephedra alkaloids.

Out of the 60 different orders in higher plants, 34 orders contain alkaloids. Amongst them the prominent orders are Campanulales, Centrospermae, Gentianales, Geraniales, Liliflorae, Ranales, Rhoedales, Rosales, Rubiales, Tubiflorae and Sapindales.

The promising families with alkaloidal content are Amaryllidaceae, Apocynaceae, Berberidaceae, Euphorbiaceae, Leguminosae, Loganiaceae, Liliaceae, Lauraceae, Menispermaceae, Papaveraceae, Ranunculaceae, Rubiaceae, Rutaceae and Solanaceae. On the other hand, the orders like Curcurbitales, Fagales, Oleales, Salicales and the families like Labiatae and Rosaceae are practically devoid of alkaloids.

Within a plant, in most of the cases, the alkaloids are highly localized and concentrated in certain morphological parts only e.g. seeds (nux vomica, areca, physostigma), roots (rauwolfia, belladonna, ashwagandha), underground stems (sanguinaria), barks (kurchi, cinchona), leaves (coca leaf, lobelia, duboisia) and fruits (conium). In some cases, like vinca and ephedra, practically every part of plant contains alkaloids. The list of crude drugs containing alkaloids as active constituents is presented here.

Properties of Alkaloids

1. Physical Properties

With few exceptions, all the alkaloids are colourless, crystalline solids with a sharp melting point or decomposition range. Some alkaloids are amorphous gums, while others like coniine, sparteine, nicotine etc. are liquid and volatile in nature. Some alkaloids are coloured in nature, e.g. betanidin is red, berberine is yellow and salts of sanguinarine are copper red in colour.

In general, the free bases of alkaloids are soluble in organic non-polar, immiscible solvents. The salts of most alkaloids are soluble in water. In contrast, free bases are insoluble in water and their salts are also very sparingly soluble in organic solvents. The alkaloids containing quaternary bases are only water soluble. Some of the pseudoalkalcids and protoalkaloids show higher solubility in water. For example, colchicine is soluble in alkaline water, acid or water and caffeine (free base) is freely soluble in water. Quinine hydrochloride is highly soluble in water i.e. 1 part of quinine hydrochloride is soluble in less than 1 part of water, while only 1 part of quinine sulphate is soluble in 1000 parts of water.

The solubility of alkaloids and their salts is useful in pharmaceutical industry for the extraction and formulation of final pharmaceutical preparations.

2. Chemical Properties

Most of the alkaloids are basic in reaction, due to the availability of lone pair of electrons on nitrogen. The basic character of the alkaloidal compound is enhanced if the adjacent functional groups are electron releasing. The alkaloid turns to be neutral or acidic when the adjacent functional groups are electron withdrawing like amide group which reduces the availability of the lone pair of electrons. But, alkaloids exhibiting basic character are very much sensitive to decomposition and cause a problem during their storage. Their salt formation with an inorganic acid prevents many a time their decomposition.

The alkaloids may contain one or more number of nitrogen and it may exist in the form as primary ($R - NH_2$), e.g. mescaline; secondary amine ($R_2 - NH$), e.g. ephedrine; tertiary amine (R_3N) e.g. atropine; and quaternary ammonium compounds [R_4N^+X] e.g. tubocurarine chloride. In the last type, their properties vary from other alkaloids, owing to quaternary nature of nitrogen.

In the natural form, the alkaloids exist either in free state, as amine or as salt with acid or alkaloid N-oxides.

Classification of Alkaloids

The various methods proposed for classification of alkaloids are as follows:

1. Pharmacological Classification

Depending on the physiological response, the alkaloids are classified under various pharmacological categories, like central nervous system stimulants or depressants, sympathomimetics, analgesics, purgatives etc. This method does not take into account chemical nature of crude drugs. Within the same drug, the individual alkaloid may exhibit different action e.g. morphine is narcotic analgesic, while codeine is mainly antitussive. In cinchona, quinine is antimalarial, while quinidine is cardiac depressant.

2. Taxonomic Classification

This method classifies the vast number of alkaloids based on their distribution in various plant families, like solanaceous or papillionaceous alkaloids. Preferably, they are grouped as per the name of the genus in which they occur, e.g. ephedra, cinchona etc. From this classification, the chemotaxonomic classification has been further derived.

3. Biosynthetic Classification

This method gives significance to the precursor from which the alkaloids are biosynthesized in the plant. Hence, the variety of alkaloids with different taxonomic distribution and physiological activities can be brought under same group, if they are derived from same precursor. e.g. all indole alkaloids from tryptophan are grouped together. The alkaloidal drugs are categorised on the fact whether they are derived from amino acid precursor as ornithine, lysine, tyrosine, phenylalanine, tryptophan etc.

4. Chemical Classification

This is the most accepted way of classification of alkaloids. The main criterion for chemical classification is the type of fundamental (normally heterocyclic) ring structure present in alkaloid. The alkaloidal drugs are broadly categorised into two divisions.

(a) Heterocyclic alkaloids (True alkaloids) are divided into twelve groups according to nature of their heterocyclic ring.

(b) Non-heterocyclic alkaloids or proto-alkaloids or biological amines or pseudoalkaloids.

The following chart indicates type of alkaloids and their occurrence in various plants along with basic chemical ring.

2. GLYCOSIDES

Glycosides are organic compounds of plant and animal origin which yield on either acidic or enzymatic hydrolysis, one or more sugars and a non-sugar residue. The non-sugar moiety is called as genin or aglycone, while the sugar components are glycones.

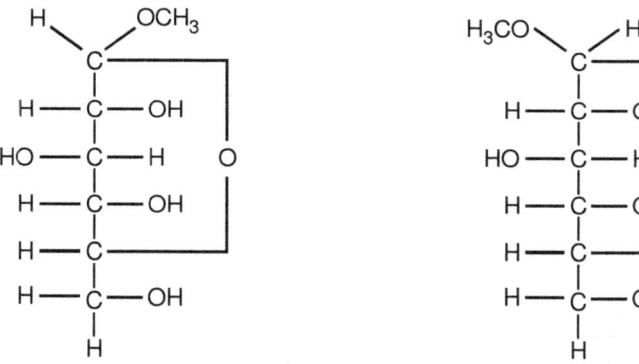

Fig. 2.1 : α-methyl glycoside   Fig. 2.2 : β-methyl glycoside

Genins or aglycones may be hydroxylic compounds like alcohols or phenol or even it may be an amine. Glycosides are acetals and thus, the condensation products of sugar and aglycone. Most commonly occurring sugars as a product of hydrolysis of glycosides are glucose, mannose and galactose. Rhamnose, digitoxose and cymarose occur rarely. Few glycosides like α, β and γ methyl glycosides and galactosides are prepared synthetically, as they are not found naturally. Thus, action of glucose on methanol produces α-methyl glycoside and β-methyl glycoside.

Pharmaceutically important glycosides are obtained from vegetable sources only. They occur in various parts of the plants like fruits, seeds, leaves and barks. Glycosides are colourless, crystalline, non-reducing, optically active compounds, usually laevo-rotatory. They are water soluble, as well as, alcohol soluble. They are hydrolysed with dilute acids and with enzymes naturally present in the same plants containing glycosides, but in different cells. Maceration, germination and other physiological conditions of the tissues can cause hydrolysis of glycosides by an enzyme.

Like alkaloids, glycosides also perform important functions in plant life, i.e., growth, regulation, protection etc. Therapeutically glycosides are important due to their aglycone content. They exhibit various types of physiological actions (Table 2.1).

Table 2.1 : Therapeutically Important Aglycone Moieties

Moiety	Physiological action
(a) Methyl salicylate from gaultheria	Analgesic
(b) Anthraquinone derivatives in senna, cascara sagrada, aloe, rhubarb	Laxative
(c) Strophanthin, digitoxin in strophanthus and digitalis respectively	Cardio-tonic
(d) Sinigrin in black mustard	Irritant
(e) Salicin in Salix species	Anti-rheumatic
(f) 18-β-glycyrrhetinic acid from liquorice	Anti-peptic ulcer
(g) Hesperidin in citrus fruits	Capillary fragility

Classification of Glycosides

The glycosides are classified on the basis of chemical nature of their aglycone moieties as follows.

1. Cyanophoric or Cyanogenetic Glycosides

They yield one molecule of hydrocyanic acid as the product of their hydrolysis.

Prunasin from *Prunus serotina* and amygdalin from bitter almond, are common examples of this group (Fig. 2.3).

2. Cardiac Glycosides

The term itself is self-explanatory, indicating that the glycosides act on cardiac muscles (heart muscles). Therapeutically, these glycosides strengthen heart muscles by increasing force of contraction and thereby, its efficiency.

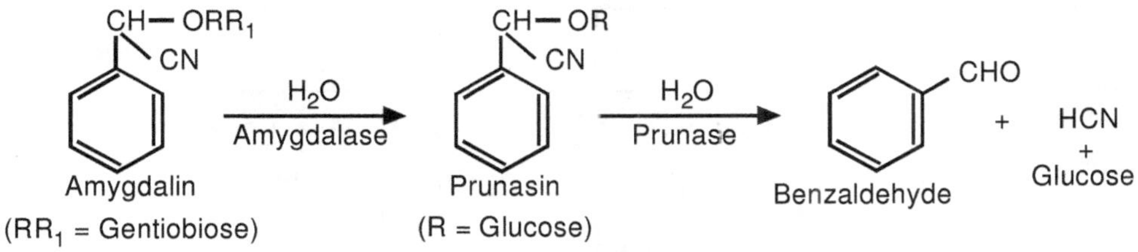

Fig. 2.3 : Structures of cyanogenetic glycosides

Cardiac glycosides can be divided into two major categories : cardenolides (C_{23}) and bufadienolides (C_{24}). Cardenolides commonly occur in the plants belonging to Apocynaceae and Scrophulariaceae, while bufadienolides are common in Liliaceae. Important examples of cardiac glycosides are purpurea glycoside from digitalis leaves; K-strophanthoside from strophanthus seed and glucoscillaren from squill bulbs.

3. Saponin Glycosides (L-Sapo-soap)

These plant glycosides on hydrolysis yield an aglycone known as sapogenin. They form colloidal, soapy solutions in water (hence named as saponin). They cause haemolysis of red blood corpuscles, even in very low concentration. If taken orally, they are less harmful. Saponins are powerful emulsifiers and good detergents. They are of two types chemically, i.e. steroidal saponins and triterpenoid saponins.

Digitonin, gitonin and digonin (digitalis seeds), sarsapogenin (sarsaparilla roots), and diosgenin (Dioscorea tubers) are some of the important steroidal saponins.

Quillaia, senega and glycyrrhiza are crude drugs containing triterpenoid glycosides.

4. Isothiocynate Glycosides

These are the sulphur containing glycosides. The examples of this group are sinigrin from black mustard, sinalbin of white mustard and gluconapin from rapeseed.

5. Phenolic Glycosides

This is the group covering largest number of glycosides available from plant sources. Depending upon the chemical structure, this group is subdivided as follows :

(i) Simple phenolic glycosides

(ii) Anthracene glycosides

(iii) Coumarin glycosides

(iv) Flavone and flavonoid glycosides

(v) Anthocyanidins and their glycosides.

The following schedule gives examples of each type alongwith their sources (Table 2.2).

Table 2.2 : Phenolic Glycosides from Plants

	Type	Aglycone	Source
(i)	Simple phenolic glycosides	Salicin	*Salix* species
		Gaultherin	Gaultheria
		Glucovanillin	*Vanilla* species

Contd...

(ii)	Anthracene glycosides	Chrysophanol	Cascara
		Aloe-emodin	Rhubarb, senna
		Rhein	Senna
		Barbaloin	Aloe
(iii)	Coumarin glycosides	Umbelliferone	Asafoetida, galbanum
		Scopoletin	Jalap, belladonna
		Aesculetin	Stramonium, tobacco
			Horse chest nut
(iv)	Flavone and flavonoid glycosides	Kaempferol	Senna
		Gentisin	Gentian and swertia
		Liquiritigetol	Liquorice
		Hespiridin	Lemon and orange peels
(v)	Anthocyanidin glycosides	Cyanidin	Rose, corniflowers
		Malvidin	Purple-grapes

Chemical Tests for Glycosides

(a) Test for Saponin glycosides :

Saponin glycosides can be tested as under:

1. Shake the powdered drug with water, formation of foam indicates the presence of saponins.
2. Aqueous solution of saponin containing drug, when added to the sample of blood, causes haemolysis.

Steroidal and triterpenoidal saponins do not respond to these tests.

(b) Test for cyanophoric glycosides :

To the powder in a test tube add little water, and suspend the piece of sodium picrate paper above the drug, trapping the top edge between the cork and the tube wall. Allow it to stand for thirty minutes. Hydrocyanic acid gets evolved and turns the picrate paper brick-red owing to the formation of sodium isopurpurate.

(c) Test for Anthraquinone glycosides :

Boil the powdered drug with dilute sulphuric acid. Filter immediately, separate the filtrate and cool. Mix the filtrate with water insoluble organic solvents like benzene, chloroform or carbon tetrachloride. Shake it well and separate the organic solvent layer. To the layer of organic solvent, add equal quantity of dilute ammonia. The layer becomes pink and finally red indicating the presence of anthraquinone derivatives.

(d) Test for cardiac glycosides : *Keller-Killiani test* :

The test consists of boiling about one gram finely powdered digitalis with 10 ml of 70 % alcohol for 3 minutes. The extract is filtered. To the filtrate is added, 5 ml of water and 0.5 ml of strong solution of lead acetate, filtered and filtrate is treated with equal volume of chloroform and evaporated to yield extract. The extractive is dissolved in glacial acetic acid and after cooling, 2 drops of ferric chloride solution are added to it. These contents are transferred to a test tube containing 2 ml of concentrated sulphuric acid. A reddish brown layer acquiring bluish green colour after standing is observed due to presence of digitoxose, at the interface and pale green colour in the upper layer (due to steroid nucleus) form in the presence of cardiac glycosides.

3. TANNINS

It constitutes high molecular weight group of very complex chemicals of plant origin. It is difficult to define them precisely. In the past, the term was applied to chemicals which were used to combine with proteins of animal hide to prevent their putrefaction and to convert them into leather. However, the compounds with low molecular weight, like gallic acid and chlorogenic acid which satisfy other properties of tannins are not covered under this class. They are categorized as *pseudotannins* and they do not respond to the goldbeater's skin test. Tannins can be broadly defined as the *derivatives of polyhydroxy benzoic acid,* capable of combining with proteins. They are further characterised as non-crystallisable, alcohol and water-soluble compounds with an acid reaction and astringent taste. They cause precipitation of proteins and alkaloids, impart dark blue or green black colour with ferric salts. When applied to smooth muscles, they cause their contraction.

Classification of Tannins

Tannins are classified into two classes, according to their behaviour on dry distillation.

1. Condensed Tannins:

These are true tannins. They are also known as non-hydrolysable tannins, phlobatannins or proanthocyanidins. They are very resistant to hydrolysis. Being related to flavonoid pigments because they are formed via derivatives of flavones, like catechin or flavan-3-ol or flavan-3, 4-diols. Unlike the hydrolysable tannins, on treatment with enzymes or mineral acids, they are polymerised or decomposed into red coloured substances called phlobaphenes, which are insoluble in water and indicate the typical brownish-red colour of many plants and drugs. On dry distillation they yield catechol. With ferric chloride tannins, these produce brownish-green colour.

They are distributed in different parts of plants. The green tea and hamamelis leaves; cinchona, cinnamon and wild cherry bark; male fern rhizome; cocoa, cola and areca seeds; pale and black catechu are rich in condensed tannins.

Depending upon the source of the tannins, various modified methods are used for extraction. Methyl alcohol, hot water, acetone and ethyl acetate are the common solvents used for extraction; the extract is filtered and dried under vacuum.

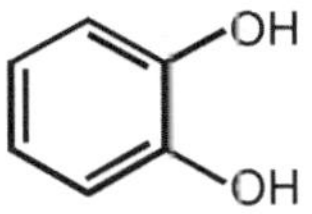

Catechol (pyrocatechol)

2. Hydrolysable Tannins:

As the name indicates, these tannins are hydrolysed by acids or enzymes quickly and the products of hydrolysis are *gallic acids* or *ellagic acid*. On dry distillation, gallic acid and other compounds get converted to *pyrogalol*. They respond to ferric chloride solution, producing blue colour. The examples of hydrolyzable tannins are gallotannin in nutgall, rhubarb and clove; ellagitannin from oak, myrobalans and pomegranate bark.

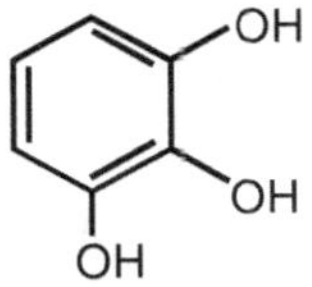

Pyrogallol (Pyrogallic acid)

Isolation of Tannins

Depending upon the source of the tannins, various modified methods are used for extraction. Methyl alcohol, hot water, acetone and ethyl acetate are the common solvents used for extraction, the extract is filtered and dried under vacuum.

Properties of Tannins

Tannins are soluble in water, alcohol, dilute alkalies, acetone and glycerol. The solutions of tannins precipitate alkaloids, heavy metals, gelatin and glycosides.

Chemical Tests for Tannins

1. With ferric chloride solution, hydrolyzable tannins give blue-black colour and condensed tannins brownish-green tint.

2. A piece of gold beater skin, when treated with dilute hydrochloric acid, ferrous sulphate and test solution of Tannin gives brown or black colour.

3. With gelatin solution (1%) containing sodium chloride (10%), tannins are precipitated out from the solution.

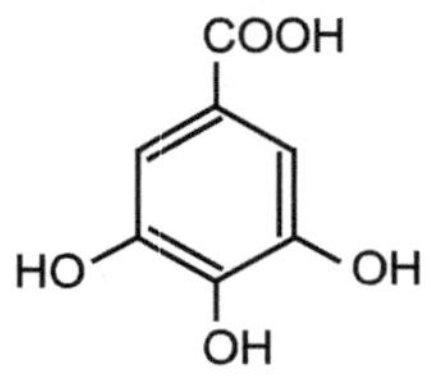

Gallic acid

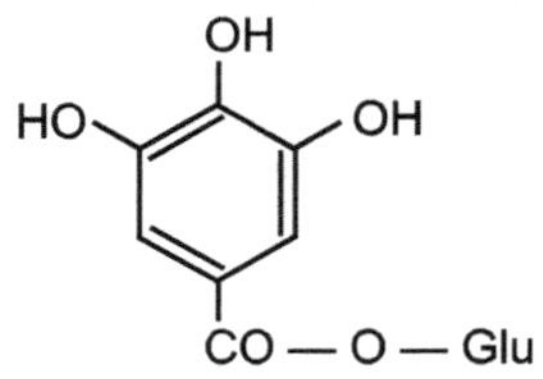

Glucogallin

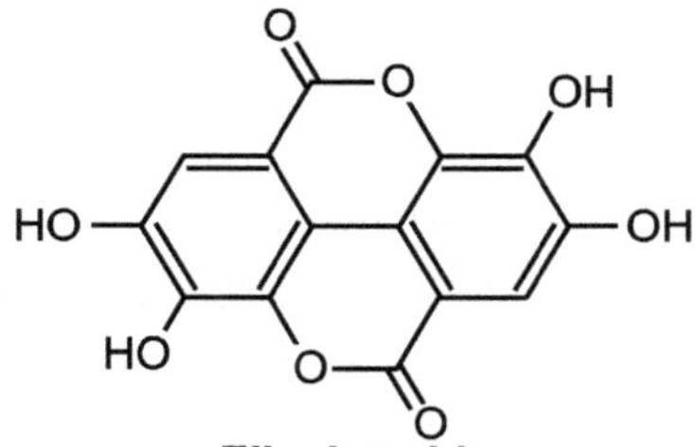

Ellagic acid

3. Pseudotannins:

These are not as such a separate group of tannins, but may be treated as subgroup because they do not obey to Goldbeater's skin test and are low molecular weight compounds. Chlorogenic acid in coffee and nux vomica, ipecacuanhic acid in ipecacuanha and catechins in cocoa are examples of pseudotannins.

The detection test for chlorogenic acid is carried out by extracting the drug with water and treating this extract with ammonia solution, followed by exposure to air, which leads slowly to formation of green colour.

❖ ❖ ❖

Chapter 3...

GLYCOSIDAL DRUGS

APAMARGA

Synonyms

Durgraha, Markati, Pratak pushpi, Markat pippali, Aghada.

Biological Source

It consists of all parts of plant *Achyranthes aspera* belonging to family Amaranthaceae.

Geographical Source

It is found spreaded all over India.

Cultivation

Not cultivated commercially, collected from wild grown plants, available throughout Maharashtra.

Collection

Seeds are collected at maturity during summer season, and other parts from September to May.

Description of Herb

It is small branched about 1 meter high herb.

Leaves	:	Leaves are oblong, hairy about 2-5 to 12 cm long.
Flowers	:	Appending in long spikes with small greenish white flowers.
Fruits	:	Small, elongated, ash coloured or greyish, similar to rice grains and are hard.
Stem	:	Stem grows straight with six to ten ridges.
Types	:	There are two types as (a) Shwet, (b) Rakta
Parts Used	:	Root, leaves, seeds, entire herb.

Fig. 3.1 : Apamarg herb with spike

Ayurvedic Properties

Rasa	:	Katu, Tikta
Vipak	:	Katu
Veerya	:	Ushana
Guna	:	Laghu, Rooksha, Tikshna
Doshaghna	:	Kaphaghana, Vatghana and Pittakara.

Chemical Constituents

It contains betain, water soluble alkaloid achyranthine, pure saponion as achyranthes saponium A & B, oleanolic acid, and oligosaccharide saponin.

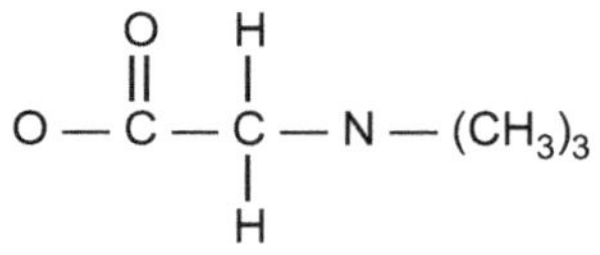

Betain

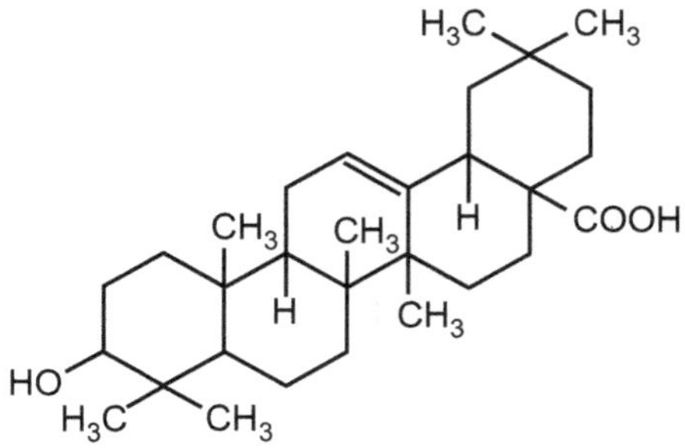

Oleanolic acid

Pharmacological Uses

It is used as Astringent diuretic, purgative and alternative.

Traditional Uses

a) Apamarga paste is used as anti-inflammatory for local application.

b) Skin conditions and Corn : The paste is applied locally along with internal consumption of decoction.

c) In cases of scorpion, snake and mouse bite its paste is used for local application.

d) Bleeding piles : Achyranthes seed paste along with rice water is useful.

e) In spleenamegaly asperakshar along with Jaggary is useful.

f) In cases of chronic fever its decoction is useful.

g) It is very useful in treetment of Leprosy.

Kalpa

Apamargakshar taila.

Dosage

Decoction : 10 to 20 ml

Kshar : 0.5 to 2 gm

Market Products

It is an ingredient of (1) **"CYSTONE-Tablets":** Himalaya Drug Company, Banglurue.

(2) **Arjin:** Alarsin Pharmaceuticals, MIDC Andheri, Mumbai.

BABACHI

Synonyms

Krushanaphala, Kushtaghani, Kushtani, Psoralea.

Biological Source

It consists of dried ripe fruits of *Psoralea corylifolia* synonym *Cullen corylifolium* belonging to family Leguminoseae.

Geographical Source

It is found throughout India as weed in waste places in Assam, Uttarpradesh, Maharashtra, Punjab and Shri Lanka.

Description of Herb

It is 0.5 to 1.5 metre annual herb.

Stem and branches are grooved, studded with glands and white hairs.

- **Leaves** : Leaves are 2.5 to 8 cm long, broadly elliptical, rounded, dotted with backglands on both surfaces, leaves are hairy; serrated margins.
- **Flowers** : Flowers are bluish purple, small, solitary in a bunch of 10 – 80, arising in axis of leaves.
- **Fruits** : Small, subglobose, black. Also arising in bunch.
- **Seeds** : Small, black, smooth with characteristic small.

   Seeds are compilotropous, non-endopermic, smooth oily and free of starch.
- **Useful Parts** : Seeds, leaves, seed oil.

Macroscopic Characters

- **Colour** : Dark chocolate to black.
- **Odour** : Non-pungent and characteristics
- **Taste** : Bitter, unpleasant and acrid
- **Size** : 3 to 5 × 2 to 3 mm
- **Shape** : Oblong, beam-shaped

Fig. 3.2 : Psoralea herb

Chemical Constituents

Psoralea fruit contains essential oil, resins, fixed oil, raffinose, coumanin compounds, psoralen isopsoralidin and cerylifolin. Recently two more compounds bavachromanol and psoralenol have been reported.

Psoralen   **Psoraledin**

Standards of Quality

Foreign organic matter ≯ 2.0%

Ayurvedic Properties

Rasa	:	Tikta, Katu
Vipak	:	Katu
Veerya	:	Ushna
Guna	:	Laghu and Rooksha
Doshaghna	:	Kaphegnana, Vataghana, Pittakar.

Pharmacological Uses

Seeds are laxative, anthelmentic, diuretic, diapheretic. Oil has powerful effect against skin infections.

Traditional Uses

It improves hair growth and complexion.

a) Major role of the drug is treatment of leucoderma. Its decoction along with jaggary or psoralea oil alongwith honey is useful.

b) In cases of scabies, seeds of psoralea and karale (bitter gourd) paste in gomutra (cow urine) is applied externally. Cavities of teeth are treated with babachi.

c) In leprosy, psoralea seed and seseam seed in proportion of 1:1 are administered daily.

d) In leprosy, psoralea oil along with beetal leaf is given internally and oil is applied externally.

e) As anthelmintic, its oil is given followed by castor oil. After 3 - 4 days proves to be good remedy.

f) It is also used as aphrodisiac and in the treatment of piles.

Kalpa

Khadiraarishta, Mahamanjishtadi kwath, Shwitrahar vati.

Dosage

Seed powder : 1 to 3 gm

Oil : For external application.

Market Products

(1) **Ludoil:** Ayulabs Pvt. Ltd., Vavdi, Rajkot, Gujrat.

(2) **Psora:** Ayulabs Pvt Ltd., Vavdi, Rajkot, Gujrat.

BRAHMI

Synonyms
Saraswati, Somvalli.

Biological Source
It consists of fresh leaves and stems of the plant *Bacopa moniera*, belonging to family Scrophulariaceae.

Geographical Source
It is prostrate succulent herb found throughout India, in wet, damp, marshy places upto 1200 m elevation.

Cultivation and Collection
Usually it is collected from the wild grown sources. Now-a-days it is also cultivated for its commercial uses. Easily cultivated by using seeds or by using succulent stems.

Description of Herb
It is succulent herb spreading on ground.

- **Stems** : Small fleshy, reddish green in colour.
- **Leaves** : Small, fleshy, alternate leaves are smooth with minute black dots.
- **Flowers** : Flowers are solitary, arising in the axil of leaves, colola is bluish, white or pink coloured.
- **Fruits** : Small ovid containing minute and numerous seeds.
- **Parts Used** : Leaves

Macroscopic Characters

- **Colour** : Green.
- **Taste** : Bitter.
- **Size** : Leaves about 2 cm.
- **Shape** : Leaves are obvate, sessile.
- **Flowers** : 1 cm in size, five petioled with one petal larger than other four.
- **Capsule** : Ovoid.

Fig. 3.3 : Bacopa Herb (Brahmi)

Chemical Constituents
Brahmi contains alkaloid brahmine, herpestine and mixture of other three alkaloids. It contains saponin as bacoside A and bacoside B. It also contains betulic acid, stigmasterol, monnierin and hersaponin. Bacoside A and B on acid hydrolysis yield triterpenoid aglycone bacogenins A and B.

Standards of Quality

Foreign organic matter	:	≯ 2.0 %
Alcohol soluble extractives	:	≮ 6.0 %
Water soluble extractives	:	≮ 22.0 %
Total ash	:	≯ 18.0 %
Acid unsoluble ash	:	≮ 06.0 %
Loss on drying	:	≯ 12.0 %

Ayurvedic Properties

Rasa	:	Tikta, Keshaya, Madhur
Vipak	:	Madhur
Veerya	:	Sweet
Guna	:	Laghu, Snigdha
Doshaghna	:	Kapha vatnashak
Prabhav	:	Unmad/Apasmar shamak (Antiepilliptic)

Pharmacological Uses

It is good nervine tonic, cardiac tonic, diuretic anticareer activity and sedative effect.

Traditional Uses

a) Liquid extract along with honey is useful in cases of insanity and epilepsy.

b) Poultice made of boiled plant is applied in bronchitis and other forms of cough.

c) In cases of demenisa, memory enhancement powder along with honey is given for local application.

e) In cases of hysteria and epilepsy along with ghee is useful and given for long term use.

Dosage

Extract: 10 ml

Powder: 0.25 to 1 gm

Infusion : 8 to 16 ml.

Kalpa

Brahmiprash, Brahmighrut, Saraswatarishta, Brahmisiddha talia.

Market Products

(1) **Geriforte:** Himalaya Drug Company, Banglurue.

(2) **Mentat:** Himalaya Drug Company, Banglurue.

(3) **Brahmi Awala Tail:** Dabur Pharmaceuticals Ltd., Faridabad, Haryana.

CHAKRAMADHU

Synonyms
Tarwat, Takala

Biological Source
It consists of the leaves, root and seeds of *Cassia tora* belonging to family leguninosae.

Geographical Source
It is found growing wild all over India, especially on dry soil in Bengal and tropical parts of India.

Description of Herb
It is an annual herb of about 0.30 to 2 metre height.

Leaves : Compound leaves, three pairs of leaflets with small gland at the base of lower leaflet. Leaves are pinnate.

Flowers : Flowers are small appearing in pair or single, yellow coloured, 1 cm in diameter.

Fruits : Appear in pods of about 15 to 30 cm long. They are slender, four sided, curved and sharp pointed.

Seeds : Grayish brown or reddish in colour, oval shaped about 20 – 30 seeds in apod.

Roots : Not well developed, tap root.

Flowers : It flowers in rainy season and bears fruits in winter season.

Parts used: Seeds, leaves and roots.

Cultivation and Collection
It is collected from wild grown plants and is not cultivated commercially.

Macroscopic Characters (Leaves)

Colour : Greenish yellow
Odour : Disagreable
Taste : Sour-sweet
Size : 10 to 12 cm long
Shape : Ovate

Fig. 3.4 : *Cassia tora* **flowering twig**

Chemical Constituents

Chakramadhu contains flavanol glycosides, oxytoxic principle, calcium, magnesium, sodium, potassium sulphate, rhein, aloe-emodin and chrysophenol.

Aloe-emodin

Ayurvedic Properties

Rasa	:	Katu
Vipale	:	Katu
Veerya	:	Ushna
Guna	:	Laghu, Rooksha
Doshaghna	:	Kapha vata shamak

Pharmacological Uses

Antiperiodic, anthelmintic

Medicinal Uses

a) In skin diseases like scabies, eczema and ringworm, root paste is applied externally.

b) For reduction of obesity, seed powder or fresh leaf juice is used.

c) Root is used as antidot for snake bite.

d) In leprosy, leaf extract is given.

e) In urticaria, seed powder along with ghee is used.

Kalp

Dadrughamivati

Dosage

Powder: 1 to 3 gm

Leaf extract : 5 to 10 mL

Market Products

1) **Mahamarichadi Tail:** Dabur India Ltd., New Delhi.

CHIRATA

Synonyms
Naditika, Nidrari, Chirayata.

Biological Source
Chirata is the entire herb of *Swertia chirata* belonging to family Gentianaceae, and contains not less than 1.3% of bitter principle of chirata.

Geographical Source
It found in India, Nepal and Bhutan. In India it grows in Kashmir, Meghalaya, Madhya Pradesh, Khasi Hills upto an altitude of 1200 – 1500 metres.

Description of Herb
Chirata is an annual herb upto 30 – 80 centimetre high.

Stem	:	Robust, branching cylindrical at base and quadrangular at the apex.
Leaves	:	Leaves are placed in opposite pairs 5 to 7.5 cm long, 1 to 2 cm broad, ovate, lanceolate with pointed tips.
Flowers	:	Numerous 2 to 3 mm broad, greenish yellow, lined with purple, white hairs.
Fruit	:	Superior, bicarpellary, unilocular, 6 mm long.
Seeds	:	Numerous reticulated ovoid seeds.
Types	:	a) Tikta, b) Ardhatikta
Part used	:	Whole plant all parts.

Cultivation and Collection
At present it is collected from wild grown plants. It can also be cultivated in temperate region. The plant is collected for medicinal purpose when the capsules are fully formed. The dried plants are made into sheaves weighing 1 kg.

Macroscopic Characters

Colour	:	Leaves, flowers and fruits: peculiar with yellowish tinge. Stems yellowish brown to purple.
Odour	:	Odourless
Taste	:	Extremely bitter
Size	:	Stems are about 6 mm broad and 1 mm in length.
Roots	:	These are brown, twisted, tapering with root lets and about 5 – 10 cm in length.

Chemical Constituents
It contains bitter yellow acid as ophelic acid, glycosides as chiratin and amorogentin, other alkaloids as gentianine and gentiocrucine. It also contains resin and tannin.

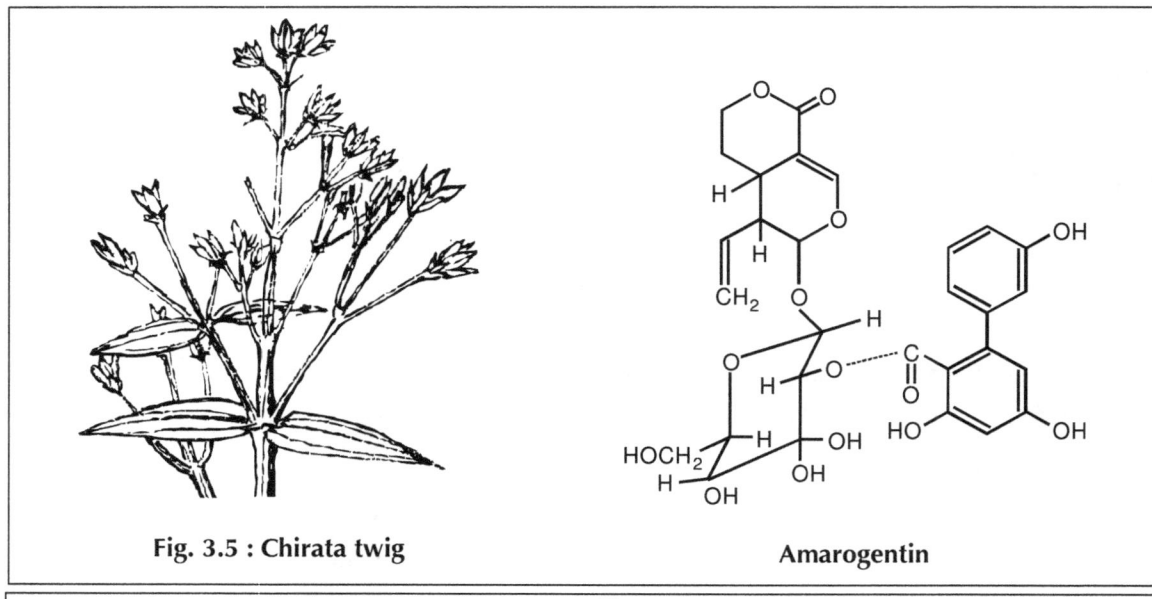

Fig. 3.5 : Chirata twig

Amarogentin

Gentianine

Standards of Quality

Alcohol Soluble Extractives (60%) : ≮ 10.1%

Test for tannin : Negative

Foreign Organic Matter : ≯ 2.0%

Acid insoluble ash : ≯ 1.0%

Ayurvedic Properties

Rasa : Tikta

Vipale : Katu

Veerya : Sheetal

Guna : Laghu, Rooksha

Doshaghna : Kaphaghana, Pittaghana, Vatkar.

Pharmacological Uses

It is used as bitter tonic, stomachic, anthelnintic, laxative, antidiarheic, antiperiodic.

Traditional Uses

a) In cases of rhumatoid anthritis, irregular fever (intermittant fever) infusion of chirata with 3 gm powder camphor, 250 mg. shilajeet and 5 gm of honey taken early morning proves to be useful.

b) Decoction of chirata, ginger, deckamali is useful in any kind of fever.

c) In hyperacidity, decoction of chirata and bhringaraj is very useful.

d) Dypepsia, pain in abdomen paste of leaves along with pepper, rock salt and asofoeteda is very useful.

Dosage

Decoction : 25 to 50 ml

Powder :   1 to 4 gm

Kalpa

Sudarshanchurna, Kirattiktadikwath, Bhuinimbadi kwath, Mahasudarshandi kwath, Medoyogsarkara kisaladi taila.

Substitutes

a) S. densifolia from Kokan plant is about 30 to 90 cm in height with decussate sessile leaves and white flowers.

b) S. Ciliata from Himalayas in Kashmir. Small herb with oblong or lanccolate leaves. Flowers are purple or dark red.

c) S. peniculata: It grows in Himalayas from Kashmir to Nepal also in Mizoram. Herb is 50 to 90 cm. Leaves are oblong lanceolate. Flowers are white in colour with two purple patches at base and long pointed capsules.

Market Products:

(1) **Sudarshan powder**

(2) **Safi:** Hamdard Laborataries, Delhi.

(3) **Diabecon:** Himalaya Drug Company, Bangalurue.

DHAMASO

Synonyms

Dusparsha, Durlabha.

Biological Source

Dhamaso consists of dried whole plant of *Fagonia indica* Burm. *Fagonia cretica* or *Fagonia arebica,* Family: Zygophyllaceae.

Geographical Source

Spain and Baleric Islands and India. In Rajasthan, Uttar Pradesh, Punjab, Cutch, Gujrat.

Macroscopic Characters

Flowers : Small pale yellow or purple. Solitory, rose coloured.

Roots : Roots are tap-roots with brownish green colour externally, while core, yellowish green. Surface is rough, with fibrous longitudinal fracture.

Leaves : Leaves are sub-sessile, oblong. Margin is entire, grey or black brown, opposite 1-3 foliate linear.

Size : 0.5 to 1.5 cm in length and 0.05 to 0.10 cm in width. Fruits are 5 mm long, 5 partite 1 seeded.

Fruits : Pentagonous, schizocarp, compressed of five compressed two valved cocci.

Cultivation and Collection

It is not cultivated commercially but collected from wild grown plants only.

Description of Herb

Dhamaso plant is about 60 cm in height. It is glabrous, woody and perennial. It is also spiny. Herb is green and much branched. It is bitter in taste and odourless. Flowering during antumn.

Fig. 3.6 : Dhamaso plant

Chemical Constituents

It is rich source of various chemicals like saponins, flavanoids, sterols and phenolic acids.

Oleanolic acid

Saponin I, Saponin II, fagogenin, genin A, genin B, oleanolic acid, diosgenin, and fagonin are the members of saponin compounds. Steroidal β-sitosterol, stigmasterol, compesterol, lanosterol are the members of another chemical compounds. Flavanoidal compounds reported in Dhamaso are kaempferol, gaeveatin, isorhamatin and quercetin-3-diglycoside. Alkaloid harmine is present.

Fatty acids like caprylic acid, oleic acid, myristic acid along with several amino acids like threonine, serine, alanin, aspartic acid are also reported in the drug.

Ayurvedic Properties

Rasa	:	Tikta
Vipale	:	Katu
Veerya	:	Sheetal
Guna	:	Laghu, Rooksha
Doshaghna	:	Kaphaghana, Pittaghana, Vatkar.

Uses of Dhamaso

Acrid, bitter, febrifuse, tonic with unflammatory. It is also anti-cancer and specifically used in breast cancer.

Traditional Uses

In the treatment of pyrexia and bleeding disorders. Leaves and twigs are used as cooling agent. Bark is used in Scabies.

Market Products

Sudarshan Churna, Durlabhi Kwath, Ushirasav, Parpatadi Kwath, Maha Vishgarbha Tail, Mahatiktaka Ghrit.

GINSENG

Synonyms

Ninjin, Pannag, Panax.

Biological Source

Ginseng is the dried root of various species of *Panax*, like *P. ginseng* (Korean ginseng), *P. japonica* (Japanese ginseng), *P. notoginseng* (Chinese ginseng) and *P. quinquefolium* (American ginseng), belonging to family Araliaceae.

Geographical Source

It grows widely in Korea, China and Russia. Presently, ginseng is commercially cultivated in Korea, China, Japan, Russia, Canada and United States of America. In India, at present it is cultivated in Kohima, Tunsang district of Nagaland. It is also available in Arunachal Pradesh.

The term *Panax* indicates curve all (*Pan and axos*), while *ginseng* is derived from Chinese words *shen sang*, which stands for manroot, because the shape of the root resembles the human body. The references about ginseng are found in ancient Chinese literature, stating its medicinal properties. Now-a-days, ginseng is considered as adaptogen. It increases non-specific resistance and defence mechanism of the body.

Cultivation and Collection

The cultivation technology adopted in Korea is briefly described.

Ginseng is propagated by means of seeds in nursery beds and then transplanted into open fields i.e. permanent beds. The ripe seeds are collected from four year old plants. They are sown in November in nursery beds. There are 3 types of nursery beds viz. Yang-Jik, To-Jik and Ban-Yang-Jik. The first type gives high quality seedlings. After attaining sufficient growth, the seedlings are dug up in the following May and transplanted to permanent beds for next 3 - 5 years. Ginseng requires clay loam or sandy loam soil. It grows at altitudes from 100 - 800 metres. The soil with high amount of potassium gives better results. About 10 - 15 seedlings are planted in one square metre. About 7 -10 days after transplantation, shades are provided to plants to protect them from excessive sunlight. Generally, use of fertilizers is avoided, but before transplantation, the soil is mixed with large amount of green grass. Periodically, weeding is done. The plants are harvested 3 - 5 years after transplantation. Generally, they are harvested between July to October. White ginseng is obtained by removing the outer layers of the roots. Red ginseng is obtained by first steaming the roots and after that they are dried. But, removal of outer layers may lead to loss of active constituents.

Macroscopic Characters

Ginseng has green coloured and oval shaped leaves with long stalk, while roots are forked shaped and light in colour. Roots are also translucent and possess stem scars.

Chemical Constituents

Ginseng contains a mixture of several saponin glycosides, belonging to triterpenoid group. They are grouped as follows :

(1) Ginsenosides;

(2) Panaxosides; and

(3) Chikusetsusaponin

Ginsenosides contain aglycone dammarol while panaxosides have oleanolic acid as aglycone. About 13 ginsenosides have been identified. Panaxosides give oleanolic acid, panaxadiol and panaxatriol on decomposition.

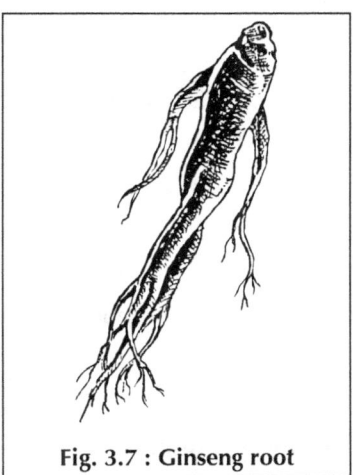

Fig. 3.7 : Ginseng root

Oleanolic acid **Panaxadiol** **Panaxatriol**

Glycosides of ginseng

Standards of Quality

Foreign organic matter	≯ 2.0%
Total ash	≯ 4.2%
Acid insoluble ash	≯ 1.0%
Sulfated ash	≯ 12.0%
Alcohol soluble extractive	≯ 14.0%

Uses

Like some of the wellknown ayurvedic medicines, ginseng has generated large interest because of its novel pharmacological actions.

An international symposium was arranged at Lugano in 1975 to discuss the analytical, pharmacological and clinical aspects of ginseng, which was sponsored by World Health Organisation.

Ginseng is an important immunomodulatory drug. It shows a wide range of activities. It increases the natural resistance (non-specific resistance) and enhances the power to overcome the illness or exastaution. It has both stimulant and sedative properties. It is used as aphrodisiac. It is believed to be useful in adrenal and thyroid dysfunctioning.

Traditional Uses

In old days, ginseng was used for a number of ailments, like curing the giddiness and prolonging life of elderly and diabetic persons. It is given as demulcent and in gastritis and aneamia.

Although, ginseng shows a low toxicity, long term use leads to poisoning, similar to that of corticosteroids.

Ginseng extracts are also used externally in cosmetics.

Market Products

Ginsec: Duphor interfran Ltd.

Korean Ginseng: Holland & Barrett.

Menergy

These are few of the well known products of ginseng in the market.

GOKHRU

Synonyms

Gokshuraka, Svadanshtra-sweet thorns, Trikantaka, Swadu kantaka.

Biological Source

It consist of dried mature fruits of plant *Tribulus terrestris* Linn, Family: Zygophyllaceae.

Description of Herb

Shrub spreads on land and covers an area of about 1 metre. It is a prostate plant. Branches spread from all the sides. Leaves similar to gram plant. Flowers small, yellow coloured with five petals. Roots 10 - 13 cm long, smokey with slightly strong smell and sweet. Flowering occurs in autumn follows by fruiting.

Macroscopic Characters

Colour	:	Greenish to grey
Odour	:	Slight aromatic
Taste	:	Bitter
Size	:	0.2 × 0.1 cm
Shape	:	Angular, oblong, funnel shaped
Fruit	:	Fruit consists of 5 - 10 woody cocci, each with two pairs of hard, sharp, divergent spines.

Two types: Bruhat goksur and laghu gokshura, Therapeutic actions are same for both.

Chemical Constituents

Two alkaloids that cause limb paralysis (staggers) in sheeps that eat it.

Alkaloids: β-carboline alkaloids harmine, harman (harmane) and norharman (norharmane). The alkaloid content of dried foliage is about 44 mg/kg. It also shows presence of other type of alkaloids such as isochinoline and pyrazol.

Volatile oil containing Thymoquinone, p-cymene and pinene

Other constituents are resin, tannin, fixed oil 3.5% and fairly large amount of nitrates.

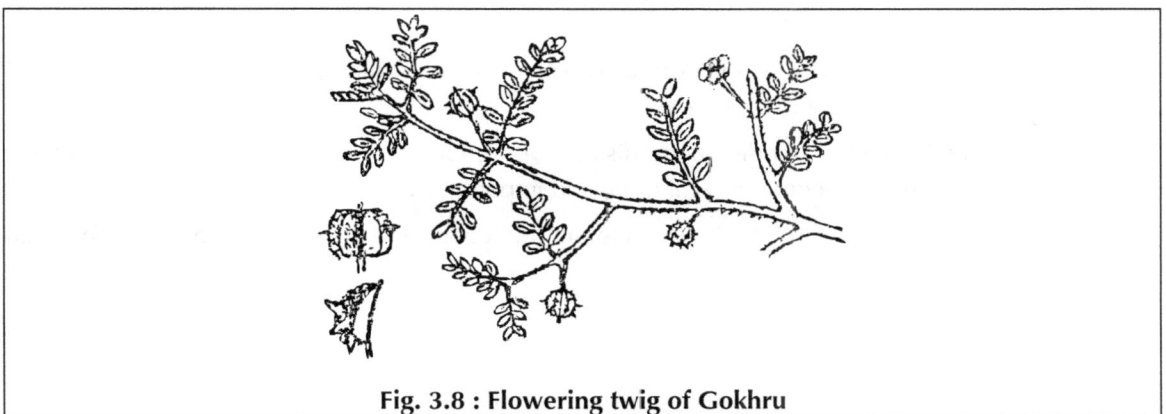

Fig. 3.8 : Flowering twig of Gokhru

Standards of Quality

Loss on Drying	:	≯ 5.0%
Foreign Organic Matter	:	≯ 2.0%
Total ash	:	≯ 11.0%
Acid in ash	:	≯ 01.0%
Water Soluble Extractives	:	≮ 15.0%
Alcohol Soluble Extractives	:	≮ 03.0%

Ayurvedic Properties

Rasa	:	Madhur
Guna	:	Guru, Snigdha
Veerya	:	Sheet
Vipak	:	Madhur

Pharmacological Effect

Circulatory system: Cardio tonic, anti inflammatory and helps in haemorrhagic disorders. Used in low appetite, piles and helminthiasis.

Digestive system: Stomachic, astringent, anthelmintic but laxative in large dose. Therefore used in low appetite, piles and helminthiasis.

Nervous system: Analgesic and vatashamak. Therefore used in neutral debility, painful conditions and vata disorders.

Respiratory system: Expectorant, therefore used for coughs and asthma.

Reproductive system: An aphrodisiac and helps in conception, useful in preventing abortion, vaginal disorders, impotency and post natal discharge.

Urinary system: Diuretic-dissolves calculi and amorphous calculi. Therefore useful urinary calculi, dysuria and cystitis.

Traditional Uses

Fresh leaves and stem powder - kept in cold water produces thick paste which is tasteless and good remedy for gonorrhoea and dysuria.

Fruits - Diuretic, antispasmodic, aphrodisiac. Decoctions good for urinary local irritations. Given for spermatorrhoea, incontinence of urine and impotency cases.

Fruits - anti-arthritic, cooling, tonic, expectorant and good for early conception. Good for renal calculi and kidney diseases.

Dosage

Fruit powder	2.5 - 5 gm
Decoction	60 - 100 ml

Market Products

1) **Bonnisan:** Himalaya Drug Company, Bangalurue

2) **Bodylotion capsule:** Jay Pronow Ayurvedic Pharmaceuticals.

Preparations: Gokshuradi churna, Avaleha, Auggulu, Kwatha, Dashamoolarista, Amrutarishta, Livomin tablets.

Trikantakadi churna, Ghruta, Laghu Pancha Mooladi kwatha, Churna.

Precautions

Contraindications: Dryness. Caution during pregnancy as foetus moves downwards.

GUDMAR

Synonyms

Madhu nashini, Merasingi, Gudmar bootee.

Biological Source

This consists of the leaves of a perennial woody climber plant known as *Gymnema sylvestre* R. Br. Family: Asclepiadaceae.

Description of Herb

Leaves: Simple, 2 to 5 cm long, opposite, ovate a elliptic covered with hairs all over the surface non-glandular trichomes are present on both surface of leaf.

Flower: Small yellow coloured in the four of umbellate cymes.

Useful part: Leaves and Roots

Cultivation

It is occasionally cultivated for medicinal purpose. Plant can be propagated through cuttings and by sowing seeds.

Collection

The leaves are collected after 1 year of cultivation. They are shade dried. The roots are collected in summer, washed and cut into pieces and dried.

Macroscopic Characters

Colour : Green

Odour : Pleasant and aromatic odour

Taste : Tasteless, bitterish

Size : 3 - 5 × 1 - 2 cm

Shape : Elliptic or ovate with acute or acuminate apex

Fig. 3.9 : Gudmar herb

The leaves when chewed have remarkable property of paralysing the taste glands for few hours against sweet and bitter taste.

Macroscopic Characters (Stem)

Colour : Greyish black (yellowish)

Odour : None

Taste : Bitter

Shape : Cylindrical

Fracture : Fibrous

Chemical Constituents

The leaves contain pentriacontane, hentriacontane, phytin, α and β chlorophylls, resin, tartaric acid, formic acid, butyric acid, mucilage inositol, quercitol, gymnemic acids (anti-sweet compounds), the mixture of triterpene saponines and arthraquinone derivatives.

The plant is reported to contain alkaloids, betain, choline and trimethylamine in the leaves. Lupeol, β-amyrin, stigmesterol are also present in the leaves.

Standards of Quality

Total ash : ≯ 15.0%
Acid insoluble ash : ≯ 06.0%
ASE : ≮ 05.0%
WSE : ≮ 20.0%
LOD : ≯ 14.0%

Ayurvedic Properties

Rasa : Kasaya, Tikta
Vipak : Katu
Veerya : Ushna
Guna : Laghu, Rooksha
Doshaghna : Kaph vat shamak

Pharmacological Action

It shows astringrnt, stomachic, stimulant, laxative and diuretic action. It causes insignificant reduction in blood sugar level hence can be used as antidiabetic. It also shows weight lowering properties.

Uses

Local : In skin disease (in leproxy)

Internal uses: Digestive system : It is used in cases of Hyper acidity, Anaemia, Jaundice, Indigestion dysentary, diarrhoea.

Circulatory system: In cases of chronic fever, rheumetism as an cardiac tonic.

Respiratory system: In cough, cold allergy rhimitis lower respiratory tract infection.

In cases of diabetis decoction is used with honey.

Traditional Uses

a) Root decoction is used in snake bite.
b) In cases of fever and cough leaves decotion is given internally.
c) It is also used as a good cardiac tonic.
d) In asthamatic conditions seed powder is used internally.
e) Leaves triturated and mixed with castor oil are applied to swollen glands.

Dosage

Decoction: 40 to 80 ml.
Powder: 1 to 3 gm
Extract: 1 to 2 gm

Kalpa

Guduchadi churna, Guduchadi kwath, Guduchiloha, Amritarishta, Guduchstaila.

Substitutes

Gymnema hersutum: *Gymnema montanum* are substituted for genuine gymnema.

Market Products

1) **Diabe :** Bacfo Pharmaceutical (India) Ltd., Defence Colony, New Delhi.

GULWEL

Synonyms

Tinospora, Giloe, Amrita, Guduchi.

Biological Source

These are the dried leaves and stem pieces of woody climber *Tinospora cordifolia*, Miers belonging to family Menispermaceae. It contains not less than 0.02 % of cordifolioside.

Geographical Source

It is found in deciduous and dry forests of India. It is spread throughout India from Kuman to Assam, Bihar, Kokan and also in Sri Lanka and Indonesia.

Cultivation and Collection

It usually grows in tropical dry areas and does not tolerate moist and humid climate. It can be grown under varying climatic conditions. It is habitated throughout tropical India ascending to an altitude of 500 metres in the temperature range of 25 to 40°C. It thrives well in almost all types of soils. Sandy loam soil, rich in organic matter with good drainage is found to be good for higher yield of crop. Propagated by using stout stem cuttings. It is cultivated at onset of monsoon during May - June.

It can be easily intercropped with neem, mango and coconut.

As it is a perennial crop, periodical weeding is carried out so as to keep the crop weed free. One manual weeding should be done to keep weeds under check in early stage of growth i.e. after 20 - 30 days and during the remaining period of crop growth. 3 - 4 weedings may be sufficient to keep weeds under check.

The plants are harvested for stem and leaves. The leaves are collected when the plants are matured enough, and the stems (stout) are collected by cutting.

The collected stems are cut into small pieces. They are made free of adhered impurities, if any, and then leaves and the stem-cuttings are shade-dried and are placed in dry places.

On an average, about 9 to 10 quintals of stems are obtained per hectare of land.

Macroscopic Characters

Colour	:	Grayish black
Odour	:	None
Taste	:	Bitter
Size	:	3 to 5 cm in length and 3 to 8 mm in diameter
Shape	:	Cylendrical
Fracture	:	Fibrous

Fig. 3.10 (a) : Gulwel herb

Fig. 3.10 (b) : Pieces of stems of Tinospora

Chemical Constituents

It consists of tinosporine, tinosporic acid, tinosporol, giloin, gilonin, berberine, syringin, cordifolioside A ($C_{22}H_{32}O_{13}$) tinosporidine, tinosporoside, tinosporaside. etc. The bitter principles identified are chasmanthin, palmarin and columbin. The stems are rich in proteins, starch, calcium and phosphorus.

Tinosporoside   Tinosporaside   Cordifolioside A

Standards of Quality

FOM	:	≯ 2.0%
ASE	:	≮ 1.5%
WSE	:	≮ 9.0%
Ash	:	≯ 10.0%
Acid insoluble ash	:	≯ 03.0%
Loss on drying	:	≯ 10.0%

Ayurvedic Properties

Rasa	:	Tikta, Katu, Kashaya
Vipak	:	Madhur
Veerya	:	Ushana
Guna	:	**Fresh:** Snigdha, Mrudu
		Dried: Ruksha, Laghu, Mrudu
Doshaghna	:	Tridoshaghana

Uses

It is used in general debility, pyrexia and skin diseases. It is effective in prevention of fibrosis. Also, used in rheumatoid arthritis, jaundice and in diabetes. It is effectively used in viral hepatitis.

Substitute : *Tinospora malabarice* is the substitute for T. corlifolia.

Traditional Uses

The drug has been used in traditional medicine since ancient times for its ability to impart youthfulness, vitality and longevity. For these qualities, it is also referred to as *'Amrita'*. Now a days, the drug is gaining popularity due to its potent immunostimulant activity. It is also referred as *"Rasayan dravya"* in Ayurveda for these properties.

Market Products

Sanjivini Gutika: Amruta Guggul, Chavanprashowleh.

Bonnisan: Himalaya Drug Company.

Runalaya: Himalaya Drug Company.

Immunocare: Bacfo Pharmaceutical (India) Ltd., New Delhi.

Dosage

Powder: 1 - 3 gm

Decoction: 40 - 80 ml

Kalp

Guduchiloha, Amritarishta, Guduche taila

KALMEGH

Synonyms
Kirayat, Bhui-nimb.

Biological Source
This consists of dried leaves. Whole plant of *Andrographis paniculata* belonging to family Acanthaceae.

Geographical Source
It is found throughout India, specifically in Maharashtra, Karnataka, Uttar Pradesh, Tamil Nadu, Andhra Pradesh and Madhya Pradesh.

Description of Herb
It is a 30 cm to 1 metre annual herb.

- **Stem** : It is quadrangular, smooth on the lower side and hairy in upper part stems are much branched.
- **Leaves** : Leaves are opposite 4 to 6 cm long and 1 to 2 cm broad, short petioled.
- **Flowers** : Small in racemes, they are whitish pink in colour. It flowers in the month of September to December.
- **Fruits** : Fruit capsules are linear, oblong or elliptic 2 cm long and 3 mm broad; newly bearing capsules are hairy, and on maturity turns smooth.
- **Seeds** : Seeds are sub-quadrate, brownish or creamy yellow.
- **Parts used** : Whole plant.

Cultivation
It is cultivated in shady waste lands under hot and humid condition. Propagation is through seeds. Vegetative propagation is also possible. After four to five months of planting, at the time of flower initiation, entire plant is harvested.

Collection of Kalmegh
The harvested material is collected, shade dried and powered.

Macroscopic Characters

- **Colour** : Leaves are dark green, while flowers are rose coloured.
- **Odour** : Odourless
- **Taste** : Intensely bitter
- **Size** : Leaves 7 × 2.5 cm, flowers 1.8 cm in length.
- **Shape** : Leaves are lanceolate and petiolate and with entire margin and acuminate apex.

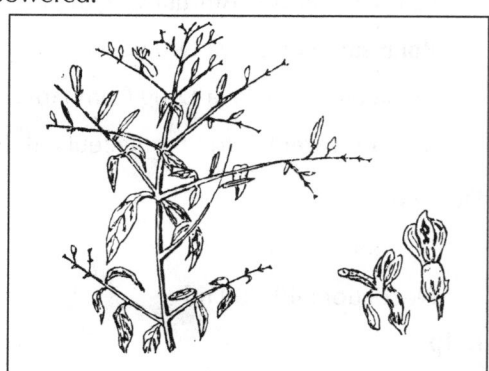

Fig. 3.11 : Kalmegh flowering twig

Chemical Constituents

Kalmegh contains bitter principles andrographolide, a bicyclic diterpenoid lactone and kalmeghin.

Andrographolide

Standards of Quality

Ash	: Not more than 20.0 %
Acid-insoluble ash	: Not more than 5.1 %
Foreign organic matter	: Not more than 2.0 %
Alcohol-soluble extractive	: Not less than 24 %
Water-soluble extractive	: Not less than 20 %

Ayurvedic Properties

Rasa	:	Tikta
Vipak	:	Katu
Veerya	:	Ushna
Guna	:	Laghu, Rooksha
Doshaghna	:	Kaphapittaghana

Pharmacological Uses

It is used as anthelmintic, bitter tonic, hepatoprotective and also as febrifuge.

Traditional Uses

(a) Chronic fever; rheumatic fever: Kept for whole night infusion of Kirayat + Camphor + Shilajeet + Honey taken early morning for seven days proved to be useful.

(b) Colitis and pari in abdomen : Swaras of kirayat along with powdered pepper, black salt and asofotordies is useful.

(c) Hyperacidity: Decotion of kirayat and bhringraj along with honey is useful.

(d) Decoction of kirayat in cases (Hareze poison)

Substitutes

As kalmegh is substituted with *Andrographis echioides*, found in tropical India and in dry districts of Maharashtra, Rajasthan and Tamil Nadu.

Kalpa

Kalmegh Taralsatwa (Liquid extract)

Dosage

Powder:	1 to 2 gm
Liquid extract:	5 to 10 ml
Decoction:	20 to 40 ml
Drawasatura:	0.5 to 1 ml

Market Products

1) **Stimuliv:** Franeo – Indian Pharmaceuticals, Mumbai – 11.
2) **Optiliv:** Envin Bioceuticals Pvt. Ltd., Saharanpur (UP).

KANHER

Synonyms

Shatkumbha, Nerium, Oleander.

Biological Source

It consists of roots and root bark of plant *Nerium indicum* belonging to family Apocynaceae.

Geographical Source

It is found in Himalayas from Kashmir to Nepal upto an altitude of 2100 m. also found in Uttarpradesh, South India and Central India.

Description of Herb

A large, evergreen milky shrub.

Leaves : 10 to 15 cm long, shortly stalked, dark green with hard midrib.

Flowers : Flowers are red or white in colour having characteristic smell, appearing in bundles.

Fruits : Appearing as 8 to 10 cm flat long pods. Containing greyish, hairy seeds. It flowers in summer and rainy season and bears fruits in winter.

Types : There are two varieties :
   (a) White flowered
   (b) Red flowered

Part used: Root, Root bark

Cultivation and Collection

It is found wild all over India, and usually collected from there. It is not cultivated for commercial purpose.

Macroscopic Characters

- **Colour** : Yellowish brown
- **Odour** : Characteristic
- **Taste** : Intensly bitter
- **Size** : 10 - 15 cm
- **Shape** : Cylindrical, elongated

Fig. 3.12 : Kanher flowering twig

Chemical Constituents

It contains toxic principles as neriodorin and karabin. Petroleum extract gives constituents as plumericin, α-amyrin, β-sitosterol; fresh leaves contains betulinic acid, ursolic acid, betulin and oleanolic acid.

Ayurvedic Properties

- **Rasa** : Katu, Tikta, Kasaya
- **Vipak** : Katu
- **Veerya** : Ushna
- **Guna** : Laghu, Rooksha, Tikshna
- **Doshaghna** : Kaphaghana, Vataghana

Pharmacological Action

All parts of plants are poisonous. It shows powerful diuretic action, cardiac tonic, shows abortifacient action. Lower dosage also shows analgeric, anti-inflammatroy and analgeric activity.

Traditional Uses

a) Paste of roots is used for external application in cases of hemorrhoids, leprosy, ulcers on penis, choncres.
b) Fresh juice of leaves used as eye drops in ophthalmic cases.
c) Decoction of leaves is used for cleaning wounds.
d) In cases of headache, root powder is used externally for application.
e) In cases of snakebites and other powerful venamous bites, root paste is applied at the site of sting, or decoction of root or leaf extract is given in small doses or according to the weight of the patient.
f) In toxic condition *ghee* is used as *antidot*.

Dosage

Powder: 30 to 125 mg

Kalp

Karviradi Talia, Karviryog.

KUTKI

Synonyms
Krushnabheda, Shatparna, Indian gentian.

Biological Source
It consists of dried rhizomes of the plant *Picrorrhiza kurroa* belonging to family Scrophulariaceae, cut in small pieces and freed from attached root-lets. It contains not less than 5.0 % of Kutkin on dried basis.

Geographical Source
It is found well distributed in the upper Himalayas from Kashmir to Sikkim – naturally also in Punjab, Uttar Pradesh and China.

Description of Herb
It is more or less hairy perennial herb.

- **Stem** : It is woody shizome, 15 to 25 cm long, covered with thin layers of leaves.
- **Leaves** : 5 to 10 cm long; serrate margins, coriaceous with rounded tips, base is narrowed into winged sheathing petioles.
- **Flowers** : 5 to 10 cm whitish, purple colour, flowers are diamorphic; appear in long spikes, ciliated.
- **Fruit** : 1.25 cm long oval shaped.
- **Roots** : 1 to 1.5 cm in diamter, 15 to 25 cm long, greyish coloured with transverse cracks; internally black coloured with strong bitter smell.

Parts used: Dried rhizomes

Cultivation and Collection
Usually it is collected from naturally growing plant. May be cultivated at an altitude of 2000 to 4500 m. It can be propagated by seeds and vegetatively by using rhizomes (stored). It bears flowers in the month of June and July and attains maturity in the month of August-September.

Macroscopic Characters

- **Colour** : The rhizomes are deep greyish-brown in colour, externally white, blackish internally with whitish-wood.
- **Odour** : Slight and unpleasant.
- **Taste** : Bitter.
- **Size** : 3 to 5 cm in length and 0.5 to 1 cm in diameter.

Fig. 3.13 : Kutki herb

Shape : Cylindrical pieces with longitudinal wrinkles and annulations at the tip.

Features : Conical buds and stems along with the roots also constitute the drug. The roots are longitudinally wrinkled with transverse cracks. Roots are grey to brown in colour. Fracture is tough.

Chemical Constituents

The drug consists of glycosides as Picroside I, Picroside II, and Kutkoside. It also contains mannitol, kutkiol, kutkisterol a bitter principle as picrorhizin is also found.

$$C_6H_5 - CH = CHCOO - \underset{\underset{CH_2OH}{|}}{\overset{\overset{OH}{|}}{C}} - \underset{OCH_3}{\text{benzene ring}} - O\text{-Glucose}$$

Kutkin

Standards of Quality

FOM	: ≯ 2.0%
ASE	: ≮ 15%
WSE	: ≮ 25.0%
Total Ash	: ≯ 6.0%
Acid Insoluble Ash	: ≮ 1.0%
LOD	: ≯ 5.0%

Ayurvedic Properties

Rasa	: Tikta
Vipak	: Katu
Veerya	: Sheet
Guna	: Laghu, Rooksha
Doshaghna	: Kaphapittaghana, Vatavardhak

Pharmacological Uses

It is bitter stomachic, laxative and in large doses cathartic, have beneficial effect in dropsy. The root is also used in liver diseases, spleenomegaly and anaemia.

Traditional Uses

(a) In Jaundise decoction of picrorrhiza along with honey or sugar.

(b) In chronic fever its decoction along with honey and pipper longum is proved to be useful.

(c) In vomitting and hicups, powder along with honey is administered.

(d) In fever, powdered picrorrhiza, sugar along with luckwarm water is useful.

(e) Powdered picrorrhiza is good authelmentic.

(f) In anaemia and cirrhosis decoction of 25 to 50 ml is used.

(g) In leprosy its decoction is useful.

Dosage

Powder: 0.5 to 1 gm

as Laxative: 1 to 3 gm

Kalp

Arogyavardhani; Katukadya taila; Tiktadikwathi; Tikatadighrut.

Adultrants

Gentiana kurroo is adultrated with Picrorrhiza kuro.

Market Products

1) **Herbohep:** Lupin Herbal Laboratory, Mumbai.

2) **Purin:** Himalaya Drug Company.

LODHRA

Synonyms

Jirnapatra, Hasti lodhra.

Biological Source

It consists of dried bark of plant *Symplocos racemosa* belonging to Family Symplocaceae.

Geographical Source

It is found in plains and lower hills of Bengal, Assam and Myanmar, forests of Chota Nagpur, in Kerala – Malabar and parts of Kokan.

Description of Herb

It is a small evergreen tree of about 5 to 7 metre in height.

Leaves	:	8 to 15 cm long and ½ to 1 cm broad, oblong elliptic, dark green above with slightly hairy midrib.
Flowers	:	Appear in racemes, small whitish at first and turn yellow later having fragrance.
Fruits	:	Fruit 1 to 1.5 cm long, hard, purplish black in colour containing 3 to 4 seeds.
Bark	:	Hard, pinkish or reddish grey in colour.
Parts used	:	Bark
Types	:	It has two types (a) Red (b) White

Macroscopic Characters (bark)

Colour	:	Pinkish, reddish
Taste	:	Astringent and bitter
Odour	:	Odourless
Size	:	10 to 15 cm in length
		2 to 3 cm in width.

Fig. 3.14 : Lodhra herb

Chemical Constituents

It contains mainly three alkaloids as loutrine, colloturine, loturidine and quinovin or kinovin.

Ayurvedic Properties

Rasa	:	Kashaya
Vipak	:	Katu
Veerya	:	Sheeta
Guna	:	Laghu, Rooksha
Doshaghna	:	Khapapittaghana

Traditional Uses

(a) In dental cases decoction of lodhra along with punarnava

(b) In leucorrhia decoction or powder lodhra along with ginger paste is useful.

(c) In inflammation, paste of bark is applied externally.

(d) In pimples, paste of bark along with coriender and calamus is applied.

(e) In chronic fever, lodhra, chandan, pippali, ativisha powder along with sugar, ghee, honey and milk is found to be useful.

Uses

Potent remedy for inflammation and cleaning uterus. It is also given in menorrhagia and uterine disorders, ulcers of vagina, miscarriage and abortion. It has cooling and astringent properties.

Dosage

Powder : 1 to 3 gm

Decocation : 50 to 100 mg

Kalp

Lodhrasav; Lodhrakwath

Market Product

(1) **Senorita:** Centour Pharmaceuticals Pvt. Ltd., Vakola Santacruz, Mumbai-55.

(2) **Brahmdine:** J & J Dechane Labs. Pvt. Ltd., Hydrabad.

(3) **Styplon:** Himalaya Drug Company, Banaglurue.

MANDUKPARNI

Synonyms
Manduki, Gotu Kola.

Biological Source
This consists of dried aerial parts of *Centella asiatica* belonging to Family Umbelliferae and contain not less than 0.5 % of asiaticoside on dried basis.

Geographical Source
It grows in wet and marshy areas in India, Sri Lanka, Indonesia, Australia upto an altitude of 650 metres.

Description of herb
It is annual or a perennial creeper.

- **Leaves** : Long petiolate. Entire, orbicular 1 to 6 cm in diameter, petiols are 7 to 15 cm in length.
- **Flowers** : Sessile flowers. Umbel Infloresence. It bears 3 – 4 pink flowers.
- **Fruits** : Small 2 to 3 cm in size.
- **Roots** : Fibrouss roots

Fig. 3.15 : Mandukparni herb

Macroscopic Characters
- **Colour** : Greyish green
- **Odour** : Characteristic
- **Taste** : Bitter and sweet
- **Useful part** : Whole plant mainly leaves.

Extra Features
The stems are red and has long internodes. At each internode it bears roots, leaves, flowers and fruits.

Ayurvedic Properties
- **Rasa** : Tikta, Keshaya
- **Vipak** : Madhur
- **Veerya** : Sheet
- **Guna** : Laghu
- **Tridoshaghana** : Mainly Kaphapittaghana

Chemical Constituents

It contains saponins as asiaticoside and madecassoside, bramhoside about 1.0% and bramhinoside glucose and rhamnose.

	R_1	R_2
Asiatic acid:	–H	–OH
Madecassic acid	–OH	–OH
Asiaticoside	–H	–O.gl.gl.Rha
Madecassoside	–OH	–O.glu.glu.Rha

Standards of Quality

Total Ash	: ≯ 24.0%
Acid Insoluble Ash	: ≯ 5.0%
FOM	: ≯ 2.0%
LOD	: ≯ 12.0%
ASE	: ≮ 6.0%
WSE	: ≮ 15.0%

Traditional Uses

As nervine tonic, sedative, anti-auxiety and anti-stress remedy.

Uses

Local – In leprosy, external application of herbal paste proves to be useful and also in wound healing.

Internal – Nervine tonic, sedative ankieolitic.

Dosage

Swaras : 10 to 20 ml

Kalp

Sarasvatarishta, Sarasvatghrut, Bhrami taila.

Market Products

1) **Gariforte:** Himalaya Drug Company, Bangalurue.
2) **Mental:** Himalaya Drug Company, Bangalurue.

MANJISHTA

Synonyms

Rakta samanga, Rakta pushpi, Indian maddar.

Biological Source

It consists of dried stems of *Rubia cordifolia* belonging to family Rubiaceae.

Geographical Source

All over India upto an altitude of 2700 metres Northwestern Himalayas, Nilgiris, mostly hilly parts of India.

Description of Herb

It is branched perennial climber.

Stem : Stems are cylindrical to quadrangular, reddish pink in colour.

Leaves : Leaves are heart shaped, 5 to 10 cm long. Its upper surface is rough, lower part is hairy, smooth with long petiole.

Flowers : Flowers are small, yellowish in colour. Scaly about 0.3 to 2.5 cm long.

Fruits : Rounded, blackish or light violet coloured with light black coloured seeds.

Roots : Reddish coloured, long about 4 to 8 cm long.

Parts used: Roots, leaves

Cultivation and Collection

Usually collected from wild grown palnts and not commercially cultivated.

Macroscopic Characters

Colour : Brown to purple coloured

Odour : None

Taste : Slightly bitter

Size : 4 to 5 cm × 0.5 cm

Shape : Stems are cylindrical, slender and wiry

Extra features : Stems have longitudinal cracks.

Fig. 3.16 : Manjishtha herb

Chemical Constituents

It contains glycosides manjisthin, purpurin, resin and red dye rubiadin, salt of lime, garacin, alizarin and xanthine.

Alizarin

Standards of Quality

Water soluble extractives	:	Not less than 20.0 %
Alcohol soluble extractives	:	Not less than 04.0 %
Ash	:	Not more than 10.0 %
Loss on drying	:	Not more than 5.0 %

Ayurvedic Properties

Rasa	:	Tikta, Kashaya, Madhur
Vipak	:	Katu
Veerya	:	Ushna
Guna	:	Guru, Rooksha
Doshaghna	:	Kapha pittaghana

Pharmacological Uses

The root is emmenagogue, astringent and diuretic.

Traditional Uses

(a) In leprosy and rhumatic conditions decoction of Manjishta, Triphala, Burberris, Neem, Picrorrhiza, Tinosporia is useful.

(b) Menstrual disorders: Infusion of 25 gm manjishta is useful.

(c) In cases of diarrhoea/dysentery, paste of manjishta and lodhra (*Symplocos racemosa*) along with honey is given.

(d) For blood purification, decoction of manjishta is very useful, it helps to gain lustre and glow of skin.

(e) Stems are used in Cobra-bite, scorpion sting.

(f) Paste made of root along with honey is applied over swelling, skin diseases in ulcers, leudoderrna, freckles and pimples.

Dosage

Decoction : 50 to 100 ml

Powder : 1 to 4 gm

Kelp

Manjishtadi kwath; Mahamanjishtadi kwath; Manjishtadi Arka; Manjishtamathana; Manjishtafant.

Adulteration

Roots of manjishta are reddish, long. They are mixed with similar long roots and are coloured with red clay or colour.

Market Products

1) **G-32:** Alarsin Pharmaceuticals, MIDC Andheri, Mumbai-93.

METHI

Synonyms

Methika, Fenugreek.

Biological Source

It consists of whole plant and seeds of *Trigonella foenum – graecum* belonging to family Leguminosae.

Geographical Source

It is found growing wild in Punjab and Kashmir and all over India.

Description of Herb

It is small annual herb found all over India.

Leaves : Leaves are small compound, 7 – 10 cm long. Entire, lanceolate or oblong, with three leaflets.

Flowers : Sessile, axillary, yellow coloured.

Fruits : Appearing in pods, 7 to 10 cm long containing 10 to 20 seeds.

Seeds : Brownish yellow, or having an oblique furrow along the part of length.

During the month of January to March it flowers and bears the pods.

Cultivation and Collection

Methika is a very familiar herb and is cultivated all over India easily. It is propagated from seeds. It is widely used as leafy vegetable hence cultivated regularly in all parts as seasonal crop.

Parts used: Whole plant, seeds

Type: Wild

The wild variety is used as fodder for farm animals (Lussar grass).

Macroscopic Characters (Seeds)

Colour : Yellowish brown or olive green

Odour : Peculiar, aromatic

Taste : Slightly bitter

Shape : Irregularly rhomboidal, oblong.

Fig. 3.17 : Methi Herb

Chemical Constituents

Seeds contain alkaloid trigoneline, choline, saponin, essential oil, prolamine, mucilage, and a colouring substance.

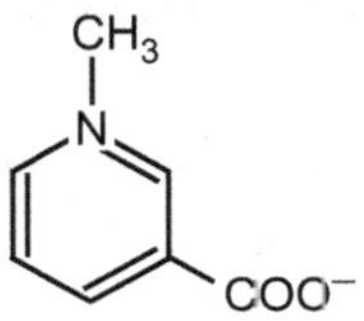

Trigoneline

Ayurvedic Properties

Rasa	:	Katu
Vipak	:	Katu
Veerya	:	Ushna
Guna	:	Laghu, Snigdha
Doshaghna	:	Vatakaphaghana, Raktpittakar.

Pharmacological Action

Demulcent, aromatic, diuretic, emollient, astringent, carminative, lactagogue.

Chemical Constituents

Fixed oil of seeds contain fatty acid. Other constituents are Palacitrin, isobutrin, monospermoside, coreopsin, and palasonin.

Standards of Quality

FOM	:	≯ 2.0%
Total ash	:	≯ 8.0%
Acid insoluble ash	:	≯ 0.5%
ASE	:	≮ 20.0%
WSE	:	≮ 25.0%
LOD	:	≯ 4.0%

Uses

It is used as anthelmintic.

Dosage

Powder: 1 to 3 gm

Traditional Uses

(a) Paste of the herb is applied to reduce swelling.

(b) Its decoction is used in treating leukorrhea.

(c) Seeds are also used as good hair tonic and its paste is applied to scalp in condition of hair loss.

(d) Seeds powder along with other herbs is used postpartum as a good galactogogue.

(e) Seeds powder is also used to reduce obesity.

(f) Daily intake of seed powder as decoction early in the morning helps for reducing sugar levels.

(g) Mucilage produced by soaking seed in water is applied locally over boils, carbuncles and abscesses.

(h) In postpartum condition it is good choice of drug as it promotes ovulation / menstrual flow, help to gain strength.

(i) In burning, micturation infusion of dried seeds along with honey is useful.

(j) In diarrhoea and dysentery, fresh extract of leaves along with juice of black resins is given.

Kalp

Methikamodak.

Market Products

1) **B.Slim Capsules:** BACFO Pharmaceuticals (India) Ltd., E-27 Defence colony, New Delhi-24.

2) **Diabetix Capsules:** Jupiter Pharmaceuticals Ltd., APC Road, Sealdah, Kolkata.

MULETHI

Synonyms

Glycyrrhiza, Liquorice root.

Biological Source

Mulethi consists of dried, unpeeled roots and stolons of *Glycyrrhiza glabra* belonging to family Leguminosae.

Geographical Source

It is commercially cultivated on a large scale in Spain, England, Sicily, Siberia, Turkistan. It is also grown in India in Punjab, Andman Island, Sindh and Sub-Himalaya tract.

Description of Herb

Mulethi is a perennial shrub growing upto 1 to 5 metres.

Roots : Roots are longer. Reddish yellow or dark brown in colour from outer side, when peeled internal colour is yellow, and is coarsely fibrous.

- **Leaves** : Leaves are compound, pinnate, alternate, leaflet are oblong shaped with 4 to 7 pairs of leaflets.
- **Flowers** : Flowers are small pale to violet in colour and papilionaceous.
- **Fruit** : These are 2 to 2.5 cm long pods containing 2 to 5 seeds with kidney shaped seeds.

Types

Glycyrrhiza glabra var. typica (Spanish liquorice)

Glycyrrhiza glabra var. glandulifera (Russian liquorice)

Glycyrrhiza glabra var violacea (Persian liquorice)

Cultivation

Propagation is done with young pieces of stolons during the month of March. The roots are harvested 3 to 4 yrs after plantation.

Part used: Peeled or unpeeled roots.

Collection

The Rhizomes and roots are dug up in October. Washed drug is sun dried.

Macroscopic Characters

- **Colour** : Unpeeled-yellowish-brown or dark brown externally, and yellowish internally, while the peeled liquorice is pale yellow in colour.
- **Odour** : Faint and characteristic.
- **Taste** : Sweet.
- **Size** : Length 20 to 50 cm and 2 cm in diameter.
- **Shape** : Cylindrical pieces which are straight may be peeled or unpeeled. Peeled liquorice is angular.
- **Fracture** : It is fibrous in the bark and splintery in wood.

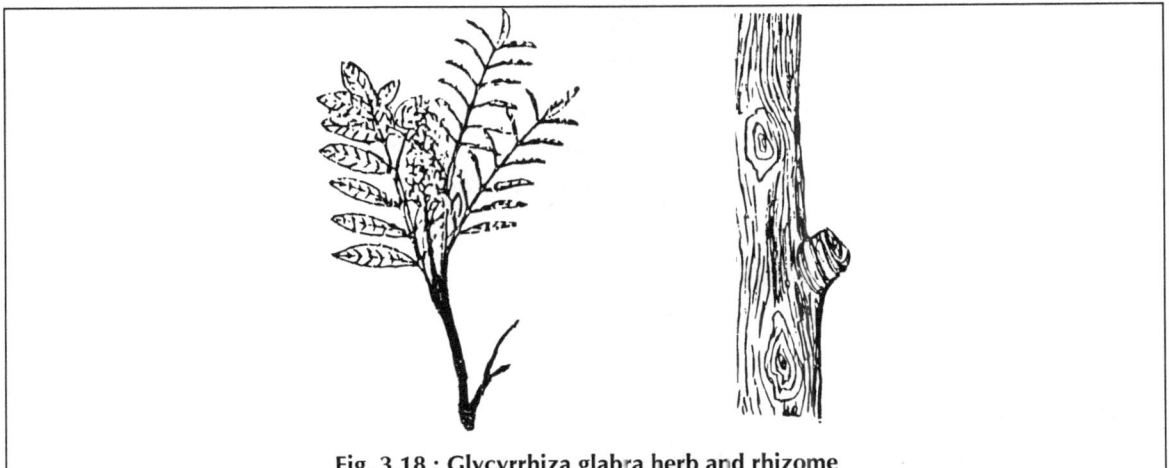

Fig. 3.18 : Glycyrrhiza glabra herb and rhizome

Chemical Constituents

The chief constituent of liquorice is glycyrrhizin which is a potassium and calcium salt of glycyrrhizinic acid. Other constituents of Liquorice are glucose; sucrose; bitter principle glycyramarin resins, asparagin and fat. Glycyrrhetinic acid is the product of Hydrolysis of glycyritizinic acid.

Standards of Quality

Ash:

    (a) Peeled drug   : not more than 6.0 %

    (b) Unpeeled drug   : not more than 10.0 %

Acid insoluble ash:

    (1) Peeled drug   : not more than 1.0 %

    (2) Unpeeled drug   : not more than 2.5 %

Water Soluble Extractions: not less than 20.0 %

Ayurvedic Properties

    Rasa   : Madhur

    Vipak   : Madhur

    Veerya   : Sheeta

    Guna   : Guru and Snigdha

    Doshaghna   : Vat pitta ghana, Kaphavardhak.

Pharmacological Uses

Liquorice shows diuretic, gentle laxative, emmenagogue action, it is used in treatment of rheumatoid arthritis, as anti-inflammatory drug.

Traditional Uses

It is used as expectorant demuleant

a) It is used with rice water.

b) In hi-cough it is administered with honey.

c) As an diuretic with milk.

Kalp

Yashtadichurna; Lavangadichurna; Karpuradichurna.

Dosage

Powder 1 to 4 gm

Adultrents

Manchurian liquorice, Russian liquorice.

Market Products

1) **Glycodin-terp-vasaka:** Alembic, Varodara

PALASH

Synonym

Triparna

Biological Source

It consists of dried seeds, flowers, gum of plant *Butea monosperma* (Syn : *Butea frondosa*) belonging to family Papilionaceae.

Geographical Source

It is found throughout India, from greater part of India, ascending to an altitude of 1000 to 1300 metres.

Description of herb

Small 13 to 15 metre high; medium size tree with crooked trunk.

Stem   : Stem uneven, bark, ash coloured

Leaves : 10 to 20 cm long; broad; compound.

Flowers : Flowers are scarlet, orange coloured in 15 cm Long inflorance; flowers velvety, corolla silvery.

Fruits : Appears in pods of about 15 to 20 cm. Long and 4 cm broad, flat, downy stalked.

Seeds   : Seeds are oval reddish black, compressed papery to somewhat thick.

Gum   : Gum is obtained by making incision on the main stem. The oozing secretion becomes gum like after exposure to air. The gum is also called as "Bengal Kino". Root bark is used to prepare ropes, and flowers are used to prepare natural colour or dye.

Flowers during spring and bears fruits in summer.

Macroscopic Characters

Colour : Reddish black

Odour : Characteristic

Taste : Astringent

Size   : 25 - 40 × 15 - 25 × 1.5 - 2 mm

Shape : Oval flat

Fig. 3.19 : Palash tree (Flowering top)

Chemical Constituents

The root of *Butea monosperma* contains glucose, glycine, aglycedise and an aromatic compound. The flower contains seven flavonoid, glucosides which are as butrin, isobutrin, coreopsin, isocoreopsin, sulfurein, monospermoside, isomonospermoside.

Standards of Quality

FOM	: ≯ 2.0%
Total ash	: ≯ 8.0%
Acid insoluble ash	: ≯ 0.5%
ASE	: ≮ 20.0%
WSE	: ≮ 25.0%
LOD	: ≯ 4.0%

Ayurvedic Properties

Rasa	:	Tikta, Katu, Kashaya
Vipak	:	Katu
Veerya	:	Ushana
Guna	:	Laghu, Rooksha
Flower	:	Madhur vipak; Sheet veerya.
Doshaghna	:	Kaphavataghana, pittakar

Pharamacological Uses

Leaves show diuretic astringent, aphrodisiac properties. Seeds are anthelmentic and laxatives, flowers are tonic.

Traditional Uses

(a) Seed paste along with milk or seed powder along with honey is useful as anthelmentic.

(b) In skin disease paste of seeds in lemon juice is applied externally is very useful.

(c) In snake bite, root paste is given internally as well as applied externally.

(d) In Arthritis, seed paste prepared in honey is applied externally.

(e) Diarrhoea – gum along with sugar is useful.

(f) In case of chronic cough leaves are chewed, juice of leaves is useful.

(g) In dysurea decoction of flowers along with 2 gm of sora is useful.

(h) Decoction of leaves is used as vaginal douche in cases of leukorrhea.

(i) Infusion of seed ash given to ladies promotes conception.

(j) In congested throat sepsis, decoction of leaves is used for gargles.

Adulterants:

These seeds are adulterated with *Butea superba* seeds which are smaller in size.

Dosage

Bark decoction	:	50 to 100 ml
Flower powder	:	3 to 6 gm
Gum resin	:	1 to 3 gm
Seed powder	:	3 to 6 gm

Kalpa

Palashbeejadi churna; Palashksharadighruta; Palashpushpaasav; Krummudgar rasa.

Market Products

1) **Lukole :** Himalaya Drug Company.
2) **J. P. Nikhar Oil:** Jamuna Pharmaceuticals, Delhi.

RASNA

Synonyms

Galanga, Chinese ginger, Lesser galangal.

Biological Source

These are the dried rhizomes of *Alpinia officinarum*, belonging to family Zingiberaceae. The rhizomes are trimmed, washed, cut into segments and dried. They contain not less than 0.5 % of volatile oil. Commercially, these are known as lesser galangal rhizomes, while the greater rhizomes are obtained from *Alpinia galanga*.

Geographical Source

It is cultivated. The drug is found throughout the Eastern Himalayas and in South West India.

Cultivation and Collection

It is a perennial herb, about 1 - 2 m in height, bearing rhizomes. The drug is collected in autumn.

Macroscopic Characters

Colour : The rhizomes are reddish-brown externally and light orange brown internally.

Odour : Characteristically aromatic.

Taste : Aromatic and pungent.

Size : The rhizomes are about 2 - 8 cm in length and 2 cm in thickness.

Shape : They are irregularly branched and marked with fine annulations.

Rhizomes are tough and have a fibrous fracture.

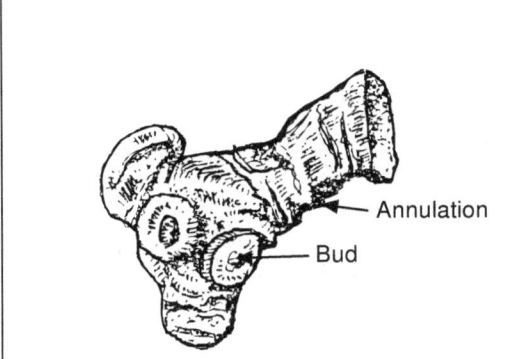

Fig. 3.20 (a) : Galanga rhizome

Fig. 3.20 (b) : Galanga herb

Chemical Constituents

The green rhizomes contain 0.6 % to 1.5 % of volatile oil. The oil contains methyl cinnamate (about 48 %), cineole (about 25 %), camphor and pinene. It also contains resin, oily pungent galangol, alpinol, yellow crystalline substance known as galangin, and di-oxyflavanol. The anti-inflammatory triterpene compounds reported are sorghumol and bochmerd.

Galangin

Standards of Quality

Foreign organic matter	: not more than 2 %
Total ash	: not more than 5 %
Acid-insoluble ash	: not more than 2 %
ASE	: ≮ 6.0%
WSE	: ≮ 13.0%
LOD	: ≯ 2.0%

Chemical Test

Shake about 1 g finely powdered rasna with 60 % alcohol for 10 minutes and filter. Put a drop on filter paper and dry it. Examine the same under ultraviolet light, a bright bluish-white fluorescence is observed.

Ayurvedic Properties

Rasa : Katu
Guna : Laghu, Tikshna
Veerya : Ushna
Vipak : Katu

Uses

Galanga is used as an aromatic, a stimulant and carminative similar to ginger. It has antibacterial properties. In India, it is used in treatment of rheumatism and catarrhal affections.

Substitute

Alpinia galanga (Java galanga or Greater galangal) is similar to the official varieties, but, less pungent. It does not contain flavonoids. The alcoholic extract does not show any fluorescence under ultraviolet light.

Market Products

Ashwagandharishta: Baidyanath, Nagpur.

GARDEN RUE

Synonyms
Sarvadanshtra, Harmal, Satap.

Biological Source
It is whole plant of *Ruta graveolens* belonging to family Rutaceae.

Geographical Source
Found all over India, indigenons to Iran.

Description of Herb
It is a small branching undershrub.

Leaves	:	Small petioled, various segments; glands over it.
Flowers	:	Appearing in inflorescence, yellow coloured, lanceolate, pectinate, abruptly clawed.
Fruits	:	Fruits are small, obtuse, pedicelled. Blackish in colour.
Parts Used	:	Whole plant, specially leaves.

Cultivation and Collection
Usually collected from wild grown. Also commonly cultivated in gardens for its medicinal properties. Can be easily propagated through seeds, but not cultivated commercially.

Macroscopic Characters

Colour	:	Leaves are green in colour.
Odour	:	Strong characteristic and disagreeable.
Taste	:	Acrid

Fig. 3.21 : Twig of Garden Rue

Chemical Constituents
It contains volatile oil consisting of ketone, methyl-n nonyl ketone, glucoside rutin and caumarin.

Standards of Quality

Total ash	:	≯ 10.0%
Acid insoluble ash	:	≯ 2.0%

Ayurvedic Properties

Rasa : Katu, Takta

Vipak : Katu

Veerya : Ushna

Guna : Laghu, Rooksha, Tikshna

Doshaghna : Kaphavataghana, pittavardhak

Pharamacological Action

Antiseptic, stimulant, emmenagogue and abortifacient. Also shows antihypertensive property.

Traditional Uses

(a) It is used as expectrant.

(b) As anthelmentic along with coriander extract.

(c) Externally its paste is used as anti-inflammatory.

(d) Its oil (volatile) is used as diuratic and emmenagogue.

(e) In fever, leaves extract is used for external application.

(f) In cough, leaf extract along with milk (decoction of leaves in milk) is found to be useful.

(g) Fresh leaf paste mixed with honey or brandy is used for external application in first stage of paralysis.

Dosage

Extract: 5 to 10 ml

Powder: 1 to 3 gm

Infusion: 10 to 20 ml

Oil: 1 to 3 drops

SHATAVARI

Synonyms

Shatmuli, Shatpadi, Narayani.

Biological Source

It consists of dried roots and the leaves of the *Asparagus racemosus* belonging to family Liliaceae.

Geographical Source

It is found all over India, especially in North India upto an altitude of 1300 to 1400 m. It is also found distributed in Africa and Australia.

Description of Herb

It is a perennial climbing shrub.

- **Stem** : Triangular, covered with recurved spines.
- **Leaves** : Leaves are linear, green, needle like, appear in bunch of 2 to 6 leaves and are 1.25 to 2.25 cm long.
- **Flowers** : It bears small fragrant white flowers in the form of simple racemes.
- **Fruits** : Small berries of red colour with 1 to 2 seeds.
- **Roots** : The roots are adventitous. Arising from main fleshy, tuberous root and tapering at both ends.

Fig. 3.22 : Shatavari roots

Macroscopic Characters

- **Colour** : Externally, roots are silver white or ash coloured and internally white coloured.
- **Odour** : Odourless
- **Taste** : Bitter followed by sweet taste
- **Shape** : Spindle shaped
- **Type** : Mahasatawa (Asparagus armentosa)

Chemical Constituents

Steroidal glycosides shatavarin I - IV, a polycyclic alkaloid, 9-10 dihydro phenanthrene derivative recemosol.

Shatavarin I

Standards of Quality

Total ash	:	≯ 05.0%
Acid insoluble ahs	:	≯ 0.6%
ASE	:	≮ 05.0%
WSE	:	≮ 34.0%
FOM	:	≯ 2.0%
LOD	:	≯ 03.0%

Ayurvedic Properties

Rasa	:	Madhur, Tikta
Vipak	:	Madhur
Veerya	:	Sheet
Guna	:	Guru, Snigdha, Mrudu
Doshaghna	:	Vaatpittaghana, Kafakar.

Substitutes

Asparagus adscendens and *Asparagns curillus* are substituted for genuine drug in North Indian Markets.

Uses

It is well established galactoguage. Antioxytoxic action has been documented. The roots also have immuno-modulatory effects.

Kalp

Shatavri kulp.

Market Products

1) **Mahanarayan tel:** Baidyanath, Nagpur.
2) **Satavrex granules:** Zandu Pharamaceutical Works, Dadar, Mumbai.

INDIAN SENNA

Synonyms

Markandi, Sonai, Tinnevelley senna, Cassia senna.

Biological Source

It consists of dried leaflets of *Cassia angustifolia or Cassia senna* belonging to family Leguminosae.

Geographical Source

Indian Senna is cultivated and collected in India. Its cultivation is mainly done in Tinnevelley, Madurai and Ramanathapuram districts of Tamil Nadu. Cultivation is attempted in Cudappa district of Andhra Pradesh, and to some extent it is collected from Kutch in Gujarat State and Rajasthan.

Description of Herb

It is a small shrub growing upto 1 or 1.5 metres.

Leaves : Leaves are compound, paripinnate, petiolate about 10 cm long bearing 5 - 8 pairs of leaflets.

Flowers : Flowers are small yellow coloured appearing in bunches.

Fruits : Fruits appears in pod. They are 3 to 8 cm long containing 5 to 8 seeds which are smooth, dark brown in colour.

Types

Arabian senna and Cassia acutifolia.

Useful parts

Leaves, fruits or pods.

Cultivation

It is a seed raise crop and is propagated by broadcasting method. First sowing is done in the month of February to March and second sowing is done in the month of October to November.

Collection

Collection of leaves is carried out after the plant is fully grown. Pods are collected when they attain maturity. So the concentration in the leaves decrease.

Macroscopic Characters

Colour : Yellowish-green

Odour : Slight

Taste : Mucilagenous, bitter and characteristic

Size : 7 to 8 mm in width and 25 to 60 mm in length

Shape : Leaves are lanceolate, entire. Apex is acute with spine at the top. Bases of the leaflets are asymmetrical with transverse lines, more prominent on lower surface, while the trichomes are present on both the surfaces.

Fig. 3.23: Indian senna twig

Chemical Constituents

Indian senna contains two anthraquinone glycosides 2 to 2.5% called as sennoside A and sennoside B. It also contains phytosterol, mucilage, resin, myricyl alcohol, salicylic acid, calcium oxalate, senna contains two napthalene glycoside and 6-hydroxy musidm glycoside.

Sennoside A

Standards of Quality

Foreign Organic Matter	:	≯ 1.0 %
Total ash	:	≯ 12.0 %
Acid insoluble ash	:	≯ 2.5 %
Moisture	:	≯ 12.0 %
Water soluble extractives	:	≮ 27.0 %

Ayurvedic Properties

Rasa	:	Katu, Tikta, Madhur, Kashaya
Vipak	:	Katu
Veerya	:	Ushana
Guna	:	Laghu, Ruksha, Tikshna
Doshaghna	:	Vatanuloman, pittashodhan

Pharmacological Uses

It is used as purgative.

Traditional Uses

(a) It is used as mild pugative (laxative)
(b) It used as anthelmintic for intestinal worms.
(c) It is also used as liver tonic or liver stimulant.
(d) Paste of dried leaves in vinegar is used in leprotic condition.

Dosage

Powder: 1 to 3 gm

Decoction: 28 to 50 ml

Storage

Collected leaves are dried under shade or indoor by spreading them in thin layer. Drying takes place in 7 - 10 days. The leaves are tossed to seperate pods. They are packed into bales under hydraulic pressure. During storage the drug should be protected from sunlight or light.

Market Products

(1) **Pursennid :** Novartis India Ltd., Sandoz House, 8th floor, Shivsagar Estate "B". Anmie Basant Raod, Worli, Mumbai – 18.

(2) **Senade:** Cipla Ltd., 289 Bellasis Road, Mumbai Central, Mumbai 8.

TALISPATRA

Synonyms

Yew, Himalayan yew, Taxus.

Biological Source

This consists of dried leaves, bark and roots of various species of *Taxus*, belonging to family Taxaceae. The four important species with parts used are as under.

1. *Taxus baccata* (English or European yew) mainly leaves.
2. *Taxus brevifolia* (Pacific yew) mainly stem bark.
3. *Taxus canadensis* (Canadian or American yew) Leaves and roots.
4. *Taxus cuspidate* (Japanese yew) leaves.

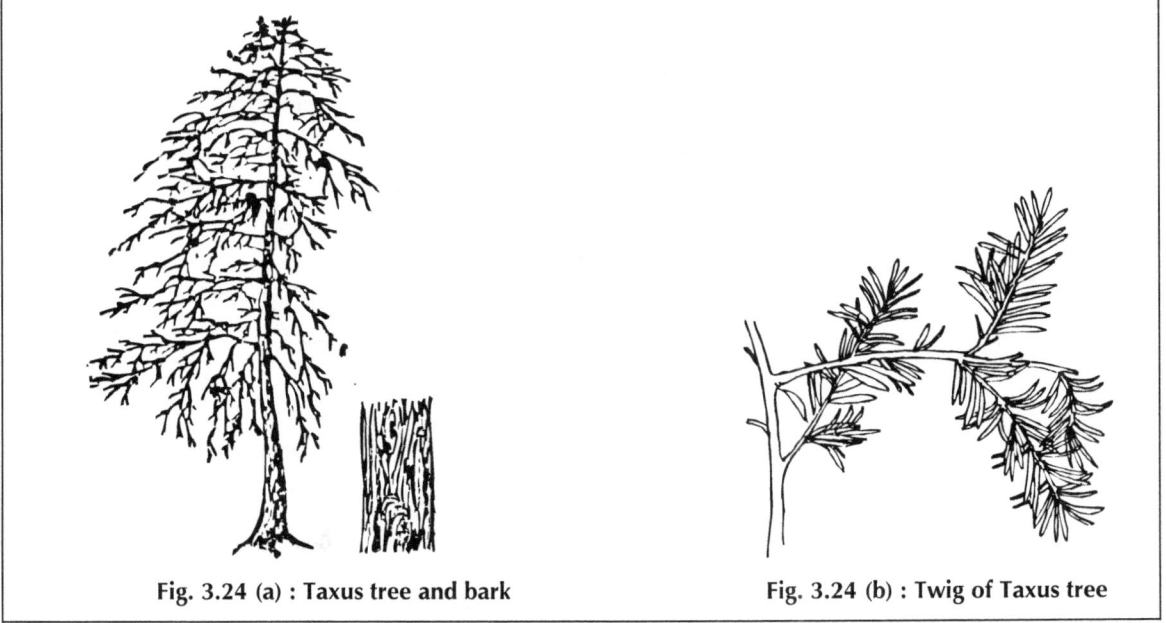

Fig. 3.24 (a) : Taxus tree and bark   Fig. 3.24 (b) : Twig of Taxus tree

Geographical Source

It is very slow growing evergreen gymnospermous tree. Found in India, Canada and America. It is reported in temperate Himalayan region of India upto an altitude of 2000 - 3500 metres.

Morphological Characters

Leaves : **Colour** : Dark shining green

Taste : Bitter

Size : 1 - 3 cm × 1 - 2 mm

Shape : Lanceolate, Flat

Extra features : Leaves are arranged spirally on the stem, leaf bases are twisted to align the leaves in two flat rows on either side of stem, except on erect leading shoots.

Bark of Taxus is thin scaly brown.

Seed cones : Each contain one seed which is 4 - 7 mm surrounded by aril. Arils get matured after 6 - 9 months.

Chemical Constituents

The main constituent Taxol is present in all parts of the plant especially in leaves, roots and bark.

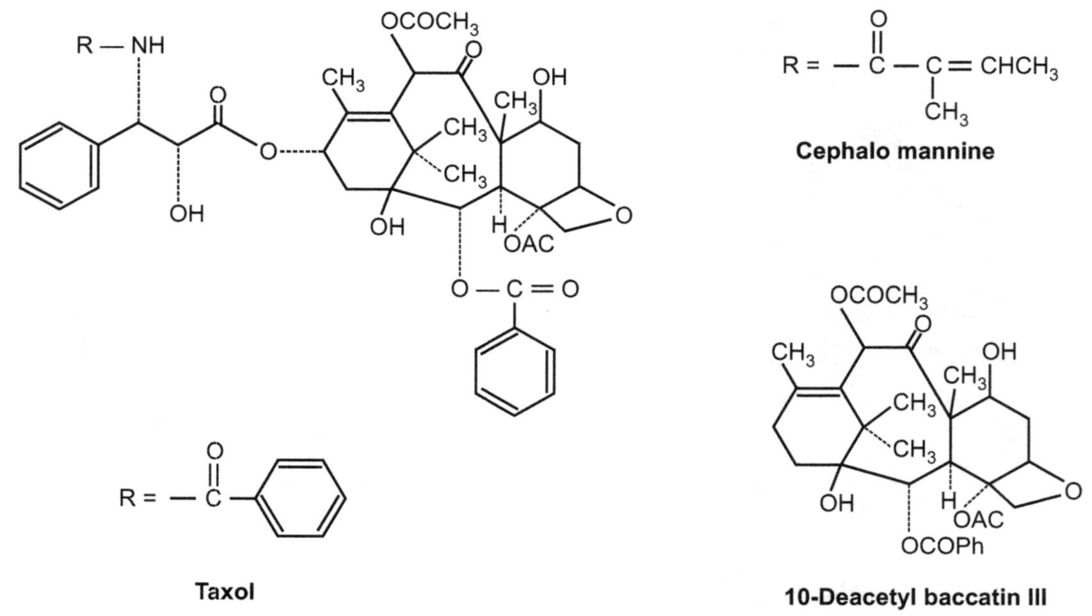

R — NH
OH
O
OCOCH3
CH3
OH
O—C=O
H
OAC
R = —C—C=CHCH3
CH3
Cephalo mannine
R = —C—
Taxol
OCOPh
10-Deacetyl baccatin III

Taxanes are the most important group of chemical constituents and uptil now 40 different Taxane compounds have been found, all of which are diterpenoid structures. Among them three most important members are Taxol, cephalomannine and 10 - deacetyl baccatin. In all species, with little variations, taxol occurs from 0.007 % to 0.01 %. Presently, it is mainly obtained from stem bark of *T. brevifolia*. But the method of isolation is tedious and like vinca, yields are also less. It needs at least 60 years old 3 - 4 trees to get 1 gm of taxol. Yields 50 - 150 mg of taxol from 1 kg dried yew bark. About 10 kg bark is available from an average tree. Considering the slow growing nature of yew tree, it has been already predicted that this will lead to severe ecological problem. Obviously alternative sources, like total synthesis or biotechnological route through tissue culture are also present under development. It has been reported that leaves contain 10-deacetyl baccatin III, which can be comparatively easily converted to Taxol. The leaves can be quickly regenerated after harvesting. Among the various yew species, most of the compounds are anticancer. The most potent compounds include Taxol (containing a rare oxetane ring and amide side chain), cephalo mannine (0.031 %), baccatin – III (0.084 %), and 10 - deacetyl baccatin III.

A derivative of Taxol, called taxotere has been reported to have better bio-availability and pharmacological properties and has been claimed as a promising anticancer agent.

Ayurvedic Properties

Rasa : Tikta

Guna : Laghu, Tikshna

Veerya : Ushna

Vipak : Madhur

Uses

The biological target of Taxol is microtubules produced from α and β-tubulin. The microtubules are responsible for the formation of mitotic spindle necessary for cell division. α and β-tubulin polymerise to give microtubules and for this process microtubule associated proteins (MAP) and guanosine triphosphate (GTP) are necessary. Taxol brings out the polymerisation to microtubules in absence of MAP and GTP. Due to this, microtubule formation is much enhanced which causes detrimental effects on dividing cells which leads to blockade of cell cycle. Eventually, multiple abnormal esters are formed from microtubules and get distributed in cytoplasm. These structures are non-functional. Taxol also inhibits cell migration thus, preventing spread of metastatic cancer cells. Taxol has been approved by USFDA for treatment of refractory ovarian cancer. It has also a promising role against non-small cell lung carcinoma, gastric and cervical cancers and also carcinomas of head, neck, prostate and colon.

Traditional Uses

Leaves and fruits are used as emmenegogue and for antispasmodic effects and also in asthma and epilepsy.

Market Products

1) **Dexofeyn:** Alarsin Pharmaceuticals, A-32 road, MIDC Andheri, Mumbai, 93.

Chapter 4...

ALKALOIDAL DRUGS

NUX VOMICA

Synonyms

Crow-fig, Semen strychni, Nux vomica seed.

Biological Source

Nux vomica consists of dried ripe seeds of *Strychnos nux vomica* Linn, Family Loganiaceae. It should contain not less than 1.2 % of total alkaloids calculated as strychnine.

Geographical Source

It is indigenous to East India and is largely collected from forests in Sri Lanka, Northern Australia and India. It is found abundantly in South India i.e. in Tamil Nadu, Kerala and on Malabar Coast. It is also available in the forests of Bihar, Orissa, Konkan, Mysore and Gorakhpur.

Cultivation and Collection

In India, the entire drug is collected from wild grown plants by the local tribal community. The nux vomica tree is found throughout the tropical area, 1300 m above the sea level. The plants are about 10 - 12 metres in height with a crooked trunk and several branches. The leaves are orange, oppositely arranged, with oval shape, entire margin and acute apex. The flowers are greenish-white and the bark is greyish to yellow. Fruits of the plants are orange yellow, berries of normal size. Each fruit contains about 4 - 5 seeds and heavy bitter pulp. The ripened fruits are collected and seeds are freed of the pulp. They are washed with water thoroughly. Unripened seeds are separated by the floating test in water. The seeds are dried on mat and packed in gunny bags for marketing. The collection of the fruit and seeds is carried out from November to February. In India, about 15,000 tones of seeds are collected annually. Seeds, pure and crude alkaloids of Nux vomica are regularly exported from India.

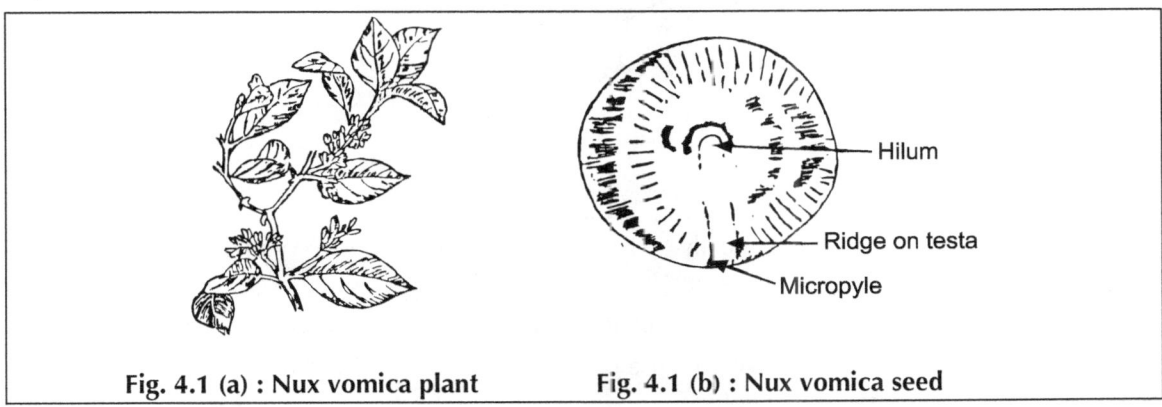

Fig. 4.1 (a) : Nux vomica plant   Fig. 4.1 (b) : Nux vomica seed

Macroscopic Characters

Colour : Greenish-brown

Odour : None

Taste : Intensely bitter

Size : Seeds are 10 to 30 mm in diameter and 4 to 6 mm in thickness.

Shape : The seeds are disc shaped, somewhat flat or irregularly bent and concavo-convex. Margin of the seeds is rounded.

Extra Features

Surface of the seeds is silky due to the radially arranged, densely covered, closely appressed unicellular lignified covering trichomes. The presence of endosperm, embryo and cotyledons can be confirmed in the L. S. of the seed.

Microscopic Characters

The epidermis consists of strongly thickened, pitted and lignified trichomes. Epidermis is followed by a layer of collapsed cells. Endosperm is characterised by thick walled polyhedral unlignified cells with plasmodesma, aleurone grains and oil globules. Calcium oxalate crystals and starch grains are absent in drug.

Chemical Constituents

Nux vomica seeds contain 1.5 - 5 % of bitter indole alkaloids. Chief constituents of nux vomica are strychnine and brucine, while vomicine, α-colubrine, pseudostrychnine and strychnicine are also present. Apart from seeds, other parts of the plant contain alkaloids. Seeds also contain 3.0 % of fat. Bark contains brucine and traces of strychnine. Wood and root of the plant also contain strychnine.

Strychnine $R_1 = R_2 = R_3 = H$

Brucine $R_1 = R_2 = ROCH_3$, $R_3 = H$

The other minor, but, chemically related alkaloids are isostrychnine, N-oxystrychnine, protostrychnine, β-colubrine and novacine.

Nux vomica also contains a glycoside viz. loganin, chlorogenic acid and fixed oil.

The alkaloids can be isolated with the use of dilute sulphuric acid and lime. Strychnine sulphate is meagerly soluble in water and alcohol.

Chemical Tests

The thin sections of nux vomica seed are defatted and the following tests are performed.

1. Stain the transverse section of nux vomica with ammonium vanadate and sulphuric acid Manddin's reagent. The endospermic cells become purple due to the presence of strychnine.
2. Stain the transverse section of nux vomica with concentrated nitric acid. Endospermic cells take yellow colour due to the presence of brucine.
3. Strychnine with sulphuric acid and potassium dichromate gives violet colour which turns to red and finally yellow.

Standards of Quality

Foreign organic matter : ≯ 1.0 %

Ash : ≯ 3.0%

Ayurvedic Properties

Rasa : Tikta

Guna : Laghu, Ruksha, Teeckshna

Veerya : Ushana

Vipak : Katu

Pharmacological Uses

Due to its bitter taste, nux vomica is used as bitter stomachic and tonic. It is a stimulant to central nervous system. It increases the blood pressure and is recommended in certain forms of cardiac failure. It stimulates respiratory and cardiovascular systems. Brucine possesses very less physiological actions and is about one-sixth in potency as compared to strychnine. But as far as the bitterness is concerned, it is four times bitter than strychnine. Brucine is used for denaturing alcohol and nonedible fats, as a standard for bitterness and as a dog poison.

It is a virulent poison producing tetanic convulsion.

Traditional Uses

Nux vomica is used in the treatment of dyspepsia and diseases of nervous system. It is also given in paralytic and neuralygic affections, mental emotion, epilepsy, in sexual importance. In epilepsy effects of nux vomica are well marked.

Substitutes and Adulterants

1. Dried seeds of *Strychnous nux blanda* Hill, are used as adulterant to nux vomica seeds. These are similar in size, pale in colour with a distinct ridge on the edge of the seeds. Nux blanda seeds are regular in shape and contain traces of alkaloids.

2. Dried seeds of *Strychnous potatorum* are another adulterant to authentic drug. The seeds are also known as clearing nuts. They are smaller and thicker with yellowish buff colour. Seeds contain diaboline and traces of strychnine and brucine.

3. The seeds of *Strychnous wallichiana* are used as substitute to nux vomica, as their alkaloidal content and composition are comparable to the genuine drug.

4. The dried seed of *Strychnous ignatii* is another allied drug. Seeds are about 2.5 cm in diameter, ovoid in shape, dark green in colour with unlignified detached trichomes. It contains 2.5 % to 3 % alkaloids of which 60 % is strychnine. The seeds are used for the manufacture of strychnine.

Market Formulation:

(1) **Visatinduka-vati:** Zandu Pharmaceutical Works Ltd., Mumbai.

(2) **Laxmivilas Ras:** Patanjali Ayurveda Ltd., Haridwar, Uttara Khand.

(3) **Navjivan Ras:** Unjha Ayurvedic Pharmacy, Unjha (Gujarat)

SARPAGANDHA

Synonyms

Rauwolfia root, Serpentina root, Rauwolfia, Chhotachand

Biological Source

Rauwolfia consists of dried roots of the plant known as *Rauwolfia serpentina* Benth, belonging to family Apocynaceae. Serpgandha contains not less than 0.15 % of reserpine and ajmalcine, calculated on dried basis.

Geographical Source

Several species of *Rauwolfia* are found distributed in the tropical regions of Asia, America and Africa. Commercially, it is produced in India, Sri Lanka, Myanmar, Thailand and America. In India, it is cultivated in Uttar Pradesh, Bihar, Orissa, Tamil Nadu, West Bengal, Karnataka, Maharashtra, and Gujarat.

Cultivation and Collection

Under wide range of climatic conditions, rauwolfia grows luxuriantly. However, it flourishes in hot humid condition and grows satisfactorily in shade. In wild state, it grows in variety of soils. But for cultivation, clay loamy soil with large amount of humus and good drainage are supposed to be ideal. The pH of the soil should be acidic and around 4. The temperature range for cultivation is 10° to 38°C. Rainfall should be in the range of 250 - 500 cm. Soils containing large amount of sand make the plants more susceptible to diseases.

In can be propagated by various methods, such as by seeds, roots, cutting, root stumps etc. The propagation from seeds is usually the method of choice. The healthy seeds are sown into the nursery beds. The rate of germination of seeds is very low, hence sufficient quantity of the seeds are sown.

Sowing is done in the month of May or at the break of monsoon. The seedlings are then transplanted in the month of August at a distance of 16 to 30 cm. The plants are provided with various chemical fertilizers and manures. The chemical fertilizers include ammonium sulphate, urea; while the manures include, generally, the bone-meal. The plants are kept free from weeds. When the plants are about 3 to 4 years old, they are uprooted. The roots are cut properly, washed so as to remove the earthy matter and dried in air.

It needs about 5 kg of seeds to produce the seedlings sufficient to cover the area of one hectare after transplantation. The average yield of roots per hectare is 1200 kg. It may vary, depending upon the soil, climatic conditions and age of the plant.

Macroscopic Characters

Colour : Root bark is greyish yellow to brown and wood, pale yellow.

Odour : Odourless

Taste : Bitter

Size : About 10 to 18 cm long and from 1 to 3 cm in diameter.

Shape : Roots are sub-cylindrical, slightly tapering and tortuous.

Fracture is short and irregular. The transversely cut surface is white, dense with finely radiating xylem.

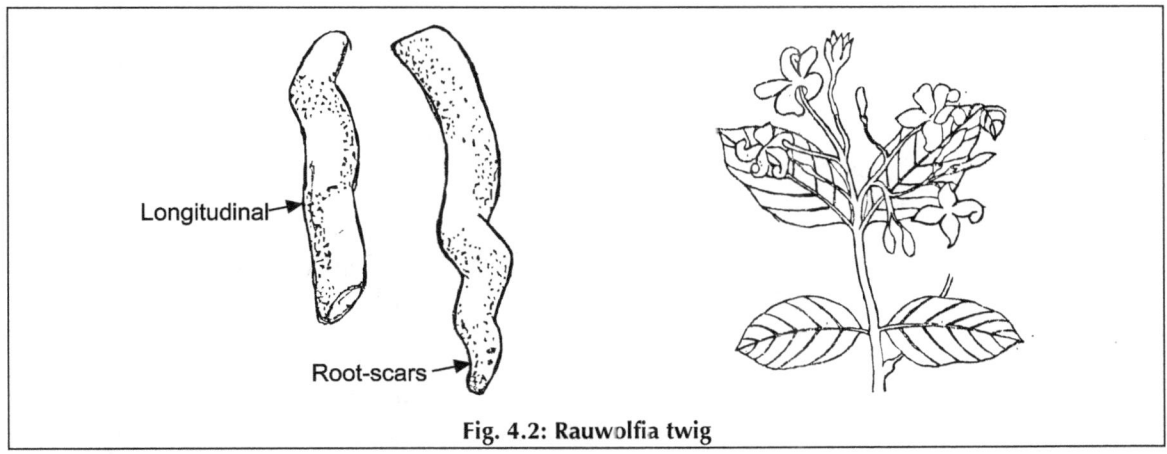

Fig. 4.2: Rauwolfia twig

Extra Features

Roots are rough with longitudinal marking and slightly wrinkled surface. Rootlets are usually absent, but few small circular root scars with tetrastichous arrangements are seen.

The cork is made up of stratified cells followed by phelloderm of few rows of parenchyma. Phloem is narrow, parenchymatous with small scattered sieve tissue. Parenchyma contains starch grains and few latex cells, with brown resinous matter. Secondary phloem contains calcium oxalate crystals. Xylem is about $4/5^{th}$ of the diameter of the root and consists of vessels, tracheids, wood parenchyma and wood fibres. Xylem vessels are elongated upto 350 µ in length and 50 µ in width and contain simple or bordered pits. Stone cells and phloem fibres are absent.

Chemical Constituents

About 30 indole alkaloids have been reported in drug and total alkaloidal content of rauwolfia roots ranges from 0.7 - 3 %, depending upon the source. Alkaloids are concentrated mostly in the bark of the roots. The alkaloids of rauwolfia are broadly classified into the following types, (a) indole alkaloids, (b) indoline alkaloids, (c) indolenine alkaloids (d) oxyindole alkaloids and (e) pseudo indoxyl alkaloids. The important alkaloid of rauwolfia is reserpine. Apart from the alkaloids, it also contains oleo-resin, phytosterol, fatty acids and sugars. The other alkaloids present in the drug are ajmaline, ajmalicine, rauwolfinine, rescinnamine, reserpinine, yohimbine, serpentine and serpentinine. The major alkaloids reserpine and rescinnamine are esters derived from methyl reserpate and trimethoxybenzoic acid in reserpine and trimethoxycinnamic acid in case of rescinnamine.

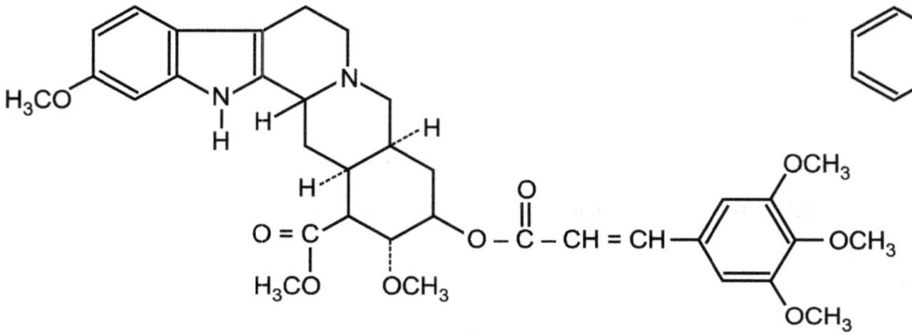

Rescinnamine

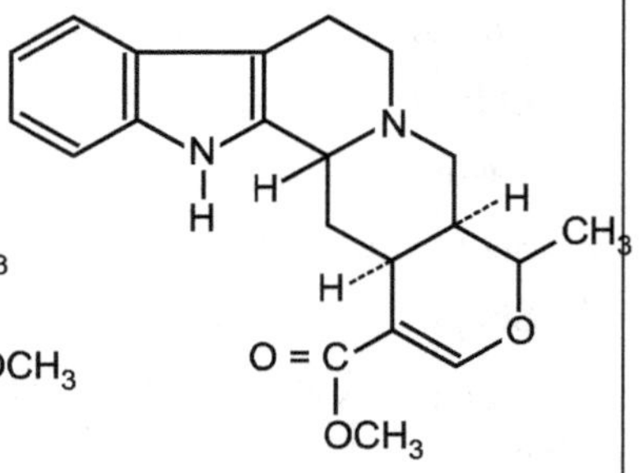

Ajmalicine

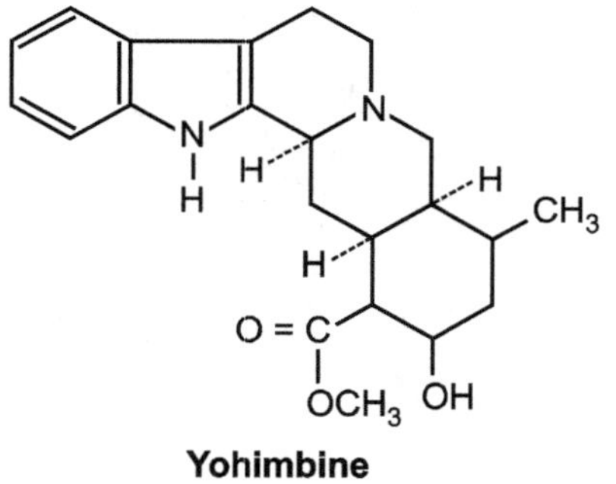

Yohimbine

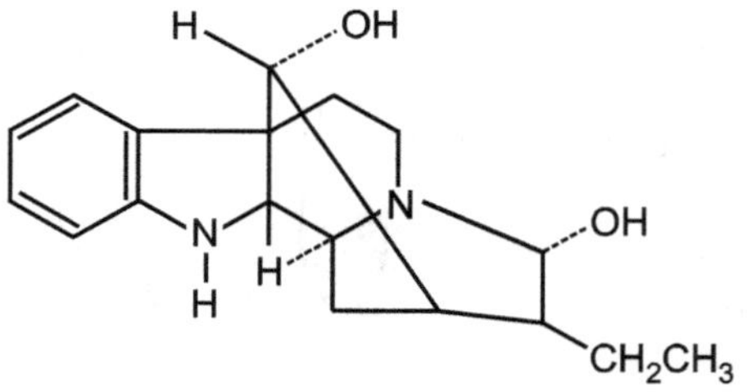

Ajmaline

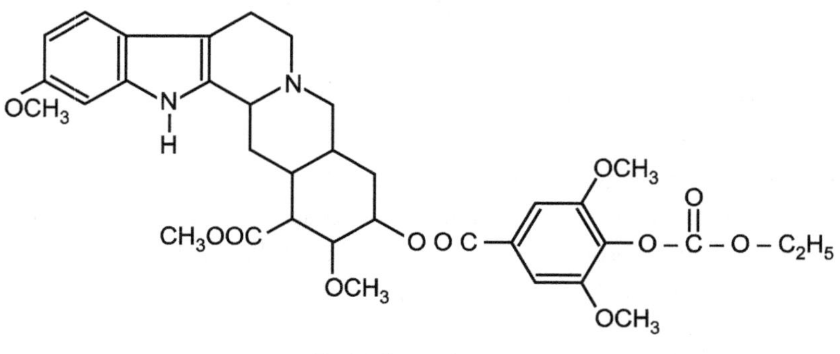

Syrosingopine

Reserpine like alkaloids is colorimetrically determined by reaction between acidic solution of alkaloids and sodium nitrite.

Chemical Tests

1. A red colouration along the medullary rays is observed when the freshly fractured surface of rauwalfia root is treated with concentrated nitric acid.

2. Reserpine shows violet red colour when treated with solution of vanillin in acetic acid.

3. Powdered ranwolfia when treated with sulphuric acid and p-di-methyl amino benzaldehyde, develops violet to red colour.

Standard of Quality

FOM	:	≯ 2.0%
ASE	:	≮ 2.0%
WSE	:	≮ 5.0%
Total ash	:	≯ 8.0 %
Acid insoluble ash	:	≯ 2.0%
LOD	:	≯ 12.0%

Ayurvedic Properties

Rasa : Tikta

Guna : Rooksha

Veerya : Ushana

Vipak : Katu

Uses

Rauwolfia is antihypertensive in activity. Among the various alkaloids of rauwolfia, reserpine, rescinnamine and ajmalicine are clinically important. Reserpine lowers the blood pressure by depleting stores of catecholamines at nerve endings. It prevents re-uptake of nor-epinephrine at storage sites, allowing enzymatic destruction of neuronal transmitter. It is used to treat mild essential hypertension and may be an effective adjunct to the treatment of more severe hypertension.

Because of the tranquillising effects, the drug is used in mild anxiety conditions and reserpine in some of the neuropsychiatric disorders.

Rescinnamine is also used as antihypertensive, but it causes mental depression in higher doses.

Deserpidine is used as antihypertensive and tranquilliser. It shows very less side effects.

Ajmalicine, though less in quantity, has the uses in treatment of circulatory diseases, in relief of obstruction of normal cerebral blood flow.

Syrosingopine shows peripheral effects similar to reserpine. It has less sedative actions and it is used for the treatment of mild or moderate hypertension.

Traditional Uses

Rauwolfia is used to increase the uterine contraction and promote expulsion of foetus. It is employed as valuable, remedy in dysentery and painful affection of the bowels, and irritative condition of central nervous system.

Allied Drugs and Substitutes

The rauwolfia species are not limited only to South East Asian region, but also found in Africa, Central and South America, New Guinea, Hawaii, New Caledonia, Australia and far east regions. It is reported that rauwolfia has about 86 different species. From the medicinal point, the most pertinent to mention here is *R. vomitoria*, which is known as African rauwolfia. It is used as a commercial source for the preparation of reserpine. The other known species of rauwolfia from Africa are *R. caffra, R. cumminsfi, R. mombasiana, R. oreogiton, R. obscura, R. rosea* and *R. volkensii*. All of them contain reserpine.

The other rauwolfia species with reserpine content are *R. tetraphylla* and *R. nitida. Catharanthus roseus* contain ajmalicine.

Pausinystalia yohimba, known as yohimbe bark, contains yohimbine, which is structurally related to reserpine.

The root bark of *Alstonia venenata* and *A. constricta* also contain reserpine. The various species of *Aspidosperma* genus contain indole alkaloids which resemble to those from rauwolfia.

The various other species with which rauwolfia is found to be substituted are *Rauwolfia tetraphylla, R. densiflora* and *R. vomitoria* (African rauwolfia). *R. densiflora* contains sclerenchyma, while *R. tetraphylla* has uniform cork, abundant sclereids and fibres, but devoid of rescinnamine. The root of *R. vomitoria* has 5 discontinued bands of sclerenchyma and very large vessels.

Market Products

1) **Serpina:** Himalaya Drug Company, Banglurue.
2) **Reserpine Tablets:** Indo-german Alkaloids Andheri, Mumbai – 93.

DARUHALDI

Synonyms

Darvi, Rasavanti, Berberis, Chitra, Indian berbery.

Biological Source

This consists of the dried roots and root bark of *Berberis aristata* DC belonging to family Berberidaceae and contain not less than 0.70 % of berberine on dry basis. Dried stems should contain not less than 0.50 % of berberine.

Geographical Source

It occurs in Assam, Bihar and Himalayas and also in Nilgiri Hills, at an altitude of 1000 – 3000 m.

Cultivation and Collection

It grows well in temperate climate. It flourishes better under moist and humid climatic conditions. The plant does not tolerate hot climate. It grows well at higher altitude between 2000 - 3000 metres above the sea-level. Well distributed rainfall in the range of 60 - 75 cm; and range of temperature from 15° - 30°C appears to be well suited to the plant. It mainly grows as rainfed crop. It grows on variety of soils, ranging from sandy alluvial loam to red lateritic loam or even dark loam soil is suitable for its growth. Propagation is carried out during spring season.

Self sown seeds are the major propagation source in nature. It can be successfully propagated vegetatively by stem cuttings. The method of raising seedlings on nursery bed and then transplanting can also be practiced. It is a perennial plant.

Daruhaldi is an erect, deciduous shrub about 1.75 to 3.5 metres in height.

Fig. 4.3 : Berberis aristata – flowering and fruiting branch

The plants are ready for harvesting after two years of plantation. The root bark is removed after its maturity. It is cut into small pieces, sun dried and stored in well closed container in dry place.

Macroscopic Characters

Colour : Pale yellowish brown
Taste : Bitter
Odour : None
Roots : Roots are cylindrical, knotty, much branched, easily separable wood is yellow.

Pieces are variable in length and thickness, bark is 0.5 to 8 cm in thickness, fracture short in bark and splintery in xylem.

Chemical Constituents

It contains number of alkaloids, ranging from 1.2 - 2 %. Roots contain maximum alkaloids as compared to stem bark. Stem bark and root bark contain berberine, barbamine, oxyberberine, palmatine and taxilamine. Roots contain berberine, barbamine, Jatrorrhizine, columbamine and oxyberberine.

Berberine

Standards of Quality

Roots

Foreign organic matter	:	≯ 2.0 %
Ethanol soluble extractives	:	≯ 2.0 %
Water soluble extractives	:	≮ 6.0 %
Ash soluble extractives	:	≮ 5.0 %
Acid insoluble ash	:	≯ 1.0 %
Loss of drugs	:	≯ 10.0 %
Mocrobial limits	:	Should comply IP limits.

Ayurvedic Properties

Rasa : Katu, Tikta
Guna : Ruksha
Veerya : Ushana
Vipak : Katu

Pharmacological Uses

It mainly possesses anti-inflammatory and antibiotic activity. It is also used as antipyretic, the plant extract is valuable in malarial fever. It is used as purgative in children; also used as blood purifier, tonic, febrifuge, anti bacterial and antidiaroheal.

The plant extract Rasaut is used externally in eye diseases and also for washing piles and swellings.

Traditional Uses

Decoctions of daruhalad is used as wash for ulcers and sores and also as antipyretic and anti diarroheal.

Market Products

Geriforte tablets

Dashang Lep

Berberin: Haffkin Biopharmaceutical Corporation Ltd., Adrarya Donde Marg, Parel, Mumbai-12.

OPIUM

Synonym

Raw opium

Biological Source

It is the dried latex obtained by incision from the unripe capsules of *Papaver somniferum* Linn., dried or partly dried by heat or spontaneous evaporation, and worked into somewhat irregularly shaped masses (natural opium) or moulded into masses of more uniform size and shape (manipulated opium). Poppy plant belongs to family Papaveraceae. It contains not less than 10 % of morphine, and not less than 2.0 % of codeine, both calculated as anhydrous morphine.

Geographical Source

India, Pakistan, Afghanistan, Turkey, Russia, China and Iran.

Cultivation, Collection and Preparation

Being a potent narcotic drug, the cultivation and other aspects of opium are governed by respective governments in different countries, including India. In India, all the activities about opium and its derivatives are controlled under Narcotic Drugs and Psychotropic Substances Act, 1985.

The genus *Papaver* has 50 different species, of which six species are found in India, viz. *P. somniferum* (Opium poppy), *P. nudicaule* (Iceland poppy), *P. rhoeas* (corn poppy), *P. orientale*, *P. argemone*, and *P. dubium*.

Poppy is an erect plant attaining 60 - 120 cm height. It is rarely branched. The leaves are linear, oblong or ovate oblong and have a dentate or serrate margin. It bears bluish white, purple or violet coloured large flowers. Accordingly, the varieties *P. somniferum* var. *glabrum*, *P. somniferum* var. *album*, *P. somniferum* var. *nigrum* are described. The second variety is cultivated in India. Indian opium is considered as the only legal source of opium to many countries including United States of America and Britain.

In India, about 54 thousand hectares of land is under opium poppy cultivation. It is under government control, and cultivation of poppy is restricted to Madhya Pradesh, Rajasthan and Uttar Pradesh.

The weather conditions affect, upto a large extent, the yield of opium. Although, temperate climate is the natural requirement of opium poppy, it can be grown with success under subtropical climate in winter season, as there is a favourable effect on yield by cold weather. But, extreme cold conditions, including frost, adversely affect the plant and ultimately yield of opium. In short, the best climatic conditions for opium poppy are cool weather without freezing temperature and cloudiness, and sufficient sunshine.

Opium poppy is grown from November to March. Propagation is done by sowing the seeds, for which 3 - 4 kg of seeds per hectare are necessary. The seeds admixed with about 3 - 4 parts of sand are sown. Opium poppy requires highly fertile, well drained loamy soil with fine sand. The soil should contain organic matter, nitrogen and should have a pH around 7. The distance between two plants maintained is usually 25 cm and the plant reaches maximum height of one metre.

Periodically, the thinning of plants is done to get uniform growth and better development. The plants are kept totally free from weeds with the use of suitable weedicides. The plant should be protected from various insect pests like cut worms, leaf minor and poppy borer. The use of manures and fertilizers markedly improve the quality and yield of opium poppy. Especially, nitrogen and phosphorus have remarkable effects on growth of plant.

After sowing, within 3 - 4 months, the plant bears flowers, which are converted to capsules within few days and attain maturity after 15 - 20 days. During the maturity period, the capsule exudes maximum latex which shows a colour change from dark green to light green. Such capsules are incised vertically in the afternoon with the help of specific needle like apparatus called 'nushtur'. It penetrates maximum upto 2 mm into the capsule. Because of incisions, latex exudes out and thickens due to cold weather in night which is eventually scrapped and collected next morning by an iron scoop called *Charpala*. The incising process is repeated for about 4 times on the same capsule with 2 days interval. The incisions must remain superficial, so as to maintain the external exudation of latex. The latex is collected in plastic containers. Then, capsules are collected and dried in open areas and further the seeds are separated by beating. The average yield of opium is about 25 - 26 kg per hectare and for seeds, it is from 4-5 quintals per hectare. Opium is exported traditionally from India.

The opium collected by this way is either exported or some of the part is further processed at Government opium factory at Ghazipur. A generalised process is outlined to cover the industrial method for extraction of alkaloids of opium.

Macroscopic Characters

Odour : Strong characteristic

Taste : Bitter

1. Indian opium: Dark brown in colour. It is found in the form of cubical pieces weighing about 900 g for marketing purposes. It is enclosed in tissue paper and is brittle and plastic in nature. Internally, it is homogenous. Depending upon the requirement, the powdered form is available in the pack of 5 to 10 kg.

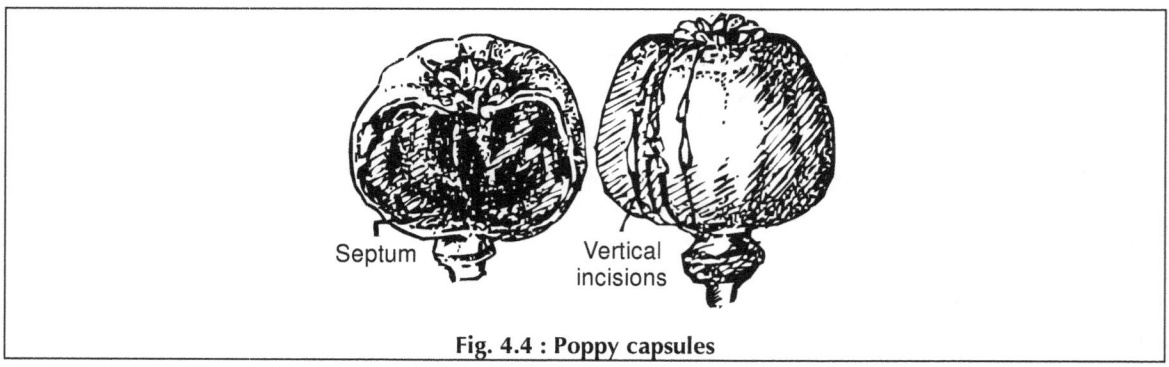

Fig. 4.4 : Poppy capsules

2. Persian opium: Dark brown in colour, found in the form of brick shaped masses, weighing 450 g. It is hygroscopic in nature, granular or nearly smooth with brittle fracture.

3. Natural Turkish or European opium: Brown or dark brown in colour. It is found in conical or rounded and somewhat flattened masses, weighing 250 to 1000 g. On keeping, it becomes hard and brittle. It is covered with poppy leaves.

4. Manipulated Turkish opium: It is chocolate brown or dark brown internally and covered with broken poppy leaves externally. The masses of this type are oval and flattened on upper and lower surface weighing about 2000 g. It is somewhat plastic or even brittle.

5. Manipulated European opium: It is dark brown in colour internally and covered with broken leaves. It is found in the form of elongated masses with rounded ends weighing 150 to 500 g. It is firm, plastic and with brittle fracture.

Chemical Constituents

The latex contains mainly the alkaloids derived from amino acids phenylalanine and tyrosine. Chemically, they are placed under benzylisoquinoline and phenanthrene types.

Narcotine (also called noscapine), narceine and papaverine belong to the former, while morphine, codeine and thebaine represent later category.

Fruits of poppy contain numerous off white coloured and minute seeds. These seeds contain 30 - 35 % drying fixed oil. Which is used commercially in oil paint industry, which is colourless, tasteless and transparent.

Morphine is monoacidic, laevorotatory phenolic alkaloid and also contains an alcoholic hydroxyl group at C (6) position. Due to presence of phenolic hydroxyl group, it is soluble in alkali hydroxides, except ammonium hydroxide. Diacetyl derivative of morphine is **heroin** which is totally synthetic and not part of opium.

Codeine (methyl morphine) is a strong monoacidic base and laevorotatory. It is soluble in water and organic solvents.

Papaverine is a weak monoacidic base and inactive optically. It is slightly soluble in organic solvents, but insoluble in water.

The other important benzylisoquinoline alkaloid narcotine which is also a weak monoacidic base and is laevorotatory, while its salts are dextrorotatory. Narcotine is soluble in acetone, benzene, chloroform, but insoluble in water, alcohol and ether.

The opium alkaloids are present as salts of meconic acid.

Protopine and hydrocotarnine are the minor alkaloids of opium. Opium also contains sugar, wax, mucilage and salts of calcium, potassium and magnesium. Opium does not contain tannins, starch and calcium oxalate.

Chemical Tests

(1) The general test to detect opium is by testing presence of meconic acid. The alkaloids are present as the salts of meconic acid. Opium is dissolved in water and to the filtrate, ferric chloride solution is added by which deep reddish purple colour is obtained, which persists even on addition of hydrochloric acid.

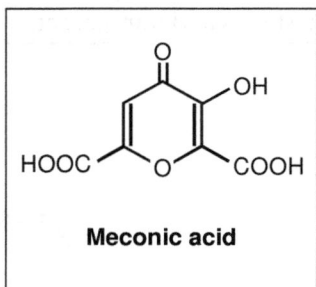

Meconic acid

(2) Morphine when sprinkled on nitric acid gives orange red colour. Codeine does not respond to this test.

(3) The treatment of morphine solution with potassium ferricyanide and ferric chloride solutions gives bluish green colour. Codeine does not respond to this test.

(4) Papaverine solution in hydrochloric acid gives a lemon yellow colour with potassium ferricyanide solution.

Standards of Quality

Thebain : ≯ 3.0%
Total ash : ≯ 6.0%
LOD : ≯ 15.0%

Ayurvedic Properties

Rasa : Rooksha, Sukshma
Guna : Kasaya
Veerya : Ushana
Vipak : Katu

Pharmaceutical Uses

Opium belongs to the category of hypnotic sedative and analgesic in which the action is mainly due to morphine. Morphine is a potent analgesic. Due to its central narcotic effects, it causes addiction. Hence, it is given only in severe pains and in those cases, when patient does not show response to other analgesics. Morphine has a biphasic action on central nervous system. It sedates the cerebrum and has a mixture of stimulation and sedation on the medulla. In the medulla, it sedates the respiratory centre, emetic centre and the cough reflex. It also stimulates chemoreceptor trigger zone in the medulla, which leads to nausea and vomitting and is considered as a side effect. Morphine also produces respiratory depression and constipation.

Codeine relieves local irritation in the bronchial tract and as an antitussive used in various cough medicines. It has mild analgesic effects, which are potent than aspirin, but only one tenth activity of that of morphine. Papaverine has relaxant effects on smooth muscles of the intestinal and bronchial tract and the blood vessels. Narcotine has a specific depressant action on cough reflex and used in the preparation of cough linctuses.

Opium alkaloids are semisynthesized like other medicinal agents. Diacetyl morphine (heroin) has more narcotic, analgesic property than morphine. By losing one molecule of water, morphine gives apomorphine which is emetic and used subcutaneously to treat poisoning cases. Hydromorphone is formed by replacing one of the hydroxyl groups and also removal of adjacent double bond. It is also a potent narcotic analgesic, but habit forming tendencies are less.

The synthetic morphine like compounds are called 'opioids', which are non habit forming, but possess the medicinal activity of morphine.

Traditional Uses

Opium is used in the treatment of diarrhoea, dysentery and cough. In Ayurvedic practice, poppy capsules are used as antiphlegmatic, to bind bowels to the capacity to perform muscular work and cause nervous excitement.

Commercial Varieties of Opium

(1) Indian opium: It is dark brown in colour and found in the form of cubical pieces weighing 900 g. It is brittle and plastic in nature. The powdered form is available as 5 - 10 kg packs. It contains 10 % anhydrous morphine.

(2) Persian opium: It is dark brown in colour and available as brick shaped masses of 450 g. It is hygroscopic, granular or smooth.

(3) Turkish opium: It is commonly called as druggists opium or soft opium. It is brown or dark brown in colour and available as conical rounded or flattened masses.

(4) Chinese opium: It comes in market in the form of flat globular cakes and contains 4 - 11 % morphine.

Different Forms of Opium

(1) **Powdered opium** : It contains 10 % anhydrous morphine with lactose, caramel and powdered cocoa husks.

(2) **Opium concentratum** : It contains different alkaloid hydrochlorides of opium in following proportions:

Anhydrous morphine	:	47.5 - 52.5 %
Codeine	:	2.5 - 5 %
Narcotine	:	16 - 22 %
Papaverine	:	2.5 - 7 %

(3) Camphorated opium tincture : It contains alcoholic solution of opium, benzoic acid, camphor, anise oil and the formulation is prepared in alcohol. It is used in treatment of diarrhoea as antiperistaltic.

Storage

Opium is preserved in a well closed container away from light.

Substitutes and Adulterants

Since the production of opium in India is under government control, it is not found to be adulterated. The adulterated forms show presence of opium capsules in powdered form, gum and sugary fruits.

Allied Plants

The various other species of poppy, which do not contain morphine are *Papaver argemone, P. dubium, P. orientate, P. bracteatum, P. strigosum, P. intermedia, P. paeoniflorum,* hybrid of *P. somniferum* and *P. orientate, P. pseudo orientale,* and plants from genera *Argemone* and *Eschscholzia* (both belonging to family Papaveraceae).

Among all these species, *P. bracteatum* has scored more importance, as it does not contain morphine, which causes addiction. The amount of total alkaloids and consequent percentage of thebaine is also very high. Because of such morphine free contents, this species is more significant as a potential new source of opiates.

Market Products

1) **Nidrodaya Ras:** Shri Bajrang Ayurved Bhawan, Guwahati, Assam.
2) **Virya Stambhan vati:** Vyas Pharmaceuticals, Indore, M.P.
3) **Kamini Dravana:** Shri. Baidyanath Ayurved Bhawan Pvt. Ltd., Kolkata (WB).

TROPANE ALKALOIDS

Tropane molecule represents the fusion of pyrrolidine and piperidine ring with common methylated nitrogen. The alkaloids containing methylated tropane nucleus are chemotaxonomic characters of family Solanaceae. Out of 10 - 12 such alkaloids of this family, therapeutic value is present only in *l*-hyoscyamine. Hyoscine and racemic form of hyoscyamine viz. atropine. They have anticholinergic effects. They are employed for different purposes. Hyoscyamine is used in parkinsonism. Hyoscine is useful as preanaesthetic in surgery and also in motion sickness. Atropine is employed to achieve paralysis of parasympathetic nerves like in treatment of eye diseases.

Family Solanaceae includes 72 genera, out of which only 8 genera viz. *Datura, Atropa, Duboisia, Hyoscyamus, Scopolia, Physoclaina, Mandrogora* and *Solandra* contain *l*-hyoscyamine, hyoscine and atropine. The species, with such alkaloids, under these genera are grouped in the following way.

1. Hyoscyamine as main alkaloid: *Datura stramonium, Atropa belladonna, A. acuminata, Duboisia myoporoides* (South Australian Strain).

2. Hyoscine as main alkaloid: *D. metel, Duboisia myoporoides* (North Australian Strain)

3. Hyoscyamine and Hyoscine (both in low quantities): *Hyoscyamus niger, Mandrogora officinarum*.

BELLADONNA HERB

Synonyms

Belladonna Leaf; Belladonnae Folium; Deadly night shade leaf (European belladonna).

Biological Source

Belladonna herb consists of dried leaves or the leaves and other aerial parts of *Atropa belladonna* Linn. (European belladonna) or *Atropa acuminata* Royle ex-Lindley (Indian belladonna) or mixture of both the species collected when the plants are in flowering condition. It belongs to family Solanaceae. It contains not less than 0.3 % of the alkaloids of belladonna herb, calculated as *l*-hyoscyamine.

Geographical Source

It is indigenous to and cultivated in England and other European countries. In India, it is found in the Western Himalayas from Simla to Kashmir and adjoining areas of Himachal Pradesh. Its chief habitat is Jammu and in forests of Sindh, and Chinab valley.

History

Because of the hallucinogenic effect of this plant, it was used as witch craft in the middle ages. In ancient times, the juice of this plant was used as a cosmetic, because of its dilatory effect on the pupil of the eye. This drug was first introduced in the London Pharmacopoeia in 1809.

Cultivation and Collection

Cultivation of belladonna at an altitude of 1400 m above the sea level is found to be satisfactory, if proper irrigation facilities are provided. It is observed that the yield per hectare can be increased substantially by proper cultivation technology. The experimental trials of applications of several fungicides and insecticides right from the treatment of the seeds up to the foliar sprays were very encouraging. Its cultivation in Jammu and Kashmir is found to be successful.

Belladonna berries are crushed to get the seeds for cultivation. Proper processing like washing and sieving is performed. Only healthy seeds are used for cultivation. Seeds are sown by broadcasting method in well prepared beds with the application of fungicide like diathon.

Sowing is done in May and July. The seedlings are ready for transplantation by the end of September. Transplanting is done by keeping certain distance between two plants and the seedlings are irrigated carefully. Fertilizers like urea, potash and superphosphate are given as per the needs. Insecticidal sprays like sevin are also tried when the plant reaches maturity. The leaves, as well as, the flowering tops are cut and sundried or dried in shade. During drying, care is taken to retain the green colour. While grading and packing for market, woolly stems and foreign organic matter are rejected. The yield per hectare is found to be 200 to 600 kg.

Macroscopic Characters

Fig. 4.5 : Belladonna herb

Colour : Leaves: Green to brownish-green
Flowers: Purple to yellowish-brown
Fruits: Green to brown

Odour : Slight and characteristic

Taste : Bitter and acrid

Size : Leaves: 5 - 25 cm long and 2.5 - 12 cm wide
Flowers: Corolla 2.5 cm long and 1.5 cm wide
Fruits: About 10 cm in diameter

Shape : Leaves: Ovate, lanceolate to broadly ovate, with acuminate apex, decurrent lamina, entire margin, petiolate, brittle and transversely broken.

Flowers: Campanulate, 5, small reflexed lobes of corolla.

Fruits : Berries, sub-globular in shape with numerous flat seeds.

Extra Features

In general, the entire drug is seen as crumpled and twisted. The dropping flowers are associated with as many pairs of leaves. The flowers are with 5 stamens, superior bilocular ovary with numerous seeds.

Microscopic Characters

Epidermal cells with slightly sinuous anticlinal wall and striated cuticle, anisocytic stomata and occasionally uniseriate multicellular covering trichomes are present. There are glandular trichomes which are uniseriate and with unicellular heads. The palisade ratio is 5 to 7.

Chemical Constituents

The total alkaloidal content of drug is 0.4 - 1 % and varies in different parts of plant, roots (0.6 %), stems (0.05 %), leaves (0.4 %), unripe and ripe berries (0.19 - 0.21 %) and seeds (0.33 %).

The main alkaloids are *l*-hyoscyamine and its racemic form atropine. The drug also contains belladonine, scopoletin (*l*-methyl aesculetin), hyoscine, pyridine and N-methyl pyrroline. The later two are the volatile bases. Homotropine is a synthetic compound and is preferred in the medical profesion as the synthetic process of atropine and hyoscyamine is very costly.

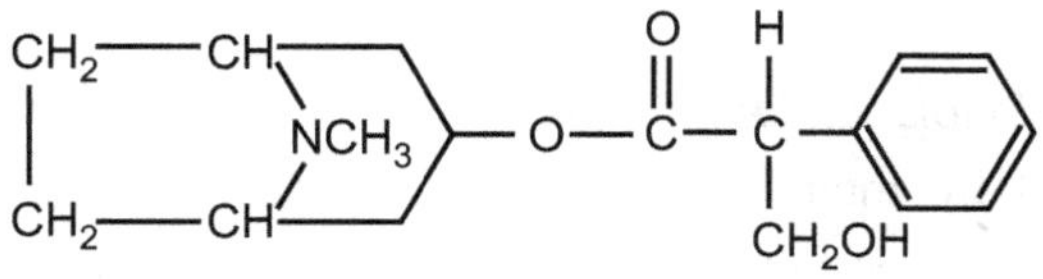

Atropine (Tropine (±) - Tropate)

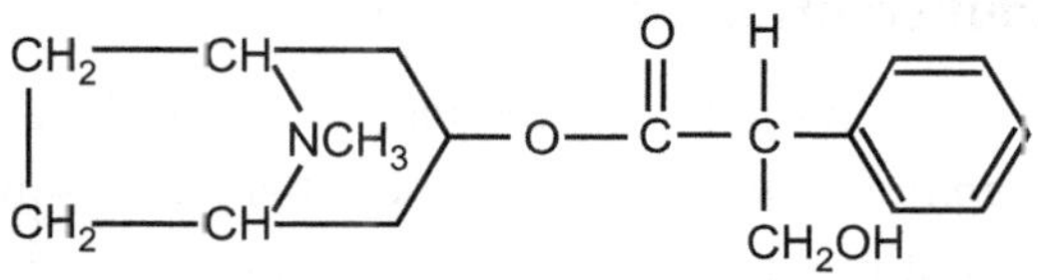

Hyoscyamine (Tropine (−) - Tropate)

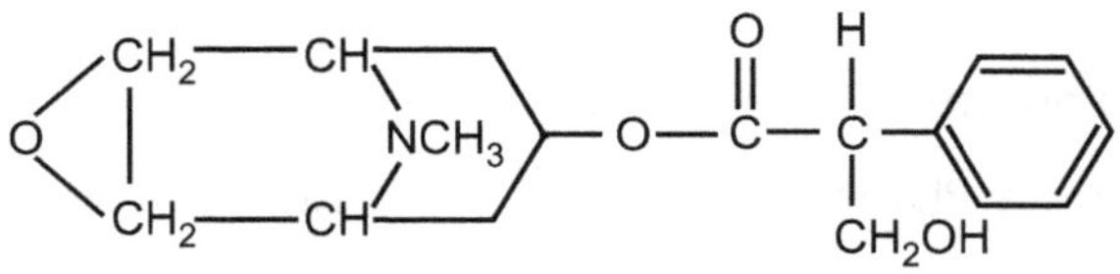

Hyoscine (Scopalamine)

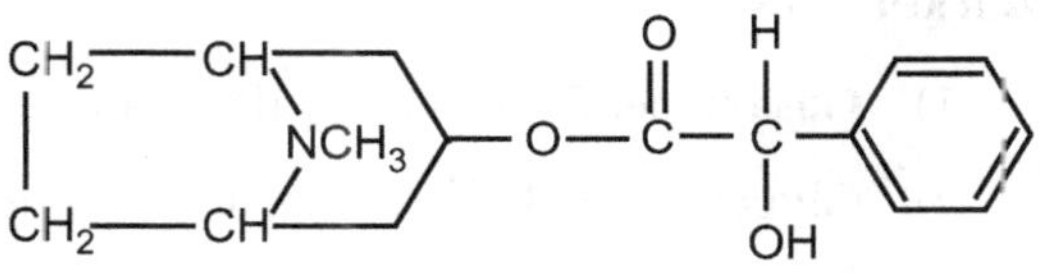

Homotropine

Standards of Quality

Total ash	: 14 %
Acid-insoluble ash	: 3 %
Foreign organic matter	: not more than 3 %

It gives Vitali - Morin reaction positive.

Ayurvedic Properties

Rasa	:	Tikta, Kath
Guna	:	Laghu, Rooksha
Veerya	:	Ushana
Vipak	:	Katu

Pharmacological Uses

It is the parasympatholytic drug with anticholinergic properties. It is used to reduce the secretions such as sweat, saliva and gastric juice and also to reduce spasm in cases of intestinal gripping due to strong purgatives. It is also used as an antidote in opium and chloral hydrate poisoning.

Traditional Use

The leaf extract is used in ophlhalmic surgery. Also used as sedatire and antispasmodic. Dried leaves are smoked as antispasmodic.

Dose

0.6 to 1 ml in the form of belladonna tincture - 4 times a day.

Adulterants and Substitutes

The drug is adulterated with the leaves of *Phytolacca americana, Solanum nigrum*, and *Ailanthus glandulosa*. Each of them is distinguished by their histological character. Idioblast is present in *Phytolacca* leaves, lamina is denser, needle shaped crystals are present and anomocytic stomata are distinct. Palisade ratio is from 2 - 4 in *S. nigrum* leaves. Clustered crystals of calcium oxalate near the veins are present in *Ailanthus* leaves. The leaves also show the presence of unicellular lignified trichomes.

Market Products

1) **Gasazyme:** Eastern drug, IIA, Earle street, Post Box No. 10454, Kolkata-26.
2) **Glycerine of Belladonna:** BPC (Lotion) Arora Pharmaceuticals Pvt. Ltd., Lawrance Road, New Delhi – 110035.
3) **Belladonna plaster:** Johnson & Johnson, Thana.

HYOSCYAMUS

Synonyms

Henbane, Hyoscyamus herb, Hyoscyamus leaves.

Biological Source

It consists of the dried leaves, or leaves and flowering tops of *Hyoscyamus niger*, belonging to family Solanaceae.

It should contain not less than 0.05 % of alkaloids of hyoscyamus, calculated as *l*-hyoscyamine. It is grown as a biennial herb.

Geographical Source

Hyoscyamus is a native of Western Asia, North Africa, Europe and India. It is cultivated in Russia, Belgium, Hungary and India.

Cultivation and Collection

The cultivation is done in temperate region at an altitude of 2400 to 3300 m. The drug is cultivated on commercial scale in England, Egypt, U.S.S.R., and Hungary. In India, it is cultivated in Kashmir to a limited extent. The method of propagation is by seeds. The small seed beds are raised and seeds are sown. The seeds require about two weeks for germination. The seedlings are transplanted in field in the month of May by keeping a distance of half metre between them and about 75 cm between two rows. The plants are kept free of weeds and occasional hoeing is also done. The crop is harvested when it reaches maturity. Under all favourable conditions, the yield of the drug per hectare is 1000 kg - 1500 kg.

Macroscopic Characters

The fresh drug has characteristic and strong odour with a bitter and acrid taste.

The leaves have about 25 cm long lamina and they are pale greyish green in colour. The shape is ovate-oblong to triangular ovate. In few cases, they may contain short petiole, otherwise they are sessile. The margin has acute triangular lobes, which are irregularly dentate. The apex is acute, the lamina is covered with glandular hair. There is the prominent midrib with pinnate venation. The flowers are funnel shaped and yellow in colour, showing purplish veins.

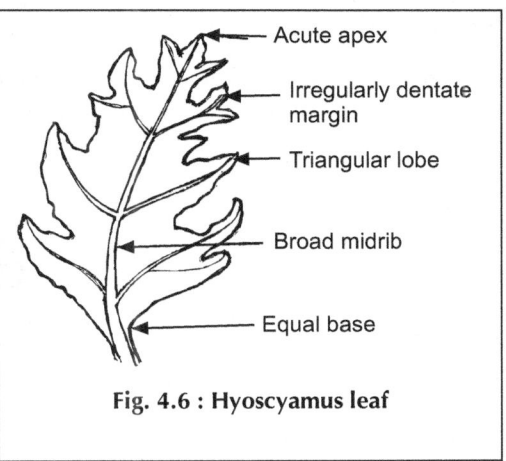

Fig. 4.6 : Hyoscyamus leaf

Microscopic Characters

The leaf is dorsiventral. Epidermis is covered with smooth cuticle and numerous glandular trichomes. Anisocytic stomata are present in epidermal layer. Palisade cells are present in a single layer but all cells contain prismatic or cluster crystals of calcium oxalate. Near the veins, sometimes, the idioblasts are present containing microspheroidal crystals. Midrib shows many bicollateral vascular bundles arranged in an arc.

Chemical Constituents

The total alkaloids present in the drug range from 0.05 - 0.15 % in which about 75 % is hyoscyamine. Atropine and hyoscine are present in fewer amount. The alkaloidal percentage is more in petiole than in the stem or lamina.

The principal alkaloid of this drug (-) hyoscyamine ($C_{17}H_{23}NO_3$) is an ester of tropic acid and tropine, and is more active than the racemic form i.e. atropine. During the extraction, it is racemized to atropine (see belladonna herb).

Chemical Test

It gives Vitali-Morin test positive in case of datura herb.

Ayurvedic Properties

Rasa : Tikta

Guna : Guru, Ruksha

Veerya : Ushna

Vipak : Katu

Pharmacological Uses

It is used to counteract gripping due to purgatives and also to relieve spasms of urinary tract. It is also sedative and used to check salivary secretion. It is an expectorant too. It is an antispasmodic and antiasthmatic.

Traditional Uses

Prescribed in mental excitement epileptic mamia, insommia, sphasmodic cough in urinary affections, irritatins of kidneys and uterus and bladder and hysteria.

Dose

Hyoscyamine sulphate - 125 – 250: 3 - 4 times a day.

CINCHONA

Synonyms

Jesuit's bark, Peruvian bark

Biological Source

It is the dried bark of the cultivated trees of *Cinchona calisaya* Wedd., *C. ledgeriana* Moens, *C. officinalis* Linn, *C. succirubra* Pav. ex-klotzsch, or of hybrids of either of the last two species with either of the first two. Cinchona belongs to family Rubiaceae. It contains not less than 6 % of total alkaloids of cinchona.

Geographical Source

India, Bolivia, Columbia, Ecuador, Peru, Tanzania, Guatemala, Indonesia and Sri Lanka are the countries where cinchona is found. In India, it is cultivated in Annamalai hills (Coimbatore district) and Nilgiri hills (Nilgiri district) in Tamil Nadu and in Darjeeling area of West Bengal.

Cultivation, Collection and Preparation

Most of the cinchona species profusely grow in sub-tropical or tropical climates at a height of about 1000 - 3000 metres. The trees, growing below this height are found to have less percentage of quinine. The rainfall conditions required are uniform (from 250 - 380 cm in a year). The favourable growth is achieved between an atmospheric temperature of 60° - 75°F. Cinchona requires light, well drained forest soil which is rich in organic matter. The acidic soil having a pH of 4.2 - 5.6 and a small amount of nitrogen are found to be most favourable for growth. Cinchona needs slopping situation, high humidity and protection from wind.

The propagation is done with either seeds or budding or layering. In West Bengal, only budding is practised and in Tamil Nadu, the budding and layering methods are applied. The seeds of cinchona are very small and light in weight. About one gramme of cinchona seeds contain 3500 seeds. They are admixed with soil during sowing. The maintenance of genetic purity causes a problem as high cross fertilization occurs in cinchona plants. This affects the yield, like in high alkaloid content giving species, such as *C. ledgeriana*, the average alkaloid content is reduced. The seeds should be immediately used for propagation as on storage they lose their viability. The germination takes place in 3 - 6 weeks. The seedlings with 2 pairs of leaves are transplanted and space of 6 - 10 cm is maintained inbetween two seedlings and 2 rows. The young seedlings are protected from direct sunlight. In forest soil, they are transplanted after 15 months of growth and preferably before heavy rainfall. A distance of 2 × 2 metres is maintained between two plants. As cinchona consists of stem, as well as root bark, the plants from 4 - 20 years of age are selected for harvesting, but the maximum alkaloidal content is found to 6 - 10 years old plants. The bark is collected by coppicing method. For this purpose, vertical incisions are made on branches, trunk of tree and these incisions are connected by horizontal circles. The bark is then stripped off and dried in sun light and further by artificial heat. The drying is done below 175°F. During drying, the bark loses up to 70 % of its weight. The care should be taken to avoid molding or fermentation during drying. The quills of drug are packed in gunny bags and marketed. The root bark is collected by uprooting the trees and bark is separated manually.

During the two world wars, Java and Indonesia lost their positions as potential producers of cinchona. After that, India has gained the prime position as producer and supplier of cinchona and quinine. By 1985 - 86, the production had reached upto 10 lakh kg of bark and about 26,000 kg of quinine salts.

Extraction of Quinine

For extraction of quinine, the bark is powdered and extracted with benzene or toluene in presence of alkali. Further, the alkaloids are extracted with dil. sulphuric acid. By bringing the acid extract to neutrality, quinine sulphate separates, as it is sparingly soluble.

Macroscopic Characters

Cinchona bark has a slight and characteristic odour, but somewhat astringent and intensely bitter taste. In general, the bark is available in the form of quills and curved pieces.

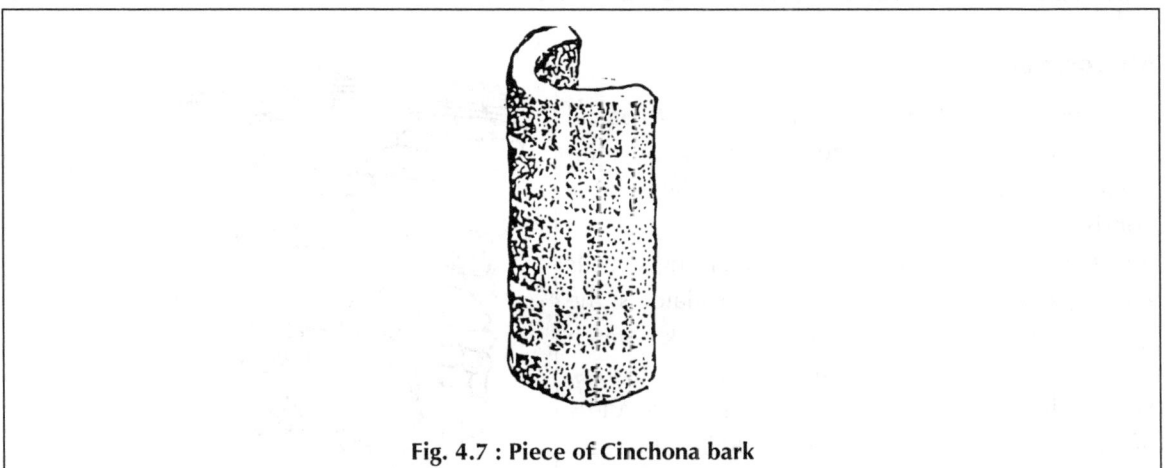

Fig. 4.7 : Piece of Cinchona bark

Stem bark: It is up to 30 cm in length and about 2 to 6 mm in thickness. The outer surface shows dull brown grey or grey colour and many a time, shows presence of mosses and lichens owing to its growth in heavy rainfall areas. The bark is rough and has transverse fissures. These fissures are different in different species. It is furrowed or wrinkled longitudinally. The outer bark in some varieties shows exfoliation. The inner surface is pale yellowish-brown to deep reddish-brown and the colour depends on the species. The fracture is short in external layers and fibrous in the inner portion.

Root bark: It occurs in length of 2 - 7 cm. The bark is curved, twisted or irregularly channelled. The outer and inner surfaces are similar in colour. The outer surface is scaly and shows depressions. The inner surface is striated.

The different commercial varieties have some special characters. *C. succirubra* is also called as red bark, while *C. ledgeriana* is referred to as yellow bark. *C. robusta* is the hybrid between *C. succirubra* and *C. officinalis*.

Table 4.1 : The Typical Characters of 4 Main Species of Cinchona

Characters	*C. calisaya*	*C. ledgeriana*	*C. officinalis*	*C. succirubra*
Size	Diameter is from 12 - 25 mm and thickness from 2 - 5 mm	Diameter is 12 - 25 mm and thickness varies from 2 - 5 mm	Diameter is upto 12 mm and thickness is upto 1.5 mm	Diameter is from 20 - 40 mm and thickness from 2 - 5 mm
Other features	Broad longitudinal fissure with transverse cracks	Broad longitudinal fissures and cracks more in number, but less deep. Some pieces show longitudinal wrinkles and reddish warts	It shows a number of transverse cracks	Well marked longitudinal wrinkles, but less number of transverse cracks. Only some pieces show reddish warts
Powder	Cinnamon brown	Cinnamon brown	Yellow	Reddish brown

Microscopic Characters

Cinchona exhibits the typical histological characters of the bark. The cork cells are thin-walled, followed by phelloderm. The cortex consists of several secretory channels and phloem fibres. Medullary rays with radially arranged cells are present. Idioblast of calcium oxalate is the specific characteristic of cinchona bark. Starch grains are present in the parenchymatous tissues. Stone cells are rarely present in the structure. A few of the cork cells are lignified. Medullary rays are 2 to 3 cells wide.

Chemical Constituents

Cinchona bark contains about 25 alkaloids, which belong to quinoline group. The important

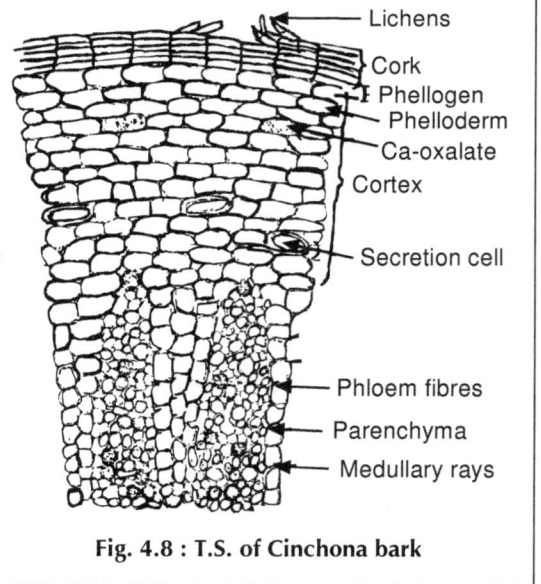

Fig. 4.8 : T.S. of Cinchona bark

alkaloids are quinine, quinidine, cinchonine and cinchonidine. The alkaloids of lesser importance are quinicine, cinchonicine hydroquinine, hydrocinchonidine and homocinchonidine. *C. succirubra* contains 5 - 7 % of total alkaloids, of which 30 % is quinine. *C. ledgeriana* yields from 6 - 10 % and, in some cases, upto 14 % of total alkaloids, with upto 75 % is quinine. *C. salisaya* has 6 - 8 % total alkaloids (about 50 % quinine).

Quinine and Quinidine form many salts, but medicinally their sulphates are more significant. Cinchonine and cinchonidine are also isomers of each other.

Apart from alkaloids, cinchona also contains quinic acid and cinchotannic acid. In the plant, the alkaloids are present as salts of these acids. Cinchotannic acid decomposes into insoluble cinchona red, due to its phlobatannin nature. Cinchona bark also contains a glycoside called quinovin, tannins and bitter essential oil.

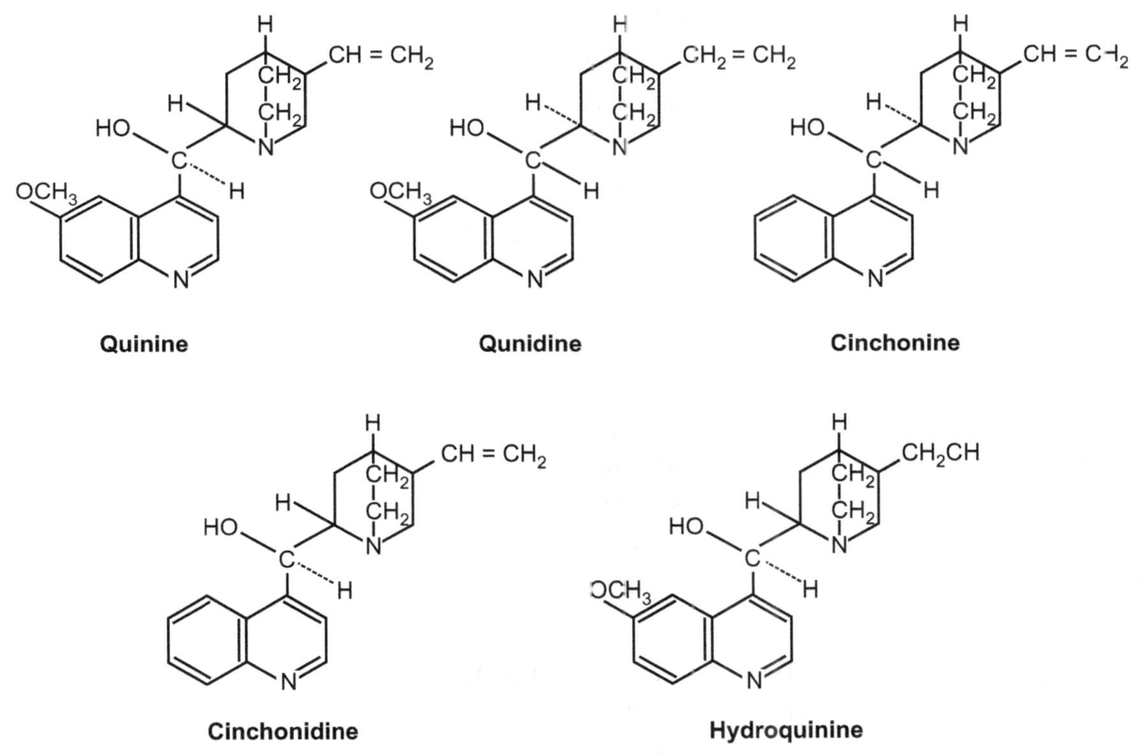

Quinine

Qunidine

Cinchonine

Cinchonidine

Hydroquinine

The alkaloid quinine occurs as bitter white crystals and it darkens when exposed to light and has fluorescent properties. It shows a strong blue fluorescence in ultra-violet light. This fluorescence is enhanced in presence of dilute sulphuric acid. Quinine forms salts with different acids. Quinine sulphate $(C_{20}H_{24}N_2O_2)_2 \cdot H_2SO_4 \cdot 2H_2O$ is important from pharmaceutical point of view. It has very less solubility in water (1 in 810 parts of water), due to which, it is suitable for oral use.

Quinidine $(C_{20}H_{24}N_2O_2)$ is similar to quinine in its physical and chemical properties and has higher water solubility. The free base is soluble in water, ethyl alcohol, methyl alcohol and chloroform.

Chemical Tests

1. Heat the powdered drug in a dried test tube with little glacial acetic acid, purple vapours are produced at the upper part of test tube.

2. Thalleoquin test: The powdered drug gives emerald green colour with bromine water and dilute ammonia solution.

3. Quinidine solution gives a white precipitate with silver nitrate solution, which is soluble in nitric acid.

Standards of Quality

Total ash	- not more than 4 %
Acid insoluble ash	- not more than 7 %
Foreign organic matter	- nor more than 2 %
ASE	- not more than 18 %
WSE	- not more than 10 %
Total phenolics	- not more than 12 %
LOD	- not more than 8 %

The UV spectrophotometric method of estimation is carried out for quinine.

Pharmacological Uses

Cinchona bark is antimalarial in nature. The cinchona preparations like cinchona extract, compound cinchona tincture etc. are also employed as bitter stomachics and antipyretics. Quinine and its salts are used in the treatment of malaria. Quinine is a protoplasmic poison, especially for protozoa like *Plasmodium vivax, P. falciparum, P. malarie and P. fatal,* and hence, used as powerful antimalarial drug.

Recently the pharmacokinetic studies on quinine have shown that it can be better used in other forms. Infusion of quinine rather than intravenous injection eliminates the risk of sudden death. Secondly, quinine in microencapsulated form has been reported to give better bioavailability.

Quinine has also been found to be highly active *in vitro* against *Trypanosoma cruzi* epimastigotes.

Quinidine is primarily a cardiac depressant and used to prevent certain arrhythmias and tachycardia. Quinidine is valuable in prevention of atrial fibrillation.

Substitutes

Cuprea bark (*Remijia pedunculata*), a coppery red coloured drug, contains quinine, quinidine and other alkaloids which resemble to those from cinchona bark. The bark contains numerous stone cells. Along with cinchona alkaloids, it also contains cupreine. False cuprea bark (*R. purdiena*) contains an alkaloid called cusconidine, traces of cinchonine, cinchonamine, but no quinine.

TEA-LEAVES

Synonym

Camellia thea

Biological Source

It contains the prepared leaves and leaf buds of *Thea sinensis* (Linne) O. kuntze, belonging to family Theaceae (Ternstroemiaceae).

Geographical Source

Large areas of land are put under cultivation of tea in India, Sri Lanka, China, Indonesia and Japan. It is available as **black tea** from India and Sri Lanka and **green tea** from China and Japan.

Black tea is obtained by fermenting the heap of fresh tea leaves and further drying with artificial heat. **Green tea** is obtained by putting tea leaves in copper pans and then drying by artificial heat.

Macroscopic Characters of Herb

It is a small evergreen shrub, when cultivated reaches to the height of 1.0 - 1.5 metres, while wild growing plants reach upto 6.0 metres. Plant is much branched and bears grey bark.

- **Leaves** : Leaves are lanceolate or elliptical, blunt at apex, base is tapering, margin is shortly serrate. Young leaves are hairy while matured leaves are glabrous.

  Leaves are smooth on both sides with prominent midrib 5 to 10 cm in length and 1 to 2 cm in width.

- **Flowers**: Flowers are solitary or in groups of 2 or 3 in the leaf axils, and drooping.
- **Colour** : Shiny green
- **Odour** : Characteristic aggreable and aromatic.
- **Taste** : Bitter and astringent.

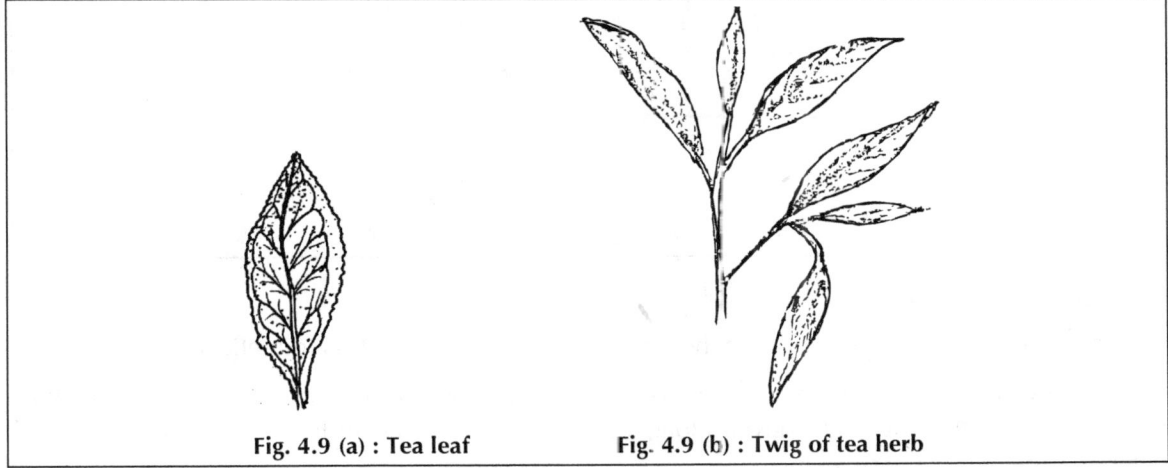

Fig. 4.9 (a) : Tea leaf   **Fig. 4.9 (b) : Twig of tea herb**

Preparation of Green Tea

It is prepared by exposing the freshly collected leaves to the air until most of the moisture is removed. Then they are roasted and stirred continuously until leaves become moist and flaccid. Then they are transferred to rolling table and rolled into balls and subjected to a pressure which removes the moisture. Then the leaves are shaken out on the copper pans and roasted again till the leaves assume dull green colour. Then the leaves are winnowed, screened and graded into various varieties.

Chemical Constituents

Tea leaves are considered as a rich source of caffeine (1 - 3 %). Caffeine is extracted from tea dust and tea leaf waste or sweepings. It also contains theobromine and theophylline in minor quantities. The colour of tea leaves is due to gallotannic acid (15 %). The agreeable odour is due to presence of a yellow volatile oil. Tea leaves also contain an enzymatic mixture called thease.

Caffeine

Chemical Tests

1. Caffeine (also the other purine alkaloids) gives **murexide colour reaction.** Caffeine is taken in a petridish to which hydrochloric acid and potassium chlorate are added and heated to dryness. A purple colour is obtained by exposing the residue to vapours of dilute ammonia. The purple colour is lost on addition of fixed alkali.

2. Caffeine also produces white precipitate with tannic acid solution.

Theobromine **Theophylline**

Pharmacological Uses

Tea is useful as a CNS stimulant in the form of beverage besides, it is a diuretic as well.

Caffeine is widely accepted and used as a central nervous system stimulant, due to its cerebral vasoconstrictor effect. It is also given along with ergotamine tartarate to potentiate the action of latter as a specific analgesic in migraine.

ASHWAGANDHA

Synonyms

Withania root, Asgandh, Winter cherry.

Biological Source

It consists of dried roots and stem bases of *Withania somnifera* (Linn.) Dunal, belonging to family Solanaceae and should contain not less than 0.02 % of total withanolide A and withaferin A on dried basis.

Geographical Source

This plant grows wildly in all dry parts and subtropical India. It occurs in Madhya Pradesh, Uttar Pradesh, Punjab plains and North Western parts of India like Gujarat and Rajasthan. It is also found in Congo, South Africa, Egypt, Morocco, Jordan, Pakistan and Afghanistan.

Cultivation, Collection and Preparation for the Market

It is reported that the plants from different sources vary in their morphological and therapeutic properties. Now-a-days, the cultivation is mainly done in Madhya Pradesh (Manasa plantations), where, about 2000 hectares are under cultivation. The propagation is done by seeds, for which about 4 - 5 kg of seeds are required per hectare. The seeds are sown in the soil which is unsuitable for other crops. The sowing is done towards June-July and during growth, no special arrangements are made for irrigation. Even the nitrogenous fertilizers lead to formation of small roots, but large foliage. Towards December or January, the plants bear flowers and fruits and during January, harvesting is initiated which lasts upto March. The roots are collected by uprooting the plant and either entire roots or the pieces thereof are dried immediately.

Macroscopic Characters

The roots show buff to grey yellow outer colour with longitudinal wrinkles. They are unbranched, straight, conical and some of them bear a crown. The root crown possesses a number of bud scars. Roots are bitter in taste and fresh roots smell similar to urine of horse (hence ashwagandha). The fracture is smooth and powdery.

Microscopic Characters

The transverse section of root shows exfoliated cork which is non-lignified with 2 - 4 layers of phellogen and about 15 - 20 rows of phelloderm. It prominently shows parts of vascular tissue like cambium, consisting of 3 - 5 layers of tangentially elongated cells, phloem region with parenchyma, sieve tubes and companion cells. Secondary xylem is hard which forms a continuous vascular ring interrupted by medullary rays. The transverse section of stem base shows pith, pericyclic fibres, xylem with tracheids, fibres, and starch grains.

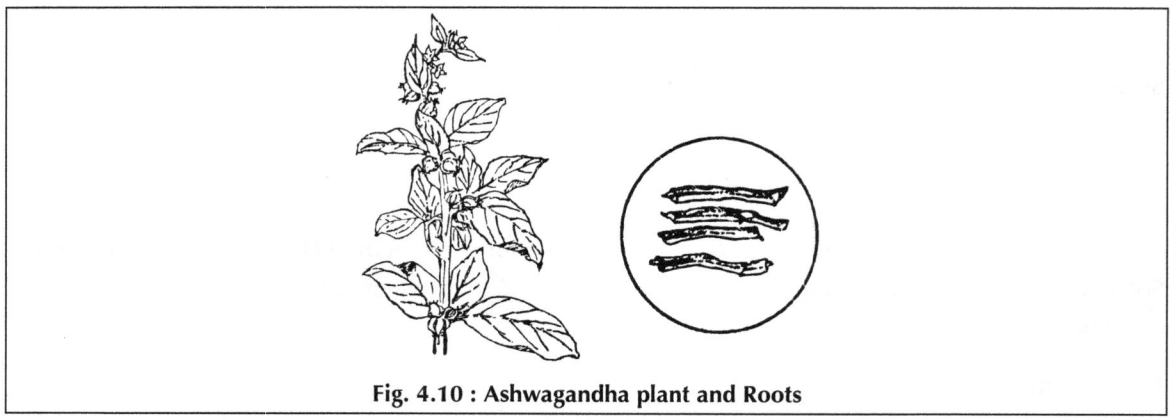

Fig. 4.10 : Ashwagandha plant and Roots

Chemical Constituents

The main constituents of ashwagandha are alkaloids and steroidal lactones. Among the various alkaloids, withanine is the main constituent. The other alkaloids are somniferine, somnine, somniferinine, withananine, pseudo-withanine, tropine, pseudo tropine, 3-α-gloyloxytropane, choline, cuscohygrine, isopelletierine, anaferine and anahydrine. Two acyl steryl glucosides viz. Sitoindoside VII and sitoindoside VIII have been isolated from roots.

Anaferine   **Dl-isopelletierine**

The leaves contain steroidal lactones, which are commonly called as "withanolides". The withanolides have C_{28} steroidal nucleus with C_9 side chain, having six membered lactone rings. Lavie *et.al*, have isolated such compounds from plants grown in Israel, India and S. Africa.

The various withanolides reported are as follows:

Steroids (withanolides) of Ashwagandha

Withaferin   **Withaferin A**

These compounds have been obtained from *W. somnifera* chemotype I.

Another series of steroidal lactones viz. withanolide E to M have been obtained from chemotype III.

The drug also contains two monohydric alcohols called somnitol and somnirol; withanic acid; a phytosterol and ipuranol; and a mixture of fatty acids containing cerotic acid, oleic acid, palmitic acid and stearic acid.

Withanolide A

Standards of Quality

Foreign organic matter	: not more than 2 %
Total ash	: not more than 7 %
Acid-insoluble ash	: not more than 1.2 %
Alcohol soluble matter	: not less than 10 %
Water soluble extraction	: not less than 15 %
Loss of Drying	: not less than 12 %

Ayurvedic Properties

Rasa	:	Madhur, Tikta
Guna	:	Laghu, Snigdha
Veerya	:	Ushna
Vipak	:	Madhur
Doshaghna	:	Vat Kaphaghna

Pharmacological Uses

Ashwagandha has sedative and hypnotic effects. It has hypotensive, respiratory, stimulant actions alongwith bradycardia. It is an immuno-modulatory agent. Sitoindoside (VII and VIII) have been shown to possess anti-stress activity. It acts as mood stabilizer, revives mind and body.

Traditional Uses

Traditionally, it has been used in the treatment of rheumatism, gout, hypertension, nervine and skin-diseases. This drug prevents bony degenerative changes in arthritic conditions. It has been widely used as sex stimulant and rejuvenator and is considered as strength and vigour promoting drug especially in geriatric cases.

The leaf extracts shows activity against *Staphylococcus aureus* and *Ranikhet virus*.

In case of insomnia, memory loss and servival debility. As a galactogogue alongwith liquorice and cows milk. Alongwith ghee and honey in cases of importance and seminal debility.

Kalpa

Ashwagandha churna, Ashwagandha rasayana, Ashwagandha ghruta, Ashwagandha arishta, Ashwagandha kwath.

Market Products

1) **Cheerup capsules :** Ayulabs Pvt. Ltd., Vavdi, Rajkot, Gujarat.
2) **Maha Narayan Taila:** Dabur India Ltd., New Delhi.

KUTJA

Synonyms

Holarrhena, Kurchi bark.

Biological Source

It is the dried stem bark of *Holarrhena antidysenterica* wall belonging to family Apocynaceae. It is collected from 8 - 10 years old plant and freed from attached wood, and peeled into small pieces. It should contain not less than 2 % of total alkaloids of kurchi.

Geographical Source

Kurchi is indigenous to India and found throughout India in parts ascending up to 1000 metres in Himalayan region. It is also found in Orissa, Assam, Uttar Pradesh and Maharashtra.

Cultivation and Collection

The drug is obtained from wild source only. For the collection of bark, the plants which are 8 - 10 years old are selected. Longitudinal and transverse incisions are made on the trunk from July to September. After detachment, the bark is separated from the wood and dried. The recurved pieces of the bark are marketed.

Macroscopical Characters

Kurchi bark appears buff to pale brown on outer surface, while slightly brownish on inner surface. The outer surface is longitudinally wrinkled and bears horizontal lenticels. The pieces are recurved with varying size and thickness. The drug shows a short and granular fracture. It has no odour, but bitter and acrid taste.

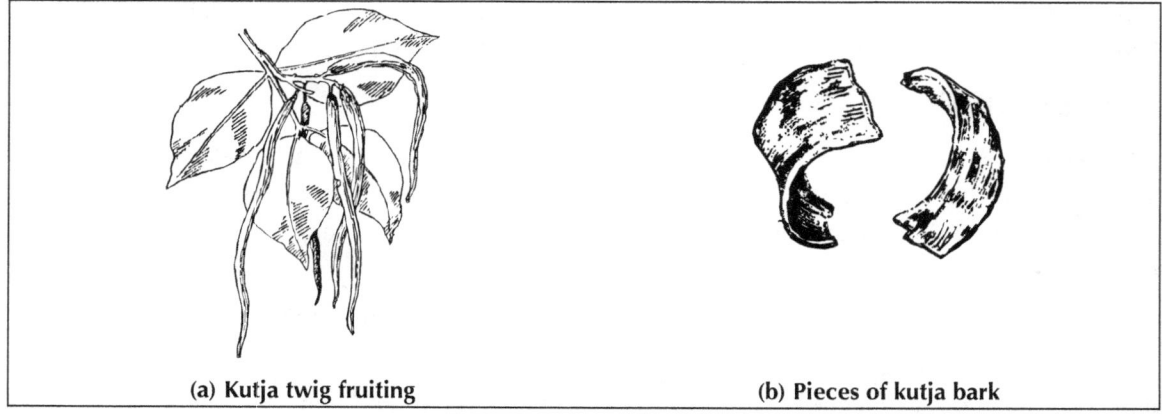

(a) Kutja twig fruiting   (b) Pieces of kutja bark

Fig. 4.11: Kutja herb and bark

Microscopic Characters

In the periderm portion, cork has both tangentially and radially elongated cells. Cork cambium has several layers. Stone cells are present in cortex, either singly or in groups or in horizontal layers. It does not show phloem fibres. Phloem contains sieve tubes, companion cells, phloem parenchyma and stone cells. Medullary rays are multiseriate. In many stone cells, prismatic calcium oxalate crystals are present.

Chemical Constituents

Kurchi contains about 25 total alkaloids (1.5 to 3 %). They are C_{21} group steroidal alkaloids. The active alkaloids are conessine (kurchicine), norconessine, isoconessine, dioxyconessine, conessimine, holarrhimine and holarrhidine.

Conessine is also present in root bark alongwith some other steroidal alkaloids.

Conessine

Standards of Quality

Acid insoluble ash	:	not more than 1 %
Alcohol (60 %) soluble	:	4 - 6 %
Foreign organic matter	:	not more than 5 %

Ayurvedic Properties

Rasa	:	Tikta, Kasaya
Guna	:	Laghu, Rooksha
Veerya	:	Sheetal
Vipak	:	Katu

Pharmacological Uses

Kurchi is antiprotozoal in activity and used to treat amoebic dysentery. Conessine is highly active against *Entamoeba histolytica*.

Traditional Uses

For the treatment of piles, intestinal worms bilions affections and bowel complaints. A traditional preparation of kurchi bark, viz. "kutajarishta" is commonly used, especially for chronic amoebiasis.

Dosage

Powder (seed) : 1 to 3 gm

Decocation: 10 to 15 gm

Kalp

Kutajarishta, Kutajaraleha, Kutajaparpati.

Adulterants

Kurchi is often adulterated with *Wrightia tinctoria* and *Wrightia tomentosa*, and can be detected by morphological and microscopic characters.

Wrightia tinctoria is available as channeled, grey in colour, torsh and brittle in natune. No pericyclic fibres and starch. Uniseriate medullary rays.

W. Tomentosa bark is yellowish with characterisitc taste. Pericyclic fibres absent.

TYLOPHORA

Synonyms

Antamul, Indian Ipecacunha.

Biological Source

This consists of dried leaves of the plant *Tylophora indica* (Syn. *Tylophora asthmatica* Weight and Arn) Family Asclepiadaceae.

Geographical Source

Tylophora occurs naturally is Andhra Pradesh, Karnataka, Konkan, Orissa and Assam upto an altitude of 100 m in the hilly region. Also found in Africa and Australia.

Macroscopic Characters

It is perennial climber and roots of which are aromatic.

Colour : Grayish green with 6 - 13 mm petioles.

Odour : Odourless

Taste : Sweetish subsequently acrid

Size : Leaves are 5 to 10 × 3 to 5 cm

Shape : Ovate or elliptic – oblong

Extra Features

Leaves are acute or acuminate at the apex, glabrous and pubescent on the lower surface, base of the leaves is cordate with petioles about 3 - 5 mm in length.

Fig. 4.12 : Tylophora herb with flowers

Chemical Constituents

Tylophora herb contains alkaloids, volatile oil, wax, resins, tannins, sterols, glycosides, and pigments. Total alkaloid content of the drug is about 0.5% and alkaloids are known as tylophorine, tylophorinine, tylophorinidine and septicine. The volalite oil content 0.25% cetyl alcohol. Quercetin, kampferol and tyloindane are the other chemicals reported in the drug.

Tylophorine

Tylophorinine

Standards of Quality

FOM	:	> 2.0%
Total ash	:	> 27.0%
Acid insoluble ash	:	> 14.5%
ASE	:	< 5.0 %
WSE	:	< 15.0 %
LOD	:	> 6.5%

Pharmacological Uses

Dried leaves are used as expectorant, diaphoretic and emetic.

Traditional Uses

In the treatment of whooping, cough, bronchitis and asthma. Tylophora is also recommended in rheumatism gout and as anti-inflammatory agent.

KANTKARI

Synonym

Vyaghri

Biological Source

Kantkari mainly consists of dried whole plant of *Solanum xanthocarpum*, Family Solanaceae.

Geographical Source

Found all-over India, luxuriously growing on waste lands. More common in xerophytic area.

The plant occurs throughout India, often in waste places, on roadsides and in open scrublands. It is a prickly, usually spreading or diffused perennial, woody at base. The young branches are densely covered with minute star-shaped hairs.

Description of Herb

It is an important ingredient of "Dushmoola" and wherein all parts of the plant are used hence all parts will be dealt in short.

It is bright green perennial plant about 2.5 metres in height, woody at the base and numerous branches (glossy green in colour). All parts bear sharp compressed straight yellow shining prickles about 1 inch in length.

Roots : Brownish yellow in colour. Plant being xerophytic root is short and covered with wrinkles on surface. It is very hard woody and flexible.

Leaves : Simple, exstipulate, petiolate, oval with stellate hairs on both surfaces.

Size : 2.5 - 7.5 × 5.10 cm

Prickles on midrib which are long, yellow and pointed.

Flowers : Extra-axillary, and pedicels are short, hairy, regular, bisexual. Violet coloured, with yellow anther. Calyx five lobed, gamosepalous, corolla purple, 1 inch in diameter, gamopetalous.

Androecium : Polyandrous, 5 filaments, short, spindle shaped, yellow coloured.

Gynoecium : Poly carpellary, superior, ovary, avoid, style short, stigma inconspicuous.

Fruit : Round, small and thorny 1.2 - 1.9 cm in diameter, yellow on whitish green in colour.

Seeds : Circular, flat, numerous, globularous and about 2 mm in size.

Fig. 4.13 : Kantkari herb

Parts used: Whole plant

Chemical Constituents

Important constituents of Kantkari are **steroidal alkaloids** namely solasodine, solasonine, solamergine and β-solamergine. While the sterols are cycloartenol, nor carpesterol and cholesterol.

Solasodine

Nor-carpesterol

Pharmacological Uses

Indigestion, intestinal worms, hypertension, common cold, cough, bronchitis, asthma, fever. When mixed with haritaki and aghada (*Achyrathus aspera*) really good for asthma.

Traditional Uses

(a) Stem flowers and fruits are bitter and carmative. All parts of plant were employed in cough, asthma and pains in chest, being used in the form of a decoction.

(b) Leaves applied locally to relieve pain.

(c) Plant credited with diuretic properties and used to cure dropsy.

(d) Juice mixed with whey and ginger given in fever.

(e) Juice of leaves, mixed with black pepper is prescribed in rheumatism.

(f) An analgesic, anti-inflammatory with antibacterial properties. Its fumes are inhaled traditionally in dental care such as dental pain.

Kantakari is mainly **expectorant** and prescribed for bronchial **asthma** and cough. It is used for several disorders like diabetis, spermatogenesis etc.

Dosage

Decoction 40 - 50 ml

VASAKA

Synonyms

Adhatoda, Adulsa, Malabar nut.

Biological Source

It consists of dried, as well as, fresh leaves of the plant *Adhatoda vasica* Nees, belonging to family Acanthaceae, and contains not less than 0.6 % of vasicine on dried basis.

Geographical Source

Vasaka is indigenous to India, where it is found in sub-Himalayan track upto an altitude of 1000 m, and in Maharashtra especially, in Konkan region. Besides India, it is found in Myanmar, Sri Lanka and Malaya.

Cultivation and Collection

The uses of vasaka have been known since old times and it is included in different formulations of ayurveda.

The plant is not cultivated on commercial scale. It is obtained from garden plants or wild sources. It can be easily propagated by stem cuttings and by seed germination. The plant is obtained in all seasons of the year. It reaches to a height of 2 - 3 metres. It is also observed that the plant favourably grows in loamy soil.

Macroscopic Characters

The drug contains stem leaf, fruit and seeds. The leaves have 10 - 30 cm length and width of 4 - 10 cm. They are petiolate and exstipulate. The shape is lanceolate. The margin is crenate with acuminate apex. There are 8 - 10 pairs of lateral veins. Taste is better and odour is characteristic.

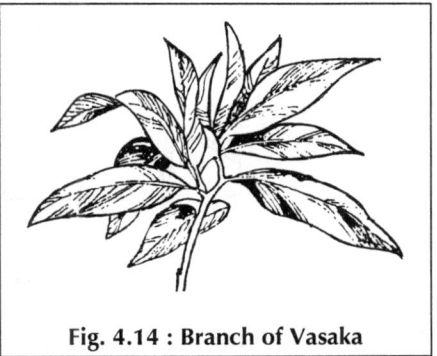

Fig. 4.14 : Branch of Vasaka

Microscopic Characters

The epidermis shows caryophyllaceous stomata with sinuous epidermal cells covering and glandular trichomes. It is a dorsiventral leaf with palisade having 2 layers of cells. 2 - 3 bicollateral vascular bundles are seen in midrib. Mesophyll contains prismatic and acicular crystals of calcium oxalate. Stomatal index is from 10.8 - 18.2 and palisade ratio from 5 - 8.5.

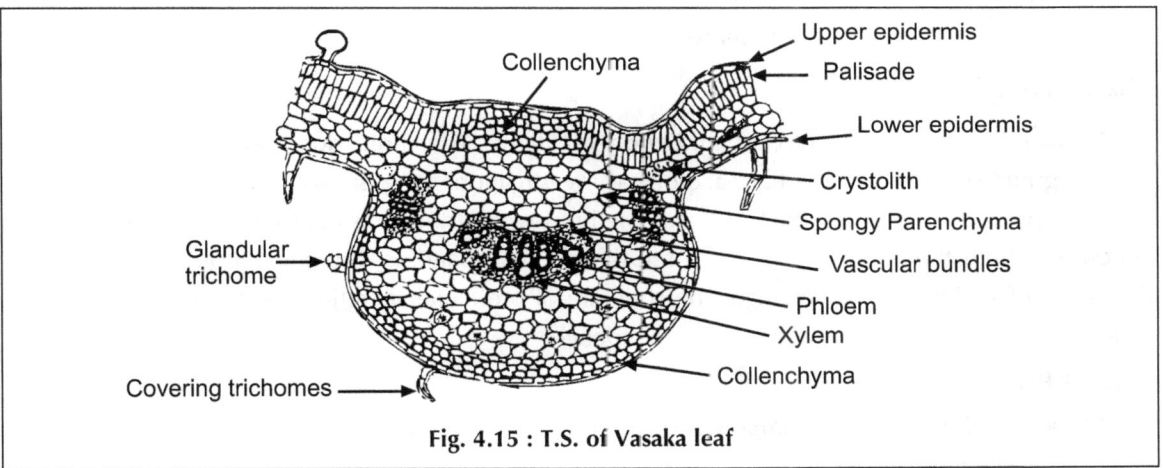

Fig. 4.15 : T.S. of Vasaka leaf

Chemical Constituents

Vasaka leaves contain quinazoline derivatives such as vasicine 2.0 to 2.5 %, vasicinone and 6-hydroxy vasicine. Biochemically, vasicine is oxidised to its ketonic derivative vasicinone, and the latter exerts main activity as bronchodilator. The drug also contains volatile oil, betain and vasakin. It is also reported that vasaka contains adhatodic acid.

Adhatodine   **Vasicol**

Standards of Quality

Foreign organic matter	:	not more than 2 %.
ASE	:	not less than 3 %
WSE	:	not less than 22 %
Total ash	:	not more than 21 %
Acid insoluble ash	:	not more than 2 %
LOD	:	not more than 12 %.

Pharmacological Uses

Vasaka is used as expectorant and bronchodilator. The large doses are irritant and cause vomitting and diarrhoea. The pharmacological investigations have shown that vasicine also shows oxytocic property similar to oxytocin and methyl ergometrine. Vasicine also shows abortificient action and both the actions are due to release of prostaglandins. Bromhexine HCl is a synthetic derivative of vasicine which changes the structure of bronchial secretions and reduces viscosity of sputum. It does not cause drowsiness or dependence.

Market Products

1) **Kasamrit Herbal:** Baidyanath, Ayurved Bhavan – Nagpur.
2) **Vasaka Capsule:** Himalaya Drug Company, Bangaluru.
3) **Vasavaleha:** Dabur Pharmaceuticals Ltd., Ghaziabad. U.P.
4) **Glycodin-terp-vasaka:** Alembic, Vadodara, Gujarath.

BHRINGRAJ

Synonyms

Eclipta, Bhangra, Maka.

Biological Source

This consists of whole plant botanically known as *Eclipta alba* (L) Hassk of family Asteraceae. It contains not less than 0.1 % wedelolactone on dried basis. (Variety with yellow flowers is botanically known as *Wedella-chinensis*).

Geographical Source

In tropical parts of world and all over India, abundant in marshy places and available in all seasons.

Description of Herb

Colour : Green to greenish brown

Odour : None

Taste : Bitter

It is a perrinial herb about 10 - 15 cm in height or a prostate plant.

Root : Cylindrical upto 7 mm in diameter, greyish with number of secondary branches.

Stem : Cylindrical or flat, node dishnet; rooting at nodes, appressed white trichomes, brownish in colour.

Fig. 4.16 : Bhringraj herb

Leaves : 3.5 cm in length. Opposite, sessile, entire, oblong, lanceolate and trichomes on both the surfaces.

Flowers : Solitary on unequal axillary peduncles, ray flowers ligulate, white disc flowers tubular, corolla four toothed, stamen five, anthers united, ovary inferior. It flowers in October November every year!

Fruits : Achenial, one seeded with narrow wing and brown in colour.

Seeds : Dark brown hairy and non-endospermic.

Cultivation and Collection

It is not cultivated commercially and is obtained from wild grown plants. It is collected in winter when the plant is in flowering state.

Chemical Constituents

Bioactive steroidal alkaloids, glycosides, resin, alkaloid ecliptine, nicotine, and flavoroid wedelo-lactone; wedelic acid, epigenin and luteolin.

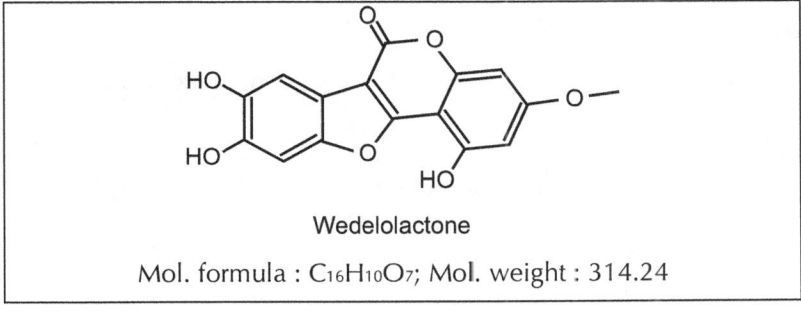

Wedelolactone

Mol. formula : $C_{16}H_{10}O_7$; Mol. weight : 314.24

Standards of Quality

Foreign organic matter	:	Not more than 5 %
Water soluble extractives	:	Not less than 15 %
Alcohol soluble extractives	:	Not less than 5 %
Ash	:	Not more than 22 %
Loss on drying	:	Not more than 15 %

Ayurvedic Properties

Rasa : Katu
Guna : Laghu, Rooksha
Veerya : Ushna
Vipak : Katu

Pharmacological Uses

It is brain tonic, used for liver-disorders, viral hepitits, skin and hair care disorders, improves complexion. It is valuable to calm the mind and memory disorders. Bhringraj strengthens spleen and is a general tonic.

Traditional Use

Paste with sesame oil is used for glandular swelling, skin diseases, head ache, toothache. It is also hair growth tonic.

Market Products

1) **Mahabringraj Tail.**

KACHNAR

Synonym

Orchid tree

Biological Source

This consists of bark, stem, leaves, seeds and flowers of the plant *Bauhinia variegate*, Family Caesalpiniaceae.

Geographical Source

It is found in sub-Himalyan tract and forests of South India, Central India and also in Myanmar.

Macroscopic Characters

Kachnar is tree with dark brown bark. Tree is about 35 feet in height while 10 - 15 feet wide. Leaves are 4-6 inches and heart shaped. Flowers are with five overlapping irregular petals having magenta, lavender or purplish blue colour in the bunches at the top of the branch. It being a member of leguminosae bears flat legumes about 12" in length.

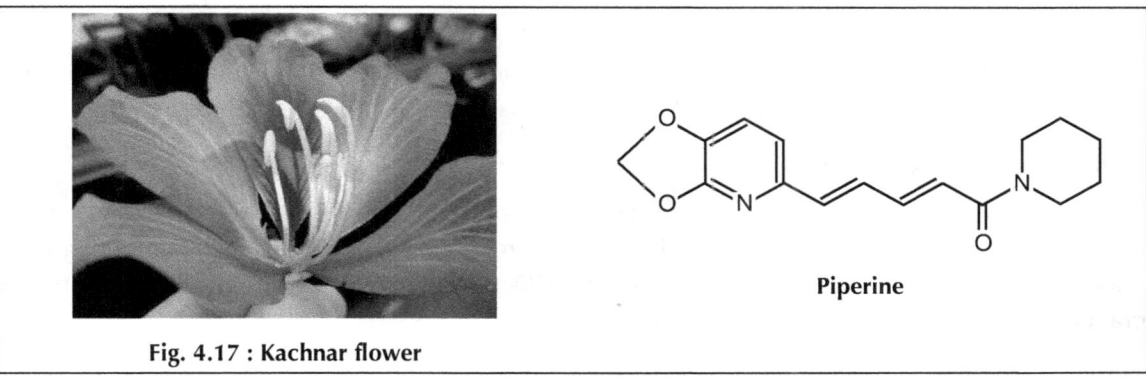

Fig. 4.17 : Kachnar flower

Chemical Constituents

Kachnar contains wide variety of chemicals i.e. Alkaloids, glycosides, vit. C, mucilage and volatile oil.

Piperine and piperlongumine are the alkaloids reported, while volatile oil contains, comphene, eugenol, gingerol. Guggulsterone is also reported in the drug.

Kanchnar seeds contains about 15.0% of fatty oil.

Ayurvedic Properties

Rasa : Kasaya
Guna : Rooksha
Veerya : Sheetal
Vipak : Katu

Pharmacological Uses

Decoction of kachnar is given in dyspepsia and flatulence. Dried buds are used in diarrhoea, worms, piles and dysentery. It is also used in malaria.

Traditional Uses

Used as astringent in salivation and sore throat. Decoction of bark is used in ulcers, skin diseases, piles and dysentery. It is also used to loose body weight and very important now-a-days to maintain the health.

PUNARNAVA

Synonyms

Rakta Punarnava, Hog weed

Biological Source

It consists of fresh, as well as, dried herb *Boerhaavia diffussa* (*B. repens*; *B. procumbens*) Linn. Nyctaginaceae. It should contain not less than 0.005 % of boervinone on dried basis.

Geographical Source

It is found wild throughout India and Sri Lanka. Punarnava is found in Himalayan valleys upto 2000 - 2500 m. The weed also grows in Malaysia, China and Africa.

Cultivation and Collection

Punarnava is not cultivated, it is very common and most troublesome weed of sandy tracts, waste-lands and road-sides. It is collected from wild grown plants only. It is abundant during rainy season and is collected in the flowering stage in October - November. It is variable, diffusely branched, and creeping herbaceous perennial.

Macroscopic Characters

Colour : Leaves: green on upper surface and whitish on lower surface

Stems: greenish-purple

Flowers: upper part pink

Odour : Odourless

Taste : Bitter

Size : Leaves are 25 - 30 mm long. Small leaves are 12 - 20 mm in length, ovate, oblong sub-orbicular and apex slightly pointed with rounded or sub-cordate base. Leaves are glabrous, rather thick in texture and petiolate. Petioles are double the length of the blade. Margin is entire.

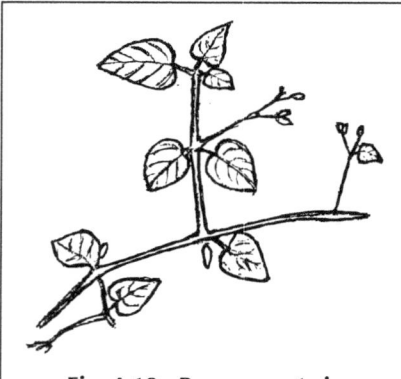

Fig. 4.18 : Punarnava twig

Stems are cylindrical, stiff and thick at the nodes. They are branched and about 1 m in length. Stems are light reddish-brown above and pale greenish below.

Flowers are internally sessile in small umbels, about 10 - 25 mm in length.

Fruits are one sided, glandular and about 0.5 cm in size.

Roots are elongated, fusiform, tapering and somewhat tuberous. Roots grow vertically downwards striking deep into the soil. They are cream or light brownish-yellow, with very soft skin. Old roots are often marked with knotty scars of fallen rootlets.

Microscopic Characters

Leaf: Epidermis shows the presence of multicellular uniseriate glandular trichomes. Cortex consists of one or two layers of collenchyma followed by few layers of parenchyma. Endodermis is distinct. Stellar part is represented by small vascular bundles, which are scattered throughout. Leaves have stomata on both the surfaces. Palisade is one layered and with small air-sac in spongy parenchyma. Calcium oxalate clusters and idioblasts are present in the mesophyll.

Chemical Constituents

Punarnava contains about 0.04 - 0.1 % of alkaloid known as punarnavine (M.P. 235°C), phenolic glycoside, punernavoside, an antifibrinolytic agent and rotenoids, boeravinone A, B, C and D. It also contains about 6 % of potassium nitrate, an oily substance and ursolic acid.

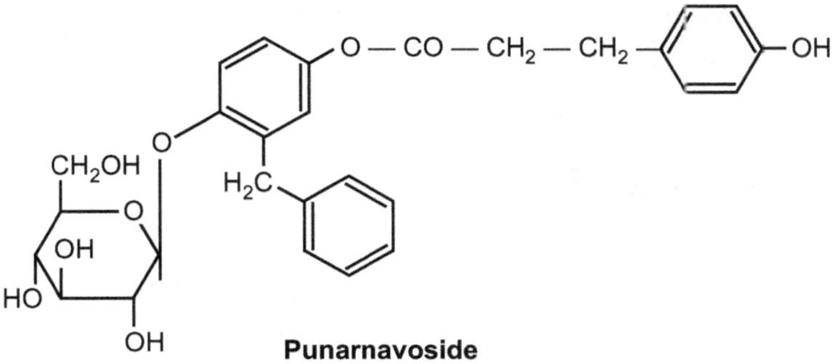

Punarnavoside

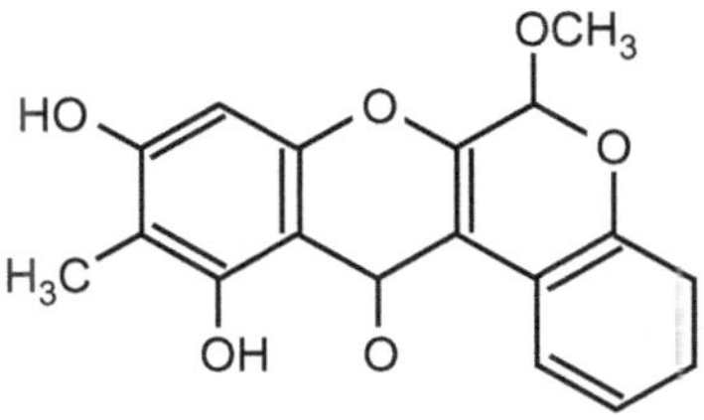

Boeravinone A

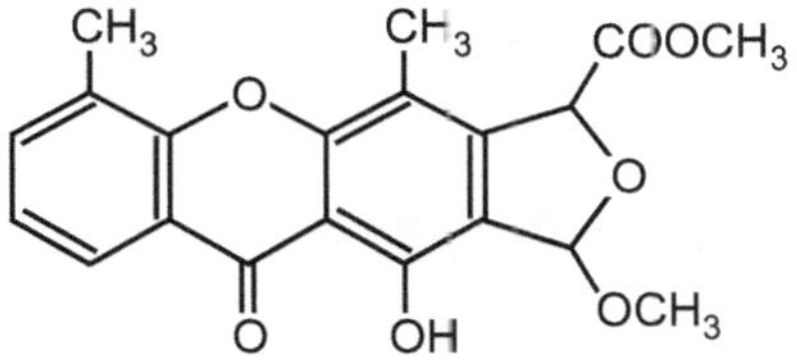

Borhavine

Standards of Quality

FOM	:	> 2.0 %
ASE	:	> 0.5 %
WSE	:	< 9.0 %
Ash	:	> 10.0 %
Acid insoluble ash	:	> 3.0 %
Loss on drying	:	> 10.0 %

Ayurvedic Properties

Rasa : Madhur
Guna : Laghu, Rooksha
Veerya : Ushna
Vipak : Madhur

Pharmacological Uses

The herb is used as diuretic and as an expectorant. Punarnava is stomachic and is prescribed in the treatment of jaundice. It is also given in the loss of digestive power, enlargement of spleen and for abdominal pains.

Substitutes

Trianthema portulacastrum, Trianthema obcordata and *T. decandra* are usually substituted for punarnava. *T. portulacastrum* has similar foliage to that of punarnava and is also known as shwet punarnava.

SHANKHPUSHPI

Synonyms

Shankhvel, Shankhini.

Biological Source

This consists of the aerial parts of the plant known as *Canscora decussata*, family Gentianaceae.

Geographical Source

Shankhpushpi is found throughout India up to an altitude of 1300 m. It is also grown in Sri Lanka and Myanmar.

Description of Herb

It is much branched, annual plant propagated by seeds. The flowering season of this plant is from October to December. The plant is cultivated in the gardens as ornamental plant for its flowers. This is an erect annual with four winged stems and half a metre in length with decussate branches. It grows well in moist situations.

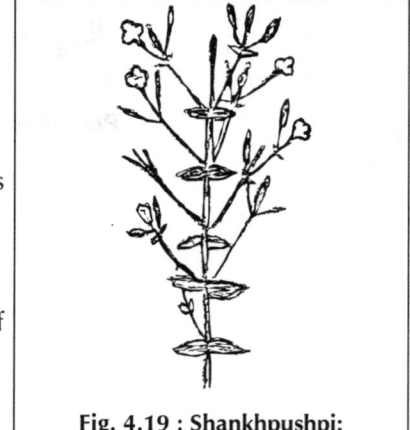

Fig. 4.19 : Shankhpushpi: *Canscora decussata herb*

Macroscopic Characters

Leaves are sessile, 2.5 - 4.0 cm in length, lanceolate, decussate with three prominent verticle lines; flowers, axilliary, solitary, white or yellowish.

Chemical Constituents

Drug is found to contain bitter substance and an oleo-resin. Two crystalline compounds have been isolated from the aqueous and alcoholic extracts of the plant. Shankhpushpi is found to contain triterpenes, alkaloids and xanthones.

Pharacological Uses

Entire plant, as well as, fresh juice is used in medicine. It is regarded as bitter alternative and nervine tonic. The fresh juice of the plant is prescribed in insanity, epilepsy, and nervous debility. Alcoholic extract possesses anti-viral activity against Ranikhet disease virus (chicks).

Substitutes

Canscora diffusa, Family: Gentianaceae distributed throughout India is used as substitute for Shankhpushpi.

There is controversy in correct identity of shankhpushpi and some scientists have identified Dwarf morning glory i.e. *Evolvulus alsinoides*, Family: Convolvulaceae and also *Convolulus pruricalis*, Family: Convolvulaceae as Shankhpushpi.

Market Products

1) **Shankhpushpi brain tonic:** Baidyanath, Nagpur.

PIPALA MUL

Synonym

Pipala-roots, Pipala mool.

Biological Source

The dried roots of *Piper-longum*, Family: Piperaceae are known as pipala mul or pipala roots in the market.

Cultivation and Collection

It is a pereunial plant cultivated from sea level to 1000 metres. Cultivated by using seed or suckers. It needs rainfall of 200 - 400 cm per annum and temperature between 10 - 15°C.

After collecting the fruits for three successive years, the whole plant is harvested by cutting the stems close to the ground and the roots are dug up. The roots and stems are washed cleaned and cut into small pieces. They are dried in the shade for 4 to 5 days. Cultivation needs temperature between 10 - 15°C.

Macroscopic Characters

Roots are cylindrical, slightly curved with swollen internodes, covered with rootless scars.

Roots are 2.5 - 5.0 cm in length and 2 - 5 mm in thickness. Dark brown in colour with pungent bitter taste, producing numbeness to tongue.

Odour: Aromatic.

The average yield of dried roots per hectare is about 500 kg.

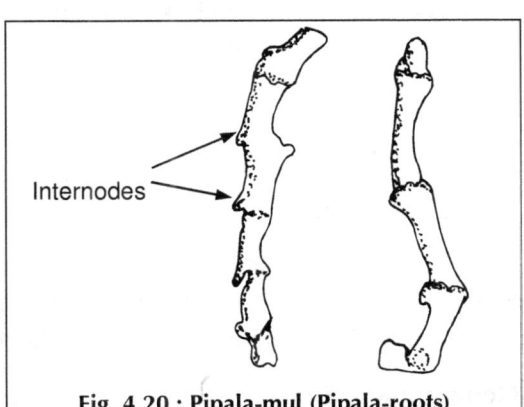

Fig. 4.20 : Pipala-mul (Pipala-roots)

Chemical Constituents

Pipala roots contain 0.15 to 0.18 % piperine, along with piplartine, triacontane and dihydro stigmesterol.

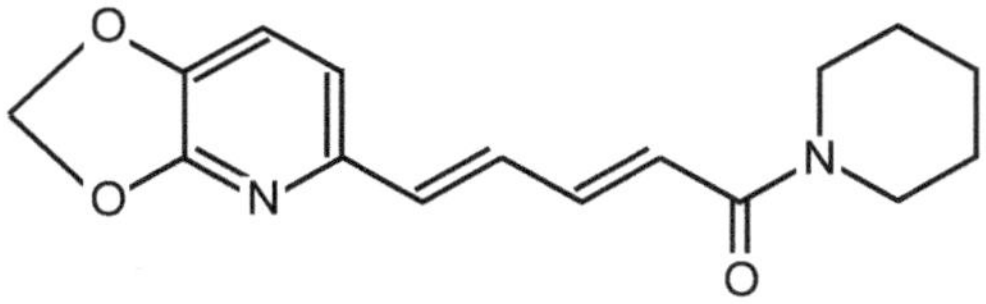

Piperine

Ayurvedic Properties

Rasa : Katu
Guna : Laghu, Snigdha
Veerya : Sheet
Vipak : Madhur

Pharmacological Uses

Pipala roots are used similar to long pepper fruits. Additioally in Ayurvedic medical practice they are also used as emmenagogue abortifacient, anthelmintic and especially for cough, bronchitis and asthma.

Traditional Uses

Alongwith honey it is prescribed for indigestion, chronic – bronchitis, chest affections, and also in asthma. Fruits are used after childbirth to check post-partum haemorrhage. Roots are also useful in enlarged spleen, in Gout and Rhumatism.

BHUI-AMLA

Introduction

It is a small annual herb, known since the ancient period of **Charaka** for its medicinal use. The fresh juice of whole plant is found to be useful in various liver disorders.

Synonym

Phyllanthus

Biological Source

It consists of all aerial parts of the plant, *Phyllanthus niruri* belonging to family Euphorbiaceae. Indian variety available is *Phyllanthus fraternus* and *Phyllanthus armarus*. It contains not less than 0.25 % of total phyllanthin and hypophyllanthin on dried basis.

Geographical Source

The plant is found growing abundantly throughout India, mainly in the states of Maharashtra, Uttar Pradesh, Punjab, Bihar, Orissa, Andhra Pradesh and some parts of Madhya Pradesh, Karnataka and Bengal. Also found in Sri Lanka.

Cultivation and Collection

It grows well under tropical climatic conditions. However, very dry temperature or very low temperature conditions are not preferred. It can grow up to 700 - 800 metres above the sea level. Suitable temperature ranging from 25 - 40°C with average humidity is desired. Well distributed rainfall in the range of 40 - 50 cm is suitable.

Bhuiamla grows in variety of soils, preferably well drained rich organic and light textured soils. It also grows well on sandy loam to calcareous soil. Soil pH should be alkaline to acidic. Even water logging soil does not show adverse effects on its growth.

Propagated well through seeds or by raising seedlings and transplanting.

The plants mature within 3 to 4 months. They are usually harvested after rainy season is over, when the amount of green leaves is in abundance. Since the active constituent is present in leaves, higher leaf mass is expected during harvesting. For harvesting, the whole plants are uprooted.

The collected whole plants are cleared of external matter and are allowed to dry in shade. The fresh juice of plant is also used in medicine.

Total yield of fresh herb per hectare is about 2 - 3 tones.

Macroscopic Characters

Colour : Green to yellowish green in colour.

Taste : Bitter

Odour : None

Stems : 1 - 1.5 cm in length and 1.4 mm in diameter stems are stout.

Leaves : Short-stalked, oblong in shape and about 5 × 3 mm in size.

(See coloured photograph at the end of book)

Fig. 4.21: Bhui-amla herb

Chemical Constituents

It contains, leucodelphimidin alkaloids, flavonoids as quercetin, astralgin, quercitrin, isoquercitrin and rutin. It also contains $\not\leq 0.25$ % of total phyllanthine and hypophyllanthine.

| Phyllanthin | Nerurin | Niruriside |

Niruriside, a carbohydrate from methanolic extract of phyllunthus niruri has shown anti-HIV activity. It is specific inhibitor of REV protein, with an IC_{50} value of 3.3 μm.

Standards of Quality

FOM	:	≯ 2.0%
ASE	:	≮ 6.0%
WSE	:	≮ 15.0%
Total ash	:	≯ 8.0%
Acid insoluble ash	:	≯ 5.0%
LOD	:	≯ 12.0%

Ayurvedic Properties

Rasa : Tikta, Kasaya, Madhur
Guna : Laghu, Rooksha
Veerya : Sheet
Vipak : Madhur

Pharmacological Uses

The drug is used as a hepatoprotective, mainly used in the treatment of viral hepatitis and various other liver disorders. It is also used as diuretic in oedema. Externally, it is used to relieve inflammation, also used as good appetiser.

Traditional Uses

Decoction of herb is given for Jaundice, costipation, dyspepsia. Fresh roots are given with rice water for menorrhagia and with milk as galactoguage. Young leaves are given in dropsical disorders and urinary complaints. Poultice is used to treat scabies, itch and skin diseases.

Market Products

1) **Ayuliv:** Ayulabs Pvt. Ltd., Gondal Road, Vavdi, Rajkot 360004.
2) **Diabicare:** Eastern Drug, IIA Earle Street, Kolkata - 26.

Chapter 5...

DRUGS CONTAINING TANNIN

AMLA

Synonyms

Amruta, Amalaki, Indian goose berry.

Biological Source

It consists of dried as well fresh fruits of *Emblica officinalis* belonging to family Euphorbiaceae. It contains not less than 1.0% w/w of gallic acid calcuatled on dry basis.

Geographical Source

It is found fluid or cultivated throughout the decidious forests of India. It is also found in Sri lanka, Myanmar.

Description of Tree

It is medium to large decidious tree with 8-18 m in height with spreading branches.

Bark	:	Greenish or ash gray to brownish in cola.
Leaves	:	Leaves are feathery with simple, small oblong pinnately arranged leaflets, glabrous and light green in colour.
Flowers	:	Flowers are small, unisexual bearing male and female flowers separately. Male flowers arises in axil of leaf in bunches while female flowers in axil of branches and are solitary. They are yellowish greenish.
Fruits	:	Fruits are fleshy, globular, with smooth surface marked with six spaced divisions. The size of fruits varies according to the variety.
Seeds	:	Seeds are 6 trygonus, very hard and smooth in appearance, normally greenish and cream in color when fresh.
Parts used	:	Fruits, root bark, leaves, flowers.

Cultivation

It is grown by seed germination. It can also be propagated by budding or cutting. It does not tolerate frost or drought. It is normally found up to an altitude of 1500 meters usually collected from wild grown plants.

Collection

Fruits are collected from full grown trees, in the month of October to February.

Macroscopic Characters

Colour : Green changing to light yellow or reddish green.

Odour : None

Taste : Sore and astrigent

Size : 1.5 to 2.5 cm in diameter.

Shape : The fruits are depressed, globose.

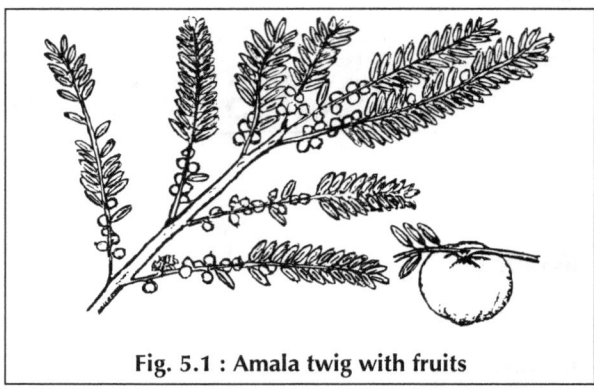

Fig. 5.1 : Amala twig with fruits

Chemical Constituents

Amla is a natural source of vitamin C; containing 600-750 mg/100 gm of fresh pulp. It also contains 5% fat, phyllemblin and 5% tannin. It is rich in minerals such as phosphorus, iron and calcium. Also contains appreciable amount of pectin. The seeds contain a fixed oil phosphatids and small quantity of essential oil with characteristic odour.

$$\begin{array}{c} O=C-H \\ | \\ HO-C-H \\ | \\ HO-C-H \\ | \\ H-C-OH \\ | \\ HO-C-H \\ | \\ CH_2OH \end{array}$$

Vitamin C (Ascorbic acid)

Standards of Quality

Foreign organic matter	:	≯ 3.0%
Alcohol soluble extractive	:	≮ 30.0%
Water soluble extractive	:	≮ 40.0%
Total ash	:	≯ 05.0%
Acid insoluble ash	:	≯ 02.0%
Loss on drying	:	≯ 12.0%

Chemical Tests

1) Transparent aqueous solution of Amla gives bluish black colour with ferric chloride solution.

2) With potassium ferrocyamide and ammonia deep-red colour is obtained.

Ayurvedic Properties

Rasa : Mukhya rasa amla, except lavan all five rasa.

Vipak : Madhur

Veerya : Sheeta

Guna : Laghu, rooksha, sheeta

Doshaghna : Tridoshghanata, Mukhyata : Pittashamak.

Pharmacological Action

Fresh fruits shows laxative, diuretic, refrigerant and stomachic action. The fruit also shows amibacterial action hence can be used in diarrhoea and dysentry. It also shows antiviral action hence can be given in cases of vital fever. It has antioxidant synergism with vitamin E.

Traditional Uses

(a) Fresh fruit juice along with cumin seeds and sugar are used in hyperacidity.

(b) Powder ash of dried fruits arrived in oil is used in scebies.

(c) In cases of diabetis fruit juice along with turmeric powder and honey is useful remedy.

(d) Urinary inconsistence along with sugarcane juice, amla juice is useful.

(e) In Hicough amla juice, honey and pipper juice are useful.

(f) OPI extracted from fruit is reported to having property of promoting hair growth.

(g) Dried fruit along with myrobalan, pipper langam is used in cases of diarrhoea and dysentery.

(h) It is largely used in Indian ancient ayurved preparation.

Ayurvedic Products

Chyawanprash, Triphalachurna, Dhatrirasayan, Bramharasayan, and Amalykayadichurna.

Dosage

Extract (juice) 10 to 20 ml

Powder: 1 to 2 gm

Market Proudcts

1) **Triphala Churna:** Baidyanath, Nagpur
2) **Triphala Churna:** Dabur India Ltd., New Delhi.
3) **Chavanprash:** Zandu Pharamceuticals, Mumbai.

AMRA-BARK

Synonyms

Mango, Aam

Biological Source

Amra consists of dried stem bark of *Mangifera indica* Linn. Family: Anacardiaceae, a tree found wild or cultivated throughout the country. It contains not less than 1.5 % of mangiferin on dried basis.

Geographical Source

It is indigenous to India and found wild as well as culturated throughout India; more than 15000 hectares land is under cultivations. It is mostly cultivated in Utter Pradesh, Madya pradesh, Tamil Nadu and Maharashtra.

Macroscopic Characters

Colour	:	Bark is greyish to dark brown externally and yellowish-white to reddish internally
Odour	:	Pleasant
Taste	:	Astringent

Fig. 5.2 : Fruiting Mango tree

Size and Shape	:	Mango bark occurs in pieces of variable size and thickness.
Extra features	:	Surface rough due to longitudinal cracks, fissures and scattered, raised lenticels.

Microscopic Characters

Mature mango bark has a wide cork consisting of tangentially elongated cells, few outer layers brown and inner lighter in colour, at few places lenticels; secondary cortex absent; secondary phloem wide, consisting of sieve elements, parenchyma and phloem fibres, traversed by medullary rays, resin canals and yellow coloured elongated; tannin sacs abundantly scattered throughout phloem; stone cells thick walled, lignified, rectangular with wide lumen starch grains and prismatic crystals of calcium oxalate present in phloem cells; phloem fibres in groups of 2-15 or more cells, long and thick walled, phloem rays 1-3 seriate, containing crystals of calcium oxalate and starch grains.

Chemical Constituents

Mango bark contains 10 - 20 % tannins, namely protocatechuic acid and catechin. Additionally it also contains mangiferin, alanine, glycine, aminobutyric acid, kinic acid and Shikimic acid. Mangiferin is a polyphenolic compound and is an antimicrobial, analgesic and antioxidant.

Mangiferin

Standards of Quality

Foreign organic matter	:	Not more than 2 %
Total ash	:	Not more than 9 %
Acid-insoluble ash	:	Not more than 2 %
Alcohol-soluble extractive	:	Not less than 20 %
Water-soluble extractive	:	Not less than 14 %

Identification by T.L.C.

TLC of the alcoholic extract on Silica gel 'G' plate using n-Butanol: Acetic acid: Water (4 : 1 : 5) shows as under:

(1) UV (366 nm) three violet spots at R_F : 0.12, 0.73 and 0.87.

(2) On exposure to Iodine vapour four yellow coloured spots appear at R_F : 0.33, 0.51, 0.74 and 0.88.

(3) On spraying with 5 % Methanolic-sulphuric acid reagent and after heating the plate at 105°C for ten minutes, three grey coloured spots appear at R_F : 0.49, 0.69 and 0.88.

Pharmacological Uses

Amra-bark is used as an astringent, antioxidant and also in the treatment of diarrhoea, dysentery and rheumatism. Fruits are edible, sweet, delicious and rich source of nutrients. Fixed oil obtained from mango-stone is valuable industrially.

ARJUNA

Synonym

Arjun bark

Biological Source

It is the direct stem bark of Terminalia arjuna belonging to family combretaceae contains not less than 0.02% of arjun genin on dried basis.

Geographical Source

Tree is common in indina peninsula. It is seen grown by sides of streams and very common in Chotta nagpur region. Also found in Himalayan plains, Bengal, Bihar, Madhya Pradesh.

Description of Tree

Arjuna is a common deciduous tree with a height of 20 to 25 m.

- **Trunk** : Growing straight about 10 to 12 ft in circumference.
- **Bark** : Outer surface is smooth, white, inner surface is reddish in colour and soft.
- **Leaves** : Leaves are subopposite, 5 to 9 cm long, oblong, often bearing glands on petiole or near the base of midrib.
- **Flowers** : Flowers are small; greenish white appearing in simple spikes.
- **Fruits** : Fruits are ovoid, vary in size, angular or winged with two to five wings, and are about 2.5 to 3 cm in diameter.
- **Part used** : Bark

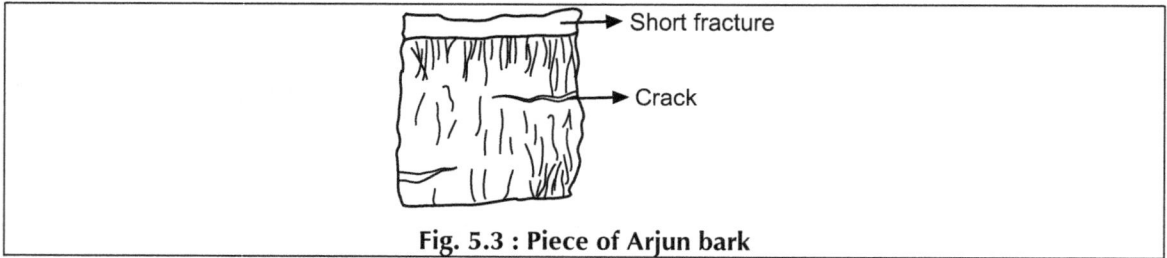

Fig. 5.3 : Piece of Arjun bark

Cultivation

Arjuna is found as naturally growing plant in the dense forests. It is very common in Baitul in Madhya Pradesh and Dehradun, Uttrakhand. Arjuna can be successfully raised by sowing seeds or by means of stumps. The seeds take about 21 days for germination. It needs moist fertile alluvial loam and rainfall in the range of 75 - 190 cm. It grows satisfactorily upto 45° C. Required rain fall 75 - 190 cm; producing 10 - 50 kg bark per tree.

Collection

Bark is collected from wild growing plants, from March to June before rainy season.

Macroscopic Characters (Bark)

- **Colour** : Colour of the outer as well as inner side of the bark is identical and is grayish brown.
- **Odour** : None
- **Taste** : Astringent
- **Size** : Piece of various sizes
- **Shape** : Flats

Extra Features

Cork gets removed due to exfoliation.

Chemical Constituents

It contains 15% tannins. It contains triterpenoid saponins, arjunolic acid, arjunic acid, arjungenin. β-sitosterol, ellagic acid and arjunic acid. The crystallisable compounds reported are arjunin and arjunetine. It also contains flavorids as arjunetin, arjunolone and arjunone. Calcium, aluminium magnesium salts and sugar are other constituents of arjuna.

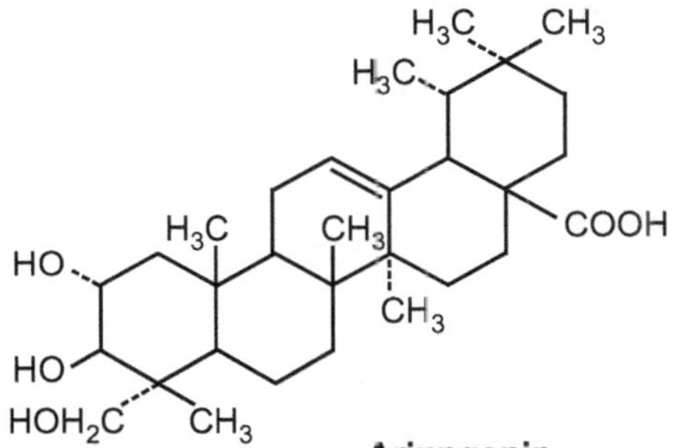

Arjungenin

Chemical Tests

Etherial extract of Arjun bark shows pinkish fluorescence under ultra violet light.

Standards of Quality

Total ash	:	≯ 20.0%
Acid insoluble ash	:	≯ 2.0%
ASE	:	≮ 20.0%
WSE	:	≮ 20.0%
FOM	:	≯ 2.0%

Ayurvedic Properties

- **Rasa** : Kashaya
- **Vipak** : Katu
- **Veerya** : Sheet

Guna	:	Laghu, rooksha
Prabhav	:	Rudhya
Doshaghna	:	Kaphaghana, pittaghana, vatvardhak.

Pharmacological Actions

It is used as cordiotonic, diuretic, febrifuge. Also used as astringent and lithontriptic.

Traditional Uses

(a) Decoction of bark is used for cleaning wounds which also helps in healing wound.

(b) In cases of fracture, powdered bark along with milk is useful and paste of the bark is applied externally.

(c) In dysentery, bark paste prepared in milk along with honey is useful.

(d) In cases like endocarditis, pericarditis, angha, decoction of bark along with cow's milk and sugar is useful.

(e) Decoction of the bark is used as good diuretic.

(f) In cases of pimples, paste of bark prepared with milk is applied externally.

(g) Ash of bark is prescribed in scorpion sting.

Dosage

Kshirpak (decoction with cow's milk)

- Swaras: 10 to 20 ml
- Decotion: 50 to 100 ml
- Powder: 3 to 6 gm

Kalpa

Arjunarishta, Arjunaghrut, Arjunkshirpak, Kakumbhadi churna.

Adultrants

Dried bark of terminalia tomelosa is used as adultrant.

Market Products

1) **Vicco vajradanti tooth powder and paste:** Vicco Laboratories, Panji, 403001. (Goa)

2) **Rikaba capsule:** Centaur Pharmaceuticals Pvt. Ltd., Vakola, Santacruz, Mumbai 55.

ASHOKA

Synonyms

Hempushpa, Sita ashok, Ashoka bark.

Biological Source

Ashoka consist of dried stem bark of plant *Saraca Indica* beloging to family Leguninosae.

Geographical Source

It is distributed in South Asia i.e. in Malaysia, Indonesia, Srilanka and all over India mainly parts of Himalaya, Khasi, Garo, Lushai hills. Also in Andaman Islands.

Description of Plant

It is evergreen small deciduous tree, found all over forest. It is about 8 to 10 m high.

Bark : From old stem is dark green in colour. On drying it is dark brown or almost black, with rough surface.

Leaves : Leaves are 8 to 10 cm long pari pinnate, oblong, lanceolate.

Flowers : Flowers are dark red or orange-yellow, appearing in bunches, are very attractive and fragrant.

Fruits (pods) : Pods are 8 to 20 cm long; 4 cm broad flat. Leathery bearing 4 to 8 oblong seeds.

Parts used : Stem bark, flowers and seeds.

Cultivation

It is frequently grown as an ornamental tree in India and is not cultivated on commercial scale. It can be easily propogated from seeds. It is found growing upto an altitude of 750 metres.

Collection

Bark is collected from wild grown plants by making transverse and longitudinal incisions.

Ayurvedic Properties

Rasa : Kashaya tikta

Vipak : Katu

Veerya : Sheeta

Guna : Laghu, Rooksha

Doshaghna : Kaphaghna, Pittaghna

Macroscopic Characters

Colour : Outer side is dark brown or black in colour. Internally it is reddish-brown with fine longitudinal straitions.

Odour : None

Taste : Astringent and bitter

Size : It occurs in various sizes upto 50 cm length and 1 cm thickness.

Shape : Appears in the form of channels.

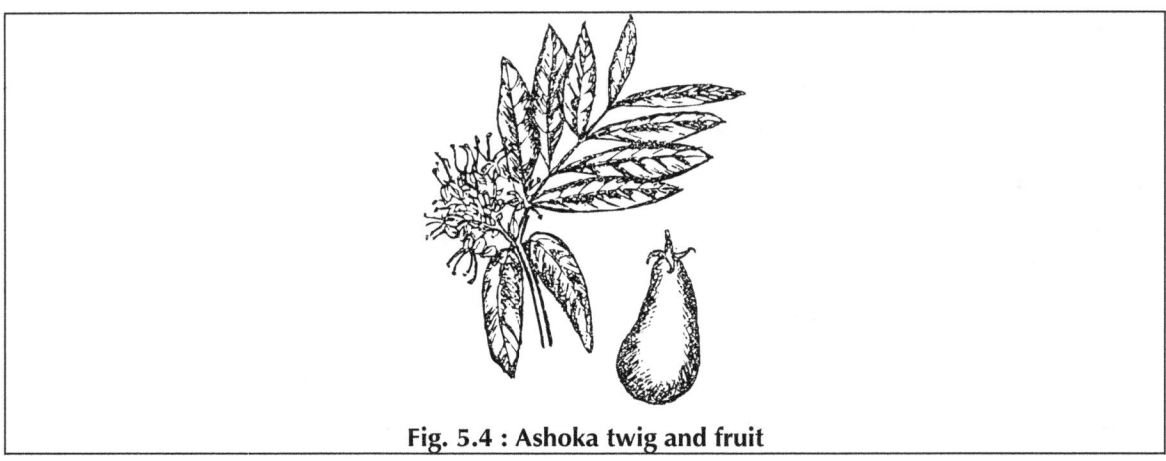

Fig. 5.4 : Ashoka twig and fruit

Extra Features

The bark is marked by bluish ash-white patches of linchens. On cutting the entire cut surface turns reddish on exposure to air.

Chemical Constituents

Bark of Ashoka contains 6% condensed haematexylin, ketosferol, saponin, organic calcium and iron compound. Bark is found to contain powerful oxytocic principle, a phenolic glycoside P_2. Leucopelargonidin and leucocyanidin have also been isolated.

Standards of Quality

Foreign organic matter : $\not> 2.0\%$

WSE : $\not< 11.4\%$

ASE (90.0%) : $\not< 15.5\%$

Ash : $\not> 11.0\%$

Acid insoluble ash : $\not> 2.0\%$

Pharmacological Uses

Bark is strongly astrignet and is a literine sedative. It also shows stimulant effect on endometrium and overian tissue and is useful in menorrhagia.

Traditional Uses

(a) Bark decotion is used in hemorrhoids and hemorrhagic dipentery.

(b) Menorrhagia bark decoction with same proportion of milk is useful.

(c) Seeds are used in dysurea and in cases of urinary calculus.

(d) In cases of leucorrhea, paste of bark along with rasonjan, honey and rice water is useful.

(e) Paste of bark is applied locally as antinflamatory.

Kalpa

Ashokarishta; Ashokaghruta; Ashokavati

Note: Bark of Ashoka should not be confused with decorative and ornamental plant Ashoka, which is botanically known as *Polyalthia longifolia* which bears white flowers.

Dosage

Bark oecoction : 20 to 40 ml

Seed powder : 1 to 3 gm

Flower powder : 1 to 2 gm

Market Products

1) **Mensocare:** Bacfo Pharmaceuticals (India) Ltd., Defence Colony, New Delhi.

BAHERA

Synonyms

Tilapurtipak, Bellaric myrobalan.

Biological Source

It consists of dried ripe fruits of the plant. *Terminalia belerica* belonging to family *Combretaceae* contains not less than 0.3% of ellagic acid.

Geographical Source

It is found all over decidous forests of Inida, in abundance in Madhya Pradesh, Uttarpradesh, Maharashtra, Punjab also in Srilanka and Malaya.

Description of Tree

A large deciduous tree of 20 to 26 m height.

Stem	:	Straight, hard dark brown coloured.
Heantwood	:	Hand
Leaves	:	Leaves 8 to 16 cm long, broadly elliptic, clustered at the end of branches; punctate on upper surface.
Petiole	:	1.5 to 2 cm long.
Flowers	:	Flowers are simple, solitary and in auxilary spikes. They are greenish yellow in colour with an odour.
Fruits	:	Fruits are 1 to 1.5 cm in diameter, brownish in colour, subglobose. Dried fruits are abscurely five angled, pulpy. Seeds are story hard.
Parts used	:	Fruits

Cultivation

Cultivation though not done on commercial scale can be cultivated by sowing seed or by transplanting raised plants (on nursery bed). It takes about 15 to 30 days for germination of seeds.

It bears simple, solitary flowers in spikes.

Collection

Matured fruits are collected and dried. Normally, it is collected from wild grown forest plants during summer.

Macroscopic Characters (Dried fruit)

- **Colour** : Dark brown to black colour.
- **Odour** : Odourless
- **Taste** : Astingent
- **Size** : 1.3 to 2 cm in length.
- **Shape** : Fruits are globular and obscurely five angled

Unripe fruit pulp is sweet to taste. Its excess dosage causes mental confusion and giddiness.

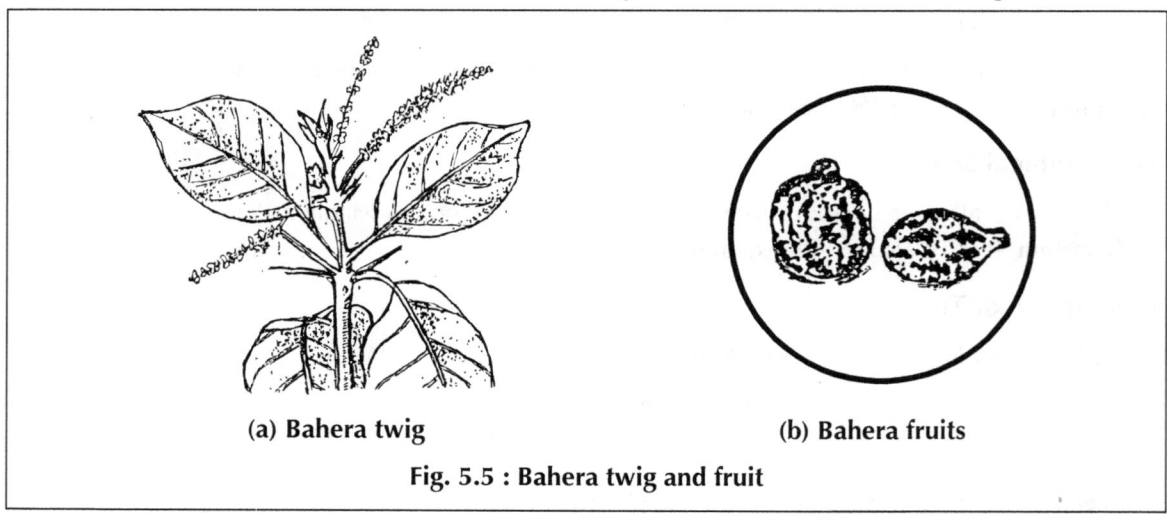

(a) Bahera twig   (b) Bahera fruits

Fig. 5.5 : Bahera twig and fruit

Ayurvedic Properties

- **Rasa** : Kasaya
- **Vipak** : Madhur
- **Veerya** : Ushna
- **Guna** : Guru, Rooksha
- **Doshaghna** : Kaphapittaghana

Chemical Constituents

The fruit contains about 20 to 30% tannins and 40 to 45 % water soluble extractives. It contains gallic acid, ellagic acid, phyllembin, ethyl gallate, and galloyl glucose. The seed contains non-edible oil. The plant producers gum.

Ellagic acid

Standards of Quality

Foreign organic matter	:	≯ 2.0%
Total ash	:	≯ 4.5%
Acid insoluble ash	:	≯ 0.2%
Alcohol soluble extractives	:	≮ 17.0%
Loss on drying	:	≯ 10.0%
Water soluble extractives	:	≯ 26.0%
Microbial limits	:	Should comply IP limits.

Pharmacological Uses

It is used as astringent, expectorant and laxative.

Traditional Uses

(a) The fruit pulp or seed oil is applied externally in rheumatism.

(b) Seed oil is used in leprosy, vitiligo and in cases of Alopecia.

(c) Dried fruit powder is applied on wound for blood clotting.

(d) Oil is used as good hair tonic.

(e) In cases of rhinitis, cough, hoarseness of voice roasted fruit pump is used.

(f) Fruit powder along with honey is useful in bronchitis.

(g) Fruit decoction with sugar is given in cases of asthama.

(h) It is constituent of 'triphala' and is used as laxative.

Dosage

Powder 1 to 3 gm

Kelpa

Bibhitak taila, triphala churna, khedisedivati, phalatrikadi kawath, kavangadivati, bibhitaksura.

Market Products

1) **Triphala Churna :** Baidyanath and Dabur Pharamaceuticals Ltd.

CATECHU

Synonyms

Dantadhawan, Gayatri, Kushtagnaha, Kattha, Catchu, Khadir.

Biological Source

It consists of dried aqueous extract prepared from the heartwood of *Acacia catechu* wild and *Acacia chundra* belonging to family Leguminosae.

Geographical Source

It is widely distributed in India from Himalayan plains to Punjab and Sikkim, Assam. It is common in dry plains.

Description of Herb

It is a moderate sized growing plant.

- **Bark** : It is nearly 1 cm thick. Dark greyish brown or whitish from outerside and reddish brown from inner side extoliating longtudinally into narrow strips. Bearing spikes (thorns) on trunk and branches.
- **Leaves** : 8 to 10 cm long, densely arranged on branchets in 30 to 40 pairs, covered with minute hairs.
- **Flowers** : Small, yellowish appearing in long racemes.
- **Fruits** : In farm of pods 5 to 10 cm long. Flat, slightly greyish with shiny tinge, have 5 to 10 rounded seeds.
- **Types** : Traditionally three types are mentioned as Khadir, Kadar(shet), Dhrimedh (vitkhadir).
- **Parts used** : Bark, extract, wood, gum.

Cultivation

For preparation of catechu, plants are grown commercially in India and Myanmar. It can be cultivated easily by sowing seeds. Moderate rainfall and any type of soil is suitable for the cultivation.

Method for Manufacture of Catechu

The trunk of trees which are more than ten years of age are cut into chips. Chips are used for extraction.

By Traditional Method: The heart wood is boiled in earthen vessels, till all soluble portion is extracted, then cooled naturally till it is converted to semisolid mass. On cooling, less soluble fraction separates out. The latter is removed as Kattha and semi-solid mass as catch.

By Modern Method: The red heart wood is cut into chips mechanically and put into extractors. The steam is passed through the drug for maximum extractors. The steam is passed through the drug for maximum extraction. The extract is concentrated under vaccume and cooled by refrigeration. It is then centrifuged to isolate cake of kattha. The cake is moulded in desired sizes and dried in proper condition.

Ayurvedic Properties

Rasa	:	Tikta kashaya
Vipak	:	Katu
Veerya	:	Sheeta
Guna	:	Laghu and Rooksha
Prabhav	:	Kushtaghana
Doshaghna	:	Pittaghana, Kaphaghana

Macroscopic Characters

Colour	:	Light brown to black
Odour	:	None
Taste	:	Very astringent
Size	:	About 2.5 - 5 cm
Shape	:	Cube or irregular fragments of broken cubes or brick shaped pieces.

Fig. 5.6 : Twig of Catechu herb and pod

Extra Features

The cubes as well as brick shaped pieces of catechu show the presence of vegetable debris and break with a short fracture. The broken pieces are angular with pale cinnamon-brown colour. It is friable and porous.

Chemical Constituents

Black catechu contains about 10 % of acacatechin. The main constituents of heartwood is catechutannic acid. The other contents of black catechu are catechu red, quercetin, gum and quercitrin. It also contains α, β, γ catchin. On dry distillation catedutannic acid gives catechol.

Catechin   **Catechol**

Standards of Quality

Ash value	: ≯ 6.0%
Acid insoluble ash	: ≯ 3.0%
Water insoluble residue	: ≮ 25.0%
Alcohol insoluble residue	: ≮ 90.0%

Pharmacological Uses

It is a powerful astringent hence, used externally for boils, skin erruptions and ulcers. It has cooling and digestive properties. Other than medicinal uses it is also used for dying, colouring, water softening, removal mercaptions from gasoline, protective agent for fishing nets and in manufacturing of ion-exchange casins.

Traditional Uses

(a) In Dental problems as well as spongy gums bleeding gums, ulceration of mouth it is used in form of paste.

(b) In pharyngitis and hoarseness of voice tonsilitis, used in form of gargles. Bark is used in sore mouth, asthama.

(c) In vitiligo and leprosy, its paste is used for local application and decoction for bathing.

(d) For internal use in leprosy. Catechu bark along with amla decoction with powder psorelon is useful.

(e) In cases of diabetes, catechu, babul paste in cow's milk along with cummin seeds and canesugar is useful.

(f) In bleeding piles, fissures decoction of catechu and triphala with ghee and acorus calamus powder is useful.

(g) In Gonorrhea, decoction with triphala powder is used.

(h) Somal decoction in cows milk is used.

(i) Chronic cough bark of catechu, beheda and clove in proportion of 4:2:1 along with honey is proved to be useful.

Dosage

    Powder   : 1 to 3 gm

    Decoction   : 40 to 80 ml

    Kadhir sar (kattha) : 0.5 to 1 gm

Kalp

Khadirarishta, Khadiradikwath, Khadiradivati, Khadiraashtak.

Market Products

1) **G-32:** Alarsin Pharmaceuticals, MIDC Andheri, Mumbai 93.

PALE CATECHU

Synonyms

Gambier, Katha.

Biological Source

It is a dried aqueous extract of the leaves and young shoots of *Uncaria gambier* Roxburgh, belonging to family Rubiaceae.

Geographical Source

The plant is indigenous to South East Asian regions like Arachipelago in Malaysia; presently, it is also cultivated in Singapore and Indonesia.

Cultivation and Collection

The cultivation is carried out in fields upto an attitude of 170 m and propagation is done by sowing seeds in damp soil. Nursery beds are raised and after 9 months, the seedlings are transplanted in open fields.

The first harvesting is done when the plant attains an height of 2 m. The plant yields the drug up to 20 years. The leaves and young shoots collected are boiled in pot called *Cauldron*, made up of wood and with iron bottom for 3 hours and decoction obtained is concentrated till it becomes a pasty mass with yellowish-green colour. This mass is moulded in cubes and dried.

Macroscopic Characters

Pale catechu occurs as reddish-brown coloured cubical mass quite friable in nature. When broken, it shows cinnamon brown colour and porous nature. The drug has no odour, but highly astringent taste which first appears bitter and then sweet. When placed in water, it shows minute acicular crystals.

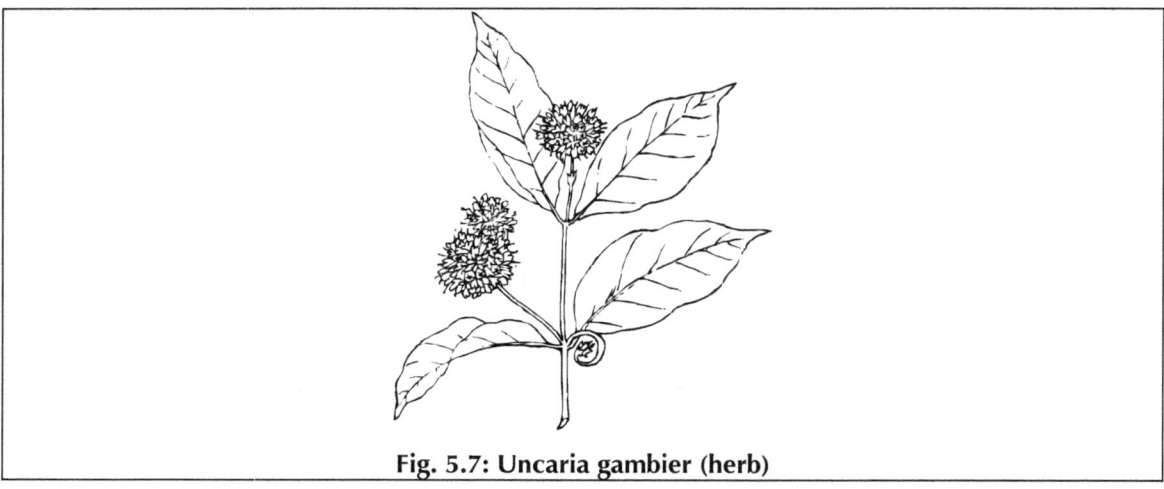

Fig. 5.7: Uncaria gambier (herb)

Chemical Constituents

The drug contains condensed tannins in the form of catechins 7 - 33 %, catechutannic acid 22 - 50 % and catechu red. The drug also contains quercetin and gambier fluorescin.

Quercetin   **Quercitrin**

Chemical Tests

(1) It gives test for catechin by dipping a match stick in hydrochloric acid and warming it near flame similar to black catechu.

(2) Test for gambier-fluorescin: The drug is extracted with alcohol and sodium hydroxide is added to extract, followed by addition of a few drops of light petroleum. The mixture is shaken and kept for sometime. Green fluorescence is observed in light petroleum layer (distinction from black catechu).

(3) Small quantity of drug is warmed with chloroform and filtered in a porcelain dish and evaporated to dryness. Due to presence of chlorophyll, it shows greenish yellow colour.

(4) With a mixture of vanillin and hydrochloric acid, it shows pink or red colour.

Uses

Gambier is used as an astringent in treatment of diarrhoea and also as a local astringent in the form of lozenges. Pale catechu is mainly used in dyeing and tanning industries, and also for protecting the fishing nets.

HARITAKI

Synonyms
Abhaya, Chetana, Pranada, Medhya, Harde.

Biological Source
It consists of dried, ripe and fully mature fruits of *Terminalia chebula* belonging to family Combretaceae.

Geographical Source
It is found all over India from Himalayan tract to West Bengal; Assam; Madhya Pradesh; Bihar, Maharashtra.

Description of Tree
It is a deciduous tree of about 20 - 30 m high.

Bark : It is dark brown in color, with rough surface, wood is hard.

Leaves : Leaves are 7 to 20 cm long, 5 to 10 cm broad. Oxate, subopposite often 6 to 8 pairs, usually acute.

Flowers : Flowers are small yellowish-white appearing in terminal spikes with offensive smell.

Fruits : They are 2.5 to 5 cm long, ellipsoidal or obovoid unriped fruits are glabrans, yellowish green in colour, and with five to six ribes when dry.

Seeds : Fruit contains single story hand seed, which is light yellow coloured and five ribbed.

Types : **(a) Bal hirdae:** Raw, Tender (immature fruits) fruits are plucked and dried which turns black are called as *Bzlhizdae*.

    (b) Rangari hardae: Medium sized yellow coloured which are usually used for colouring.

    (c) Survari hardae: Full grown, riped, blakish fruits.

Parts used: Fruits

Cultivation
Usually it is not cultivated and is found wild growing at an altitude of 1800 m. The trees are moderate sized crowned with spreading branches. It bears yellowish white flowers in the terminal spikes.

Collection
Fruits are collected from wild grown forest plants and no more cultivated.

Macroscopic Characters (Fruits)

Colour : Fruits are yellowish brown.

Odour : Odourless

Taste : Astringent, slightly bitter and sweetish at the end.

Size : 20 to 25 mm long and 15 to 25 mm wide

Shape : Orate and wrinkled longitudinally.

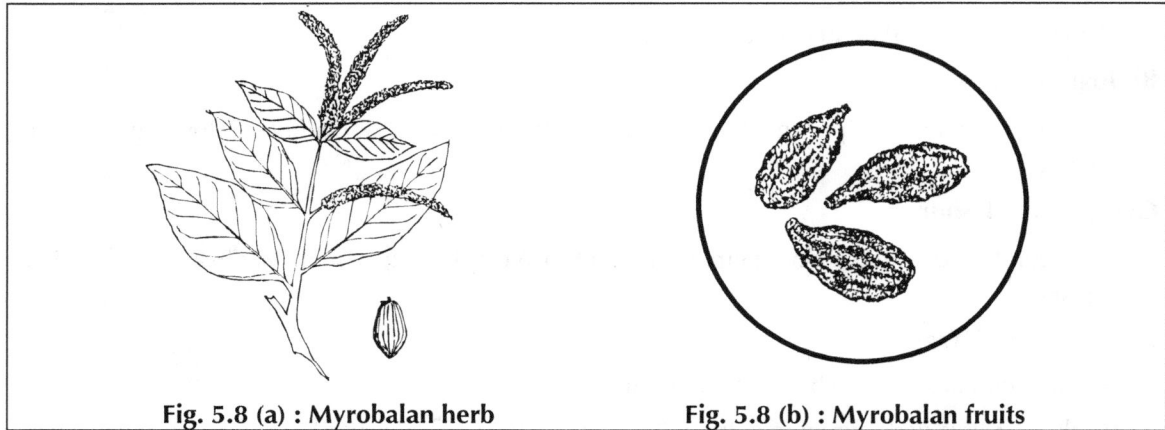

Fig. 5.8 (a) : Myrobalan herb Fig. 5.8 (b) : Myrobalan fruits

Extra Features

Fruits are hard with single seed and five to six wrinkles when dry. The pulp of the fruit is non-adherent to the seed.

Chemical Constituents

Myrobalan fruits are main source of tannins. Along with it, it also contains chebulagic, chebulinic, ellagic, and gallic acids. Haritaki also contains glucose sorbitol, resin, anthraquinone principle. During maturation amount of tannins decreases whereas the acidic content of fruits increases.

Chebulic acid

Standards of Quality

Foreign organic matter	:	≯ 2.0%
Total ash	:	≯ 5.5%
Acid insoluble ash	:	≯ 0.5%
Loss on dry	:	≯ 9.0%
Alcohol soluble extractive	:	≮ 40.0%
Water soluble extractive	:	≮ 56.0%

Ayurvedic Properties

Rasa : Except lavan; panchanasa, Main kasayarasa.

Vipak : Madhur

Veerya : Ushana

Guna : Laghu, rooksha

Prabhav : Tridoshahan

Pharmacological Action

Haritaki is mainly used as astringent. Laxative stomachie is also an anthelmentic.

Traditional Uses

(a) In rheunatic condition haritaki along with jaggari is useful.

(b) In cases of diarrhoea and colitis, its powder along with butter milk is useful.

(c) In hyperacidity, haritaki powder along with black resins and sugar is proved to be useful.

(d) In diabetic condition, triphala powder along with turmeric and sugar is used.

(e) In asthamatic condition and bronchitis, powder of hairda and behda along with honey are used.

(f) In opthalmatic conditions (conjuctivities, trichome etc.), triphala powder is used to clean eyes and along with that powder triphala is administered internally with ghee and honey.

(g) In hyperperspiration, paste of myrobalan is applied to body before bath.

(h) Obesity decotion of Triphala along with honey is useful (for weightless).

Dosage

Powder : 1 to 2 gm

As laxative : 3 to 6 gm

Decoction: 50 to 100 ml

Kalpa

Abhayamodak, Abhayarishta, Pathyadivati, Pathyadikawth, Vagryaritaki, Dantiharitkei, Chitrakharitakti etc.

Market Product

1) **Triphala Churna** from most of Aurvedic manufacturers.

PTEROCARPUS

Synonyms

Bijasal; Indian kino tree, Malabar kino.

Biological Source

It consists of the dried juice of the plant *Pterocarpus marsupium* belonging to family Leguminosae.

Geographical Distribution

It is found in hilly regions of Gujarat, Madhya Pradesh, Uttar Pradesh, Bihar and Orissa. It is also found in forests of Karnataka, Kerala, West Bengal and Assam.

Description of Tree

It is a 30 m high, very attractive tree.

Bark	: Bark is greyish in colour with longitudinal cracks on it.
Leaves	: Compound leaves with 5 to 7 leaflets, elliptical with wavy margins.
Flowers	: Yellow flowers, appearing in large dense bunches with fragrance.
Fruits	: 2 to 5 cm long and 4 to 5 cm diameter flat pods containing 1 to 2 seeds which are hard. The heart wood of this tree is golden yellow when damp, turning darker or bluish on exposure.
Parts used	: Bark, leaves, dried juice (kino gum)

Cultivation and Collection

It is a deciduous plant of mansoon forests not cultivated. Scientifically, tree is 15 - 18 m in height and 1.8 to 2.4 m in grith, with long vertical cracks. The tree bark yields reddish gum, obtained by making vertical incisions on the stem bark collected and dried or by collecting the naturally oozed gum from the tree.

Ayurvedic Properties

Rasa	: Kasaya, Tikta
Vipak	: Katu
Veerya	: Sheeta
Guna	: Laghu, Rooksha
Doshaghna	: Kapha pitta shamak

Macroscopic Characters (Kino gum)

Colour	: Ruby-red
Odour	: Odourless
Taste	: Astringent

Size   :   3 - 10 mm granules

Shape :   Angular grains

Fig. 5.9 : Pterocarpus plant in flowering

Extra Features

The pieces of kino are angular, glistening, transparent, breaking with vitreous fracture. It is partly soluble in water (about 80 - 90 %), completely soluble in alcohol (90 %).

Chemical Constituents

Kino contains about 70 - 80 % of kinotannic acid, kino-red, k-pyrocatechin, resin and gallic acid. Kino-red is anhydride of kinoin. Kinoin is an insoluble phlobapheneol, kinotannic acid is glucosidal tannin, the heartwood gave isoliquiritigenin, liquiritigenin and pterostilbine, the sap wood shows presence of pterostilbene.

Chemical Tests

1) With clear aqueous solution mineral acid produces precipitate.
2) With potassium hydroxide solutions violet colour is produced.

Standards of Quality

Moisture content   :   ≯ 15.0%
Total ash   :   ≯ 02.0%
Alcohol soluble extractives : ≮ 20.0%

Pharmacological Uses

It is Astringent, alternative, hypoglyceraic. The decoction of bark shows hypocholesterolemic effect.

Traditional Uses

(a) Leaf paste or paste of bark is used to apply exteranally as antiinflammatory, in cases of leprosy and hair growth tonic.

(b) In case of toothach, kino (gum) is used as antiinflammatory.

(c) In diarrhoea, dyseatery bark gum along with rice water is useful.

(d) Bark powder or gum along with milk and canesugar is used as tonic.

(e) Decoction of bark is useful in cases of rheumatism.

(f) To control sugar level in urine and blood, decoction of bark is very useful.

(g) In pain and inflammation and also in case of bone fracture, decoction in milk along with sugar is used.

Dosage

Decoction : 40 to 80 ml

Powder : 1 to 3 gm

Juice : 1 to 2 gm

Market Product

1) **Disoma:** Growel Pharmaceuticals, Talkatora Industrial Estate, Lucknow.

SHIRISH

Synonyms

Madhupushpa, Sirish, Albizia, Rain tree.

Biological Source

This consists of dried bark and leaves of the plant known as *Albizzia lebbek* belonging to family Mimoceae.

Geographical Source

The plant is found throughout India upto an altitude of 1000 metres above sea level also in Himalayas. It is indigenous to India.

Description of Tree

It is 17 to 20 metres high green tree.

Leaves : Compound, hairy with 4 to 8 pairs of leaflets, leaflets are green, dark, shinny.

Bark : Dark brown, greenish black, with rough covering. Odourless and bitter acid in taste.

Flowers : Greenish yellow, fragrent and delicate.

Fruits : Appear in pods of 15 to 30 cm and 1.5 to 3 cm broad, flat long with 6 to 10 hard seeds.

Seeds : Flat, roundish oval, greyish in colour.

Types : (a) Shweta: Its bark and stem are whitish in colour.

(b) Krushna: The dark brown to greenish black.

Fig. 5.10 : Flowering twig of Shirish

Macroscopical Characters

Colour : Bark is dark brown to greenish black in colour.

Odour : Odourless

Taste : Bitter and acrid

Texture : Rough

Parts used: Bark, seeds, leaves and flowers

Cultivation and Collection

The plant is also cultivated in some parts of India.

Ayurvedic Properties

Rasa : Kashaya, Tikta, Madhur

Vipak : Katu

Veerya : Alpa ushna

Guna : Laghu, Rooksha, Teekshna

Prabhav : Vishaghana

Doshaghna : Vata, pitta, kaphaghna

Chemical Constituents

Tannins and pseudatanins, echinocystic acid, γ-sitosterol, albigenic acid, are found in the part of plants. Oleanolic acid, ectinocystic acid are reported in seeds.

γ-sitosterol

Standards of Quality

Moisture content	: ≯ 15%
Total ash	: ≯ 2.0%
Alcohol soluble extractive	: ≮ 20.0%

Pharmacological Uses

It shows insecticidal anticancer (epidermal carcinoma) activity, it also shows hypocholesterolemic hypoglycemic activity and antiprotozoal activity.

Albizia reduces the release of histamines through stabilizing effect on mast cells, mildly. Suppresses activity of T-lymphocytes reducing the level of allergy inducing antibodies. Powdered leaves mixed with sesame are applied in psoriasis as well as eczema patches and imparts significant improvement in the texture of skin. It is also used as good remedy in bronchitis and gum inflammation.

Traditional Uses

(a) In gum inflammation and dental problems, gargles with bark decoction is useful.

(b) As antiinflammatory, seed paste is applied externally.

(c) In Leuchorria, bark decoction with same proportion of cows ghee is given.

(d) In cases of night blindness, leaves juice is used as eye drops.

(e) In snakebite and all cases of poison, bark decoction along with seed powder is useful.

(f) Bark paste is applied externally in cases of leprosy and as skin tonner.

Dosage

Powder	:	2 to 4 gm
Decoction	:	30 to 50 ml
Swaras	:	10 to 20 ml

Kalp

Mahashinishagad, Shirisharista, Dashang lep.

GALLS

Synonyms

Tannic acid, Tannin, Gallotannic acid, Nutgalls.

Biological Source

Galls are pathological outgrowths, formed on young twigs of *Quircus infectoria* (Oak tree), belonging to family Fagaceae. The galls are formed due to egg deposition by gall wasp: *Adleria gallaetinctoriae*.

Chinese galls are formed by an aphis, *Schlechtendalia chinensis* on the tree of *Rhus chinensis*, belonging to family Anacardiaceae and they are used for isolations of Tannic acid.

It is said that galls are collected in August and September every year. Technical and medicinal use of galls was known to ancient greeks since 450 B.C.

Geographical Source

Galls are obtained mainly from Aleppo in Asiatic Turkey, Syria, Cyperus, Greece and Perisa.

Description of Galls

Tannic acid is yellowish white to light brown shining powder. It has an astringent taste and no odour. It is amorphous and light in weight, it darkens on storage.

Solubility: Tannic acid is soluble in water and alcohol, but insoluble in most organic solvents.

Method of Preparations

Galls contains about 50-70% of Tannic acid. The galls are powdered and extracted with alcohol-ether mixture. The extract thus obtained is treated with water. Ethereal part separates out and evaporates. Alcohol-water part contains tannic acid. It is further concentrated into vacuum dryer to remove water at low temparature. It is purified by washing with organic solvents and dried.

Macroscopic Characters

- **Colour :** Galls are externally bluish green or olive green in colour and pale buff internally.
- **Odour :** Odourless
- **Taste :** Astringent followed by sweet taste.
- **Size :** 10 - 30 mm in diameter.
- **Shape :** Sub-spherical in shape with short basal stalk.

Extra Features

They are hard to touch, sink in water, absorb water, get enlarged and become soft. About 2 to 4 gm each in weight. Blunt conical projections are present on galls, which are 10 to 15 in number.

Chemical Constituents

Tannic acid is hydrolysable tannin corresponding to complexity of pentadigalloyl glucose ($C_{76}H_{52}O_{46}$) composed of gallic acid and glucose. Tannic acid is incompatible with alkaloids, gelatin, albumin, alkalis and iron salts.

Tannic acid

Chemical Tests

1) With freshly prepared ferric chloride solution it produces bluish-black colour.
2) Solution of gelatin gets precipitated with Tannic acid.

Uses

It is used as an astringent for mucous membrane of mouth and throat hence employed for sore throat and receding gums. In the form of suppositories, it is effective in the treatment of piles. Tannic acid is also used as an antidote for poisoning due to alkaloids, heavy metals, and some glycosides.

Storage

It should be stored in well closed containers, away from light and in cool place.

Market Product

1) **S.G. Paint:** Centaur Pharmaceutical Pvt. Ltd., Vakola, Santacruz, Mumbai 55.

BIBLIOGRAPHY

1. Herbal Drugs in Indian Pharmaceutical Industry, 1979 S. L. Kapoor, R. Mitra. Economic Botany Information Service, National Botanical Research Institute, LUCKNOW 226601.
2. CRC Hand book of Ayurvedic Medicinal plants, L. D. Kapoor, Taylor and Francis, CRC Press USA.
3. Text book of Pharmacognosy, Second Edition, 2012, M. K. Gupta, P. K. Sharma, Pragati Prakashan, Pragati Bhavan, 240 W. K. Raod, Meerat, 250 001.
4. Pharmacognosy IV, V, VI, VII, 2013, S. B. Gokhale, A. P. Purohit, C. K. Kokate, Nirali Prakashan, Abhyudaya Pragati, 1312, Shivaji Nagar, Off J. M. Road, Pune, 411005.
5. CRC Handbook of Ayurvedic Medicinal Plants, L. D. Kapoor, Taylor and Francis, CRC Press, USA.
6. Indian Pharmacopocia Vol. I - IV, 6th Edition, 1996, Ministry of Health, Govt. of India, New Delhi.
7. Pharmacognosy, C. K. Kokate, A. P. Purohit, S. B. Gokhale, 48th Edition, 2012, Nirali Prakashan, Pune 5.
8. Pharmacognosy Phytochemistry of medicinal plants, Jean Bruneton, 2nd Edition, 1999. Intercept Ltd. London.
9. Pharmacognosy, Trease GE and Evans W. C. 12th Edition 1983, Bailliere Tindall U. K.
10. Pharmacognosy, Tyler E. E. Brady Lyn R and Robbers J. E. Ninth edition, 1988 Burger, Minneapolis, Minnesota. U.S.A.
11. Text book of Pharmacognosy, Wallis T.E., 5th Edition 1967, J & A Churchill Ltd. London (U.K.)
12. Medicinal Plants of India Vol. I, 1976, ICMR, New Delhi.
13. Glossary of Indian Medicinal Plants, Chopra R. N., Chopra, J. C. and Nayar S. I., 1956, CSIR, New Delhi.
14. Wealth of India – Raw Material Series, 1948-1976, Council of Scientific and Industrial Research, New Delhi.
15. Indian Materia-Medica Vol. I & II, Third Edition, reprint 2009, Popular Prakashan, Mahalaxmi, Mumbai 26.
16. Herbal drugs in Indian Pharmaceutical Industry, 1979, S. L. Kapoor and R. Mitra, Economic Botany Information Service, National Botanical Research Institute, Lucknow 226601.

APPENDICES

(A) MANUFACTURERS OF PHYTOCHEMICALS AND PHYTOPHARMACEUTICALS IN INDIA

- **Abhinivs Natural Extracts**
  D/1-3, Ajit Nagar, Nr. Jain Mandir, J. B. Nagar, Andheri (E), Mumbai 400 059. Phone : 91-22-28321509, Mob: 9821337965. E-mail: vvrmurthy@rec-all.com

- **Alarsin**
  Alarsin House, A/32, Road No. 3, Opp. ESIS Hospital, Andheri (E), Mumbai – 400093, Maharashtra. Phone : 022-28216836, 28387804, Fax: 28384116.

- **Alembic Limited**
  Alembic Road, Vadodara – 390003, Gujarat. Phone: 0265-380550, 380880, Fax: 382134, 382934, E-mail: info@alembic.co.in, Website: www.alembic-india.com

- **Anil Starch Product Ltd.**
  Anil Road, Post Box No. 10009, Ahmedabad – 380025. Phone : 91-79-22-123222, Fax: 91-79-22110731.

- **Aristo Pharamceuticals Ltd.**
  23A, Shah Industrial Estate, Off Veera Desai Raod, Andheri (E), Mumbai – 400053, Maharashtra. Phone: 022-26730001-6, Fax: 022-26734792, E-mail: aristo@vsnl.com

- **Arjuna Natural Extracts Ltd.**
  Keders Centre, Bypass Road, Aluva-683 101 (Kerala) Phone : 0484-2622612, 2622204.

- **Astra-IDL Ltd.**
  32/1-2, Crescent Raod, Crescent Towers, Bangalurae - 560001, Phone: 080-22256941, 22256942, Fax: 080-22252894, E-mail: omprakash_o@yahoo.com, Website: www.nnsc@satyan.net.in

- **Atul Ltd.**
  Po: Atul Pharama Division, Dist. Valsad, Gujrat - 396020. Phone: -2632-233474, 230183; Fax: 233053. E-mail: pi@atul.co.in, Website : www.atul.co.in

- **Aurobindo Pharma Ltd.**
  248/3RT, 1st Floor, SR Nagar, Hyderabad – 500038. Phone: 2270658, 2271824, 2271217. Fax: 040 – 2270843.

- **Aventis Pasteur India Pvt. Ltd.**
  Chaitanya-1, Chaman Farm Village, Bund Road, Gadaipur, Chattarpur, New Delhi – 110030. Phone: 011-26658111/4, Fax: 26658181, E-mail: pmsindia@del2.vsnl.net.in, Website: www.aventis.com

- **Bajaj Pharmaceuticals (Bombay) Pvt. Ltd.**
  14/15, Faiz-E-Edros, 1st Floor, 37/373, Narsi Natha Street, Mumbai – 400009, Maharashtra. Phone: 022-3439275, 3412066, Fax: 3410863, E-mail: boghani.jk@mailexite.co

- **Bayer Pharmaceuticals Pvt. Ltd.**
  1st Floor, Bayer Corporate Office, Kolshet Road, Thane – 400607, Maharashtra. Phone: 022-25311234, 25455234, Fax: 25455080.
- **Bilt Biochemicals Ltd.**
  Tower 'C', 1st India Place, Mehravli - Gurgaon Raod. Gurgaon – 122 002, Phone: 0124-5099214 (O), 2804263 (F), Fax: -124-2804263. E-mail: citrabilt@bilt.com, Web: www.solanschemtech.com
- **Blue Cross Laboratories Ltd.**
  Peninsula Chambers, P.O. Box 16360, Lower Parel. Mumbai-400013, Maharashtra. Phone: 022-4638000, Fax: 4638120, E-mail:nhi@bluecrosslabs.com
- **Bombay Tablet Mfg. Co. Pvt. Ltd.**
  Plot No. 909, GIDC, Sector 28, Gandhinagar – 382028, Gujarat. Phone: 02712-22240, 22234, Fax: 273-6, E-mail : btmco@vsnl.com
- **C. Abhaykumar & Co.**
  Gopal Niwas, 127 Princess Street, (S.G. Marg), Mumbai 02. Phone: 2208 6397, 2200 4479, 5637 9314. Fax: 022-2208 5189. E-mail: caco@bom3.vsnl.net.in, Website: www.cabhay.com
- **C. J. Gelatine Products Ltd.**
  Tokersi Jivraj Wadi, Acharya Donde Marg, Sewree, Mumbai - 400015. Phone: 241317790, 24131609, 24135811, Fax: 022-24133193.
- **Cadila Healthcare Ltd.**
  Zydus Tower, Satellite Cross Road, Sarkhej-Gandhinagar Highway, Ahmedabad-380015, Gujarat. Phone: 079-6770100 (20 line), Fax : 079-26732363. E-mail: prp@vsnl.com
- **Camlin Limited**
  Camlin House, J.B. Nagar, Andheri (E), Mumbai-400059. Maharashtra. Phone: 022-8360302-6, Fax: 8216688, 8366579, E-mail: pharma@camlin.com, Website: www.camlin.com
- **Chaitanya Biological Pvt. Ltd.**
  Survey No. 75/02, Malkapur By-pass, N.H. No. 6, At+post+Aluka=malkapur, Dist: Buldara - 443101, Maharashtra. Phone: 07267-223433, 223239, 222523, Fax: 223433, 223570, E-mail : chaitbio@rediffmail.com, Web: www.chaitanyabio.com
- **Chemiloids**
  40-15-14, Brindavan Colony, Venkateswarapuram, Labbipet, Vijayawada – 520010 (A.P.). Phone: 2473468, 2476561, 2474521, Fax: 091-0866-2475278, 091-0866-2470207, E-mail: impex@md3vsnl.net.in, Website: www.lailagroup.com
- **Cipla Limited**
  289, Belasis Road, Mumbai Central, Mumbai – 400008, Maharashtra. Phone: 022-3095521, 3082891, Fax: 3070013, 3070393, Website: www.cipla.com
- **Dabur Pharmaceuticals Ltd.**
  Plot No. 22, Site IV, Sahibabad Ind. Area, Sahibabad, Ghaziabad – 201010, Uttar Pradesh, Phone: 0120-2777901-25, Fax: 2777833, Website: www.dabur.com
- **Deccan Phyto Chemicals**
  309, Kabra Complex, 61, M.G. Road, Secunderabad - 500003. Andhra Pradesh. Phone: 040-27710117, Fax: 27710337, E-mail: alkaloid@hd1.vsnl.net.in

- **Dey's Medical Stores (Mfg.) Ltd.**
  Exports Divisions, 17, Collin Lane, 3rd Floor, Kolkata – 700016, West Bengal. Phone: 033-22444103, 22440989, Fax: 22476332, 22452348.

- **Dolphin Laboratories Ltd.**
  A/2, Jitendra Estate, Opp. Sangam Talkies, Andheri-Kurla Road, Andheri (E), Mumbai-400093. Phone: 022-28221695, 28362988, Fax: 022-28213602, E-mail: dolphinb@bom.vsnl.net.in, Website: dolphinlab.com

- **Dr. Reddy's Laboratories Ltd.**
  7-1-27, Ameerpet, Hyderabad – 500016, Andhra Pradesh. Phone: 040-23731946, 23351012, Fax: 040-23731955, 23351011, E-mail: krao@drreddys.com

- **E. Merk (India) Ltd.**
  Shivsagar Estate "A", Dr. Annie Besant Raod, Worli, Mumbai-400018. Phone: 24964855, Fax: 24954590, E-mail: lab.mktg@marck.co.in

- **Eli Lilly & Company (India) Pvt. Ltd.**
  Plot 92, Section 32, Gurgaon – 122001, Harayana. Phone: 0124-2823000-1, Fax: 22823011-2.

- **Elite Pharma Pvt. Ltd.**
  Plot No. 1210/11/12, Phase III, Vatva, GIDC, Ahmedabad – 382445, Gujarat. Phone: 079-25831668, Telefax: 25832998, E-mail: eppl@wilnetonline.net

- **Emerck India Ltd.**
  801, 8th Floor, Swastik Chambers, Chembur, Mumbai – 400 071. Phone: 25226865.

- **Enzyme India Pvt. Ltd.**
  7, Briethapet Road, Vepery, Chennai – 600 007. Phone: 044 – 52066364, 25611463, Fax: 25610869. E-mail: enzymeindia@eth.net, Website: www.indiaenzyme.com

- **Farmachem**
  G-24, Solari-II, Opp. L&T Gate No. 6, 46/48, Saki Vihar Road, Saki Naka, Mumbai – 400 070, Maharashtra. Phone: 022-26287961, 26244219, Fax: 26287931, E-mail: farmachem9@vsnl.net.in

- **FDC Ltd.**
  142-48, S. V. Road, Jogeshwari (W), Mumbai – 400 102, Maharashtra. Phone: 26780652, 26782653, Fax: 26780967, E-mail: fdc.exp@bom.net.in, Website: www.fdcindia.com

- **Flavours India (Pvt.) Ltd.**
  C-5, 14 & 23, PIPDIC, Industrial Estate, Mettupalayam, Pondicherry – 605 010.

- **G. R. Exports Ltd.**
  C/o German Remedies Limited
  M. Vasanji Raod, Andheri (E), Mumbai – 400 093. Phone: 022-28387932, 28370370, Fax: 022-28344386, E-mail: grexports@netscape.net, Website: germanremedies.com

- **Geno Pharmaceuticals Ltd.**
  Pharmaceutical Complex, Karaswada, Mapusa – 403526, Goa. Phone: 0832-2255216-7, Fax: 2255215, E-mail: geno@goal.vsnl.net.in

- **Glaxo India Ltd.**
  House of Kaydees, No. 260, National Highway No. 8, Isanpur, Narol, Ahmedabad-382 405, Gujarat. Phone: 097-5393753, 5350678, Fax: 079-5324143.
- **Glaxo Smithkline Consumer Healthcare Ltd.**
  DLF Plaza Tower, DLF City-I, Gurgaon - 122002, Haryana. Phone: 0124-2540700-3, Fax: 2540728, E-mail: nicholas.j.massey@gsk.com, Website: www.gsk.com
- **Global Bulk Drugs & Fine Chemical Pvt. Ltd.**
  5-9-30, Basheer Bagh Palace Colony, Hyderabad - 500 063, Andhra Pradesh. Phone: 040-23226719, Fax: 23226878, 23221265, E-mail: globalbd@satyam.net.in, Website: www.gbdfc.com
- **Gufic Limited**
  Gufic Building, Subhash Raod, 'A', Vile Parle (E), Mumbai - 400 057, Maharashtra. Phone: 022-28344523, 28346253, Fax: 28369008, E-mail: gufic@bom2.vsnl.net.in
- **Gujarat Organics Ltd.**
  3A, Vadodarawala mansion, B1, Dr. A. B. Road, Worli, Mumbai – 400 018, Phone: 022 – 24938687, Fax: 24974886, E-mail: gujorg@vsnl.com, Website: www.gujaratorganics.com
- **Gujarat Themis Biosyn Ltd.**
  3rd Floor, Arvind Chambers, Western Express Highway, Sai Service Compound, Andheri (E), Mumbai – 400 069, Maharashtra. Phone: 022-28347789, 28221538, Fax: 28377261.
- **Herbochem**
  38 & 39, Technocrats Indl. Estate Balanagar, Hyderbad – 500 061. Phone: 040 – 23078059, 23077331, Fax: 040 – 23078059, E-mail herbochem_india@yahoo.com.
- **Herbs Medica**
  251-B, Nahar & Seth Industrial Estate, Pannalal Compound, L.B.S. Marg, Bhandup (W), Mumbai – 400 080. Phone: 564326 / 55988142. E-mail: herbs_medica@yaholl.com
- **Himachal Pharmaceutical Industries**
  E-71, Focal Point, Ludhinana- 141 010 (Punjab)
- **Himalaya Drug Company**
  Makali, Bangalurue - 562123, Karnataka. Phone: 080-28394885, 28397823, Fax: 28396057, E-mail: hdcintl@vsnl.com
- **Himedia Laboratories Pvt. Ltd.**
  A-406, Bhaveshwar Plaza, LBS Marg, Mumbai – 400 086. Phone: 25003747/0970, Fax: 022-2500 5764/2468, E-mail: info@himedialabs.com, Websidte: www.himedialabs.com.
- **Hindustan Antibiotics Ltd.**
  Pimpri, Pune – 411018, Maharashtra, Phone: 020-27476522, 27476511-3, Fax: 27472327, E-mail: hapune@pn3.vsnl.net.in, Website: www.hindustanbiotics.com
- **Hindustan Pharmaceuticals**
  911-12, Siddharth Complex, RC Dutt Road, Alkapuri, Vadodara – 390 007, Gujrat. Phone: 0265-22332567, 22334202, Fax: 22339460, E-mail: info@hindustanpharmaceuticals.com
- **Indian Drugs & Botanical Herbs Co. (Regd.)**
  103, Ram Nagar, Krishna Nagar, Delhi – 110051. Phones: 22423579, 22432443, Fax: 2217985, 22411813.

- **Indian Gum Industries Ltd.**
  A-401, Navbharat Estates, Zakaria Bunder Road, Sewri West, Mumbai - 400015. Phone: 22-24158059, Fax: 24158074.
- **Indian National Drug Co. Pvt. Ltd.**
  5/2, Dr. S.C. Banerjee Road, Formerly Beleghata Main Raod, Kolkata – 700085, West Bengal. Phone: 033-23505551, 2357524, Fax: 23520958.
- **Indo-German Laboratories**
  407, Gulab, 237, P.D'Mello Road, Mumbai-400001, Maharashtra. Phone: 022-22611345, 22610778, Fax: 22622482, E-mail: igl_m@vsnl.com
- **Indo-phyto Chemical Pvt. Ltd.**
  F 2/2, Vasant Vihar, New Delhi, 110057, Phone : 011 26144573.
- **Indo-German Alkaloids**
  Inga Building, Mahakali Raod, Andheri (E), Mumbai - 400013. E-mail: ingalabs@bom3.vsnl.net.in
- **IPCA Laboratories Ltd.**
  International Division, International House, 48-Kandivli Indl. Estate, Kandavli (W), Mumbai – 400067. Phone: 022-28686097, 6098, Fax: 022-2886613, 22873914. E-mail : ipca@ipca.co.in, Website: ipca.co.in
- **J&J Dechane Laboratories Pvt. Ltd.**
  4-1-316, Bank Street, Hyderabad - 500001, Andhra Pradesh. Phone: 040-24753537, 23753538/39, Fax: 24753131, E-mail: dechane@eth.net, Website: www.dechane.com
- **Johnson & Johnson Ltd.**
  30, Forjett Street, Mumbai - 400036, Maharashtra. Phone: 022-23861431, Fax: 23898940, 23801744, E-mail: sbamboat@jnjin.jnj.com
- **Kothari Phytochemicals International**
  766, Anna Nagar, Madurai - 625 020 (T.N.). Phone: 0452-5392451/2/3/7/8/9, Fax: 0452-2534138, E-mail: kothariphyto@eth.net, kothariphyto@mantraonline.com, Website: www.chemcals-india.com
- **Lupin Laboratories Ltd.**
  159, CST Road, Kalina, Santacruz (E), Mumbai - 400098, Maharashtra. Phone: 022-6525730, Fax: 022-26525726, 22-23961, E-mail: atulgore@lupinindia.com, Website: www.lupinworld.com.
- **Macleods Pharmaceuticals Pvt. Ltd.**
  Atlanta Arcade, 3rd Floor, marol Church Raod, Andheri (E), Mumbai – 400059, Maharashtra. Phone: 022-28214636/7, Fax: 28216599, E-mail: macleods@vsnl.com
- **Maize Products**
  P.O. Kathwada, Maize Products, Ahmedabad-382430, Gujarat. Phone: 079-22871581, 22871585, Fax: 079-22872438, E-mail: bmt@maizeproducts.com, Website: maizeproducts.com
- **Malviya Chemicals and Pharmaceuticals Pvt. Ltd.**
  Plot No. 34-A/2, Site 4, Sahibabad, Ghaziabad - 201010. Uttar Pradesh. Phone: 0575-2770976, 2770540, Fax: 2771735, E_mail: malviya@del2.vsnl.net.in

- **Manak Citrus Products Pvt. Ltd.**
  P.O. Utran, Tal. Erandol Tal., Dist. Jalgaon – 425 117. (Maharashtra). Phone: 2576-240070, Fax: 02576-240070.

- **Marine Chemicals**
  Deepa Bldgs., Santo Gopalan Road, Chullickal, Cochin – 682005 (Kerala). Phone: (0484) 2227241, 2223703, 2220802, E-mail: merion@md2.vsnl.net.in, Internet: www.keralanet.com / meron.nsf.

- **Martin & Harris Laboratories Ltd.**
  Appejay Chambers, Wallace Street, Fort, Mumbai – 400001, Maharashtra. Phone: 022-22076853, Fax: 22072625, E-mail : bombay@martinandharris.com

- **Medley Pharmaceuticals Pvt. Ltd.**
  Medley House, D-2, MIDC Area, Andheri (E), Mumbai 4000093, Maharashtra. Phone: 022-28346025, 4495-6, Fax: 044-28204453, E-mail: medpharm@bom2.vsnl.net.in, Website: www.medleylab.com

- **Mentha & Allied Products Ltd.**
  Munshi Niketan, 1/10, Asafali Raod, New Delhi-110002. Phone: 011-23231614, 23238356, Fax: 011-23231189, E-mail: mentha@del12.vsnl.net.in, Website: mentha.com

- **Natural Products**
  6/7, B.H. Complex, IInd Floor, Near Utkarsh Petrol Pump, Kareli Baug, Vadodara – 390018.

- **Nicholas Piramal India Ltd.**
  100, Centre Point, Dr. Babasaheb Ambedkar Road, Parel, Mumbai-400012, Maharashtra. Phone: 022-24134653, Fax: 24134649, E-mail vshah@pel.co.in, mhshaikh@pel.co.in

- **Novartis India Ltd.**
  Sandoz House, 8th Floor, Shiv Sagar Estate 'B', Dr. Annie Besant Road, Worli, Mumbai - 400018, Maharashtra. Phone: 022-24988888, Extn. 4830, Fax: 24973938, E-mail: ranjit.shahani@group.novartis.com

- **Nulife Pharmaceuticals**
  203, Pleasant Appartments, 15th Lane, Prabhat Road, Pune 411 004, Maharashtra. Phone: 020-25676473, 25678942, Fax: 25678872, E-mail: nulife@vsnl.com

- **Pfizer Ltd**
  Pfizer Centre, 5, Patel Estate, S. V. Road, Jogeshwari (W), Mumbai – 400 102, Maharashtra. Phone: 022-26785511, Fax: 022-26788459, E-mail: lianne.price@pfizer.com, Website: www.pfizer,com, www.pfizerindia.com

- **Procter and Gamble Hygiene & Health Care Ltd.**
  507, Mahalaxmi Chambers, 5th Floor, 22, Bhulabhai Desai Road, Mumbai – 400026, Maharashtra. Phone: 022-24964900, Fax: 24963215, E-mail: patel.bv@pg.com, kelly.e1@pg.com

- **Protein Products of India Ltd.**
  Sandynalla, Sholur Town panchayat, Ootacamund - 643 237, Dist. Nilgiri (Tamil Nadu). Phone: 22762, 22436, 22442.

- **Ranbaxy Laboratories Limited**
  Paonta Sahib, District: Sirmour Himachal Pradesh 173025. Phone: 91-1704-222834, 222720, Fax: 91-1704-223492, 222832, Mob: 09816100495, E-mail: ankush.vig@ranbaxy.com, Website: http://www.ranbaxy.com

- **Raptakos, Brett & Co. Ltd.**
  47, Dr. Annie Besant Road, Worli, Mumbai – 400025, Maharashtra. Phone: 022-24934251, Fax: 24950341, 24933747, E-mail: rbclcom@bom2.vsnl.net.in, Website: www.raptakos.com

- **S.D. Fine Chem. Ltd.**
  315-317, T.V. Industrial Estate, 248, Worli Road, P. B. No. 19160, Worli, Mumbai – 400025. Phone: 91-22-24959898, 24959898, Fax: 91-22-24937232, E-mail: purchase@sdfine.com, Website: www.sdfine.com

- **Sarabhai M Chemicals**
  (Division of Ambalal Sarabhai Enterprises Ltd.), Gorwa Raod, P. B. No. 3580, Vadodara-390007 (Gujarat). Phone: 2382433, 2380262, 2382498, Fax: 0265-2382498, 2381163.

- **Serum Institute of India Ltd.**
  13/375, Khara Niwas, Guru Nanak Nagar, Shankar Seth Road, Pune - 411 042, Maharashtra. Phone: 020-26346963, 26342053, Fax: 26345184/07, E-mail: serummgr@pn3.vsnl.net.in

- **South India Research Institute Pvt. Ltd.**
  Venkateswarapuram P.O., Brindavan Colony, Labbipet, Vijayawada - 520010 (Ap.P). Phone: 91-866-2471282-83-84, Fax: 866-2477363, E-mail: sirifact@md3.vsnl.net.in

- **Standard Essential Oil Distillers**
  84/113, Affim Kothi Crossing, Near Railway Under Bridge, Kanpur - 208 003 (U.P.)

- **Synthozyme Labs Pvt. Ltd.**
  G-1, Add. MIDC Estate, P. B. No. 106, Jalgoan - 425003, Maharashtra. Phone: 0257-2212111-4, Fax: 2212115, E-mail: ramsynth@bom6.vsnl.net.in

- **The Himalaya Drug Company**
  Makali, Bangalurue-562123, Phone: 080-23714444, Fax: 23714480, E-mail: write.to.us@himalaya.ac, Website: www.himalayahealthcare.com

- **The Pharmaceuticals Products of India Ltd.**
  Plot No. D-306, TTC Indl. Area, Turbhe, MIDC, Navi Mumbai - 400 705. Phone: 022-27630056, 27632328, Fax: 27619447.

- **Torrent Labs. Ltd.**
  Torrent House, Near Dinesh Hall, Ashram Raod, Ahmedabad - 380009.

- **Toshniwal Drugs & Pharma (Pvt.) Ltd.**
  4/16-B, Asaf Ali Road, New Delhi – 110 002, Phone: 011-23261585, 27421585, Fax: 2745185, E-mail: toshniwals@vsnl.com

- **Unichem Laboratories Ltd.**
  Mahalaxmi Chambers 2nd Floor, 22, Bhulabhai Desai Road, Mumbai - 400026, Maharashtra. Phone: 022-24968402/4, Fax: 24950450, E-mail: pamody@unichemindia.com

- **Unisankyo Limited**

  No. 392, Sagar Society, Plot No. 84, Banjara Hills, Hyderabad - 500034, Andhra Pradesh. Phone: 040-26510116/7, Fax: 23542213/4, E-mail: mak@hd.unisankyo.com

- **USV Limited**

  B.S.D. Marg, Govandi Station road, Govandi, Mumbai - 400088, Maharashtra. Phone: 022-25564048/51, Fax: 25515608, 25584025, E-mail: international@usv.co.in

- **Varalakshmi Starch Industries Ltd.**

  No. 8, Gandhi Raod, Salem - 636 007 (Tamil Nadu). Phone: 0427-2412854, 2416851, 2416852, Fax: 0427-2418854, 2416852, E-mail: vsil@vsnl.com

- **Wockhardt Ltd.**

  Wockhardt Towers, C-3, G Block, Bandra Kurla Complex, Bandra (E), Mumbai - 400051, Maharashtra. Phone: 022-26534444, 26523333, Fax: 26523355, E-mail: jpalamittam@wockhardtin.com, Website: www.wockardtin.com

- **Yogi Ayurvedic Products Pvt. Ltd.**

  Camel House, Nashik-Pune Raod, Nahsik - 422011, Maharashtra. Phone: 2594231/2, Fax: 2595698, E-mail: sonia.singht@sarda.co.in

- **Zandu Pharmaceutical Works Ltd.**

  70, Gokhale Road South, Dadar (W), Mumbai - 400025, Maharashtra. Phone: 022-24307021, 24304517, Fax: 24375491, E-mail: parikhdm@hotmail.com

- **Zydus Cadila Heathcare Ltd.**

  Zydus Tower, 5th Floor, Satellite Cross Road, Ahmedabad - 380015, Gujarat. Phone: 079-26770100, Fax: 26732365/7, E-mail: pandita@zyduscadila.com, Website: www.cadila-zydus.com

(B) GLOSSARY OF IMPORTANT AYURVEDIC TERMS

- **Antrika kotha-prasaman:** Intestinal antiseptic.
- **Anulomana:** Carminative, having the power to relieve flatulence and associated colic.
- **Anuvasan:** A drug that causes the body to be soft, unctuous and strong.
- **Arshoghan:** A drug that cures piles or hemorrhoids.
- **Abha:** Lustrous.
- **Ajeernaghna:** One which corrects indigestion.
- **Agnideepti, aghnivardhaka:** That which stimulates the factors of gastrointestinal digestion.
- **Aguru:** Light (not heavy).
- **Angamardaprashamana:** Anodyne/analgesic.
- **Apacheeghna:** That which resolves glandular enlargement.
- **Apasmaaraghna:** Anti-epileptic.
- **Garbhapatana:** That which induces abortion.
- **Graahi:** That which binds the bowel (astringent).
- **Jantughna, jantunaashanee:** Anthelmintic, antimicrobial.
- **Jwaraghna, jwarahara, jwaravegav, naashaka:** Antipyretic and febrifuge.
- **Kaamalaghna, kaamalaahara:** That which cures jaundice.
- **Kanthashodhana:** That which cleans the throat.
- **Kaasaghna, kaasahara:** Antitussive.
- **Kashaaya:** Astringent.
- **Katu:** Pungent or bitter taste.
- **Nidrajanan:** Hypnotic: a drug that brings sleep
- **Paandughna, paanduhara:** Antianemic
- **Pitta sarak:** Cholagogue; a drug that causes secretion of bile.
- **Pleeharogaghna, pleehodarahara:** Indicated in splenomegaly.
- **Prativisha:** An antidote for poisons.
- **Punarnavaa:** Self-renewing, rejuvenating.
- **Rakta bhar samak:** a vasodilator.
- **Rakta bhar vardhak:** A vasoconstrictor.
- **Raktakrit:** Hematinic.
- **Raktapittaghna:** Indicated in the therapy of hemorrhagic diathesis.

- **Raktapittastambhana:** Hemostatic.
- **Raktavardhaka:** Hematinic.
- **Rasaayana, rasaayanee:** Rejuvenator.
- **Rochaka :** An agent that promotes appetite.
- **Sangraahi:** That which binds the bowels (usually an astringent).
- **Vaajeekara:** Aphrodisiac.
- **Vaataghna:** Indicated in diseases of the nervous system.
- **Vaataghni, vaatapotha:** Anti-vaatic.
- **Vaman:** Emetic.
- **Vastirogaghni:** Said to cure diseases of the urinary system (particularly of the bladder).
- **Virechanaee, virechan:** Purgative.
- **Viriaya:** Aphrodisiac.
- **Vishahara, vishaghna:** Antidote for poisons.
- **Vranaapaha, vranaghna:** Indicated in the treatment of wounds.
- **Yonidoshaghna:** That which is said to cure uterine disorders.

(C) SYNONYMS IN VARIOUS INDIAN LANGUAGES

Key to Abbreviations Used

A.	Ar/abic	B.	Bengali;	En.	English;	Fr.	French;G. Gujrati;
Gr.	German;	H.	Hindi;	It.	Italian;	K.	Kannada; M. Malylam;
Mr.	Marathi;	Or.	Oriyan;	P.	Punjabi;	S.	Sanskrit; Tm. Tamil;
T.	Telugu.	Tr.	Turkish				

AMLA
- S. Amalaki
- En. Emblic-myrobalan
- Ar. Amlag
- B. Amla, Amlaki
- Fr. Eblique officinale
- Gr. Grave myrobalane
- G. Ambala, Anvala
- H. Amla, Amlika, Aonla
- It. Embelica
- K. Amalaka, Nelli
- M. Nelli
- Mr. Avala
- Or. Aunla
- Tm. Nellikai
- T. Usirikai
- Tr. Amlac

APAMARG
- B. Apang
- E. Staff tree
- G. Aghado
- H. Lalgira
- M. Ceruktaladi
- Mr. Aghada
- P. Kutri
- T. Uttareni
- Tm. Nayarivi
- U. Chirichita

ASHOKA
- B. Ashoka
- G. Asopalara
- H. Ashoka
- K. Ashoka
- Mr. Ashoka
- S. Ashoka
- Tm. Asogam
- Or. Oshoko

ASHWAGANDHA
- B. Ashwagandha
- G. Asan
- H. Asgand
- M. Amnkkiram
- K. Hiremaddinegida
- Mr. Askandha
- S. Ashvagandha
- Tm. Ashvagandi
- T. Asvtgandhis
- P. Asagand

ARJUNA
- B. Arjun
- G. Arjunsadra
- H. Arjun
- M. Venmarutti
- K. Holematti
- Mr. Arjun
- S. Arjuna
- Tm. Attumarudu
- T. Tellamaddicittu
- P. Arjan
- Or. Arjuno

BABCHI
- B. Lalakasturi
- En. Psoralea
- G. Bavachi
- H. Babchi
- M. Bavachi
- K. Babchi
- Mr. Bavchi
- S. Karpokarishi
- Tm. Kalagija
- T. Kalagija
- P. Babchi
- Or. Bakuchi

BEHRA
- B. Behra
- G. Behedo
- H. Behera
- K. Shantimara
- M. Thannikkai
- Mr. Beheda
- S. Bahira
- Tm. Akkam
- T. Tandra

BLACK CATECHU
- B. Khaer
- G. Katho
- H. Kathha
- K. Cachu
- M. Karianali
- Mr. Kaat
- S. Khadira
- Tm. Karum-Kali
- T. Chandra
- P. Kher
- Or. Khaira
- Gr. Catechu akazie
- Fr. Cachoutier
- It. Acacia dicachou

BHUI-AMLA
- B. Bhui amala
- E. Phyllanthus
- S. Bhumi Omalka
- H. Jangali amla
- Mr. Bhue avala
- Tm. Kizharelli

BHRANGRAJ
- S. Bhrigaraja
- E. Eclipta
- B. Kesuti, Keshori
- G. Bhangra
- H. Mochkand
- K. Garagadasoppu
- M. Kyonni
- Mr. Maka
- Or. Kesarda
- P. Bhangra
- Tm. Garuga, Kaikeshi
- T. Galagara

BRAHMI
- S. Jal/Neer brahmi
- M. Brahmi
- H. Brahmi
- B. Brahmi sak
- K. Niru brahmi
- T. Neer Brahmi

BELLADONNA
- B. Yebruj
- H. Sag angur
- Mr. Girbuti
- P. Bantamaku
- S. Suchi
- Gr. Wolaskirche
- Fr. Atrope
- It. Solano insano

CENTELLA ASIATICA
- S. Manduki, **Mandunk parni**
- En. Indian penny work
- B. Potari, Tholkhuri
- Fr. Berilaequa
- Gr. Wassernable
- G. Barmi
- H. Brahma, Manduki
- It. Centela asiatice
- K. Tutti
- M. Mutti, Kutakan
- Mr. Mandukparni
- P. Arara
- Tm. Vallarei
- T. Brahmi

CHAKRAMADHU
- B. Chakunda
- H. Chakund
- G. Kovariya
- H. Chakunda
- E. Foetid cassia
- G. Kovariya
- Mr. Takata
- T. Tantemu
- U. Tenuwar

CHIRATA
- B. Chitrata
- H. Chirayata
- K. Nelabedu
- Mr. Chiraita
- S. Kirata-tkta
- Tm. Nila vembu
- T. Nila vem
- P. Charaita

DARUHALAD
- B. Daruharidra
- G. Daruhaldar
- H. Daruhaldi
- K. Dodde Marad resin
- M. Daruhalad

DHAMASO
- S. Durlabha
- E. Khorasoni thorn
- H. Dhamasa
- G. Dhamaso
- Mr. Dhamasa
- P. Dama
- T. Chittigara

GARDEN RUE
- B. Ispand
- H. Sata p
- Tm. Aruveda
- S. Somlata
- T. Aruda
- K. Sabbu

GOKHRU
- B. Gokhru
- H. Cholagokhru
- K. Negalu
- M. Neringil
- Mr. Lahangokharu
- S. Gokshura
- Tm. Nerunji
- T. Palleru
- P. Lotak
- Or. Gokhuru
- Gr. Echter burzel
- Fr. Tribule terrestre
- It. Tribolo basapie

GUDMAR
- B. Merasingi
- E. Gymnena
- G. Mardasingi
- H. Gudmar
- K. Sennegeraschambu
- Mr. Kalikardodi
- S. Meshashringi
- T. Podapatri
- Tm. Adigam

HYOSCYAMUS (Henbane)
- B. Korasani ajowan
- H. Khurasani ajavayan
- Mr. Khorasani owa
- S. Yavani, Parasikaya
- Tm. Korusanai
- T. Karashanivamam

KANTAKARI
- S. Kantakari
- H. Kateli
- B. Kantakari
- Mr. Bluee ringani
- Tm. Kadamgattiri
- T. challa mulaga
- M. Kantankateri
- P. Kandiari

KACHNAR
- S. Kovidura
- H. Kachnar
- B. Rakth kanchan
- Tm. Sagapu-manchori
- T. Mandora
- S. Kovidara

KALMEGH
- B. Kalmegh
- G. Kariytu
- K. Nelaberu
- H. Kiryat
- Tm. Kiryat
- Mr. Olikirayat
- S. Kirata
- Tm. Nilavembu
- T. Nelavembu
- En. Great chiretta

KANHER
- B. Karabi
- H. Kaner
- Tm. Alari
- Mr. Kanher
- S. Karavira
- T. Karavirum
- M. Karavirum
- U. Karavirum

KUTJA (Kurchi)
- B. Kurchi
- G. Kadachhal
- H. Kaureya kuvachi
- K. Kodamuriki
- M. Kadagapala
- Mr. Kuda saal
- S. Kutja
- Tm. Krukkalami palsi
- T. Kodisapala

LIQUORICE (Glycyrrhiza)
- B. Jasthi-Medhu
- G. Jethimadha
- H. **Mulethi**
- K. Jhthahimhuram
- Mr. Jeshtamadh
- S. Jashta madhu
- Tm. Atimadhuram
- T. Atimadhuramu
- Gr. Echtes sussholz
- Fr. Regulisse
- It. Dolce radice

LODHRA
- B. Lodhar
- E. Lodh tree
- H. Lodh
- S. Lodhra
- T. Lodhuga
- Tm. Velli

MANJISHTA
- B. Manjit
- E. Indian madar
- G. Manjeeth
- H. Manjeeth
- K. Manjushta
- Mr. Manjishta
- T. Tamalvatti
- Tm. Manditta

METHI
- B. Methi
- E. Fenugreek
- G. Methi
- H. Methi
- K. Menthya
- M. Ventayam
- Mr. Methi
- P. Methi
- S. Methika
- T. Mentulu
- Tm. Vendaya
- U. Methi

MYROBALAN
- B. Haritaki
- G. Hirdo
- H. Harana
- K. Alate, Harade
- Tm. Divya
- Mr. Hirda
- S. **Haritaki**
- Tm. Kadukkai
- T. Karitaki
- P. Har
- Or. Haridra
- Gr. Mirobalanenbaum
- Fr. Myrobalan belleric
- It. Mirobalano

NUX-VOMICA
- B. Kuchila
- G. Zeri-Kachuo
- H. Kuchla
- K. Kasar-kena
- M. Kanjiram
- Mr. Kuchala
- S. Vishamushti
- Tm. Yettiraman
- T. Mustimanu
- P. Kagophale
- Or. Kachila
- Gr. Brechnussbaum
- Fr. Vomiquier
- It. Nocevomica

OPIUM
- B. Poostodheri
- G. Afin
- H. Afim
- K. Afeemu
- M. Apeem
- Mr. Aphoo
- S. Naranga
- Tm. Apin, Abhni
- T. Nallamandu
- P. Afim
- Or. Afima
- Gr. Schlafmohr
- Fr. Pavot
- It. Papavero

PALASH
- B. Palas
- E. Bastand teak
- H. Dhas
- Mr. Palas
- T. Maduga

PALE CATECHU
- B. Papri, khayar
- H. Kath, kutha

- M. Gambier
- Mr. Kath
- S. Khadir
- Tm. Ankudu- kurna
- T. Ankudu - kurra

PICRORRHIZA
- B. Katki
- G. Kadu
- H. Kutki, kuru
- M. Katu khur- obani
- Mr. **Kutki**
- S. Katuka
- Tm. Kitchli
- T. Katukuroni
- P. Karru

PIPLAMOOL
- B. Piplaimool
- G. Pippri mool
- H. Piplamool
- K. Hippaliberu
- M. Tippali mulum
- Mr. Pimpali
- Tm. Kandan Tippali
- T. Tippalikatte

PTEROCARPUS
- B. Pistal
- G. Biyo
- H. Bijasal
- M. Veng
- Mr. Asan, Dhorbenla
- S. Honne
- Tm. Vengai
- T. Yeggi

PUNARNAVA
- B. Sabunba
- G. Lalsabuni
- H. Lalsabunooch

- K. Muchchu-joni
- Mr. Pandhari-punernava
- S. Punernavi
- Tm. Sharunai
- T. Galijeru

RASANA
- S. Sugandhamula kulanjan
- En. Galangale, Siamese, ginger
- Ar. Khawalngan
- B. Kulanjan
- Fr. Galanga
- Gr. Galgant
- G. Kulinjan
- H. Kulanjan, Kulinjan
- It. Alpinia
- K. Kumbarasme
- M. Kolinji, Aratta
- Mr. Kulinjan
- Tm. Perarathei
- T. Dumparastramu
- Tr. Havlican

RAUWOLFIA
- B. Chandra
- G. Sarpagandho
- H. Chhotachand
- M. **Sarpagandha**
- Mr. Sarpagandha
- S. Punernavi
- Tm. Govannamilpuri
- T. Patala agandhi

SENNA
- B. MethSonamnkhi
- G. Nat-kisana
- H. Sena-ka-patta
- K. Nilavaka
- Mr. Sonamukdi
- T. Sunamikhi

SHANKHAPUSHPI
- B. Dankuni
- G. Shankhaphuli
- Mr. Shankhvel
- S. Shankhapushpi

SHATAVARI
- B. Shatamuli
- H. Satawar
- M. Shatawali
- Mr. Shatavari
- S. Shatmuli, Tagar
- Tm. Shimaishdavari
- T. Challagadda

SHIRISH
- S. Shirish
- H. Siris
- B. Siris gach
- Tm. Vagai
- T. Dirasana

TAXUS
- B. Sugandh, Bhirmie
- H. Thuneer, Biemi, Kash
- Mr. Barmi
- S. **Talispatra**
- Tm. Thalizopathari

TEA - LEAVES
- H. Chay
- P. Chai
- B. Cha
- Mr. Chaha
- Tm. Thayilai
- Tel. Theyaku

TINOSPORA
- B. Gurach, Giloe
- H. Gilo
- M. Sittamrytu
- Mr. **Gulvel**
- S. Guduchi, Amrita
- Tm. Sindil
- T. Somida

TYLOPHORA
- B. Antamul
- E. Indian Ipeacuna
- H. Antamul
- Mr. Anta mool
- M. Vallipala
- Tm. Nayppa lai
- T. Vettipale

VASAKA
- B. Bakas
- G. Adsoge
- H. Arusha
- K. Adusoge
- M. Adalodagam
- Mr. Adulsa
- S. Vasa
- Tm. Adatodai
- T. Addasaramu

INDICES

1. BIOLOGICAL INDEX

Acacia catechu, 5.14
Achyranthis aspara, 3.1
Adhatoda vasica, 4.38
Albizzia lebbek, 5.24
Alexandrian senna, 1.3
α-Amyrin, 3.27, 3.19
Andrographis echioides, 3.26
Andrographis paniculata, 3.24
Atropa acuminata, 1.3, 4.17
Atropa belladonna, 1.3, 1.2, 4.17
Bacopa moniera, 3.5
Bauhinia variegate, 4.42
Berberis aristata, 4.8
Boerhavia diffusa, 4.44
Boerhavia procumbens, 4.44
Boerhavia repens, 4.44
Canscora decussata, 4.46
Cassia acutifolia, 1.3
Cassia angustifolia, 1.3
Cassia tora, 3.7
Centella asiatiea, 3.32
Cinchona calisaya, 4.22
Cinchona ledgeriane, 4.22
Cinchona officinalis, 4.22
Cinchona succirbra, 4.22
Cullen corylifolia, 3.3

α-Colibrine, 4.2
Datura innoxia, 1.2
Datura stramonium, 1.2, 1.3
Digitalis purpurea, 1.3
Digitalis thapsi, 1.3
Eclipta alba, 4.40
Emblica officinalis, 5.1
Erythroxylon coca, 1.3
Erythroxylon traxillense, 1.3
Evolvulus alsinoides, 4.46
Fagonia arabiea, 3.11
Fagonia cretica, 3.11
Fagonia indica, 3.11
Gentiana kurroe, 3.30
Glycyrrhiza glabra, 3.38
Glycyrrhiza glandulifera, 3.38
Gymnema hersutum, 3.21
Gymnema montatum, 3.21
Gymnema sylvestre, 3.18
Holarrhena antidysentrica, 4.32
Hyoscyamas niger, 1.2, 4.20
Indian Senna, 1.3
Mangifera indica, 5.4
Nerium indicum, 3.26
Panax ginseng, 3.14
Panax japonica, 3.14

Panax notoginseng, 3.14

Panax quinquefolium, 3.14

Papaver nudicaule, 4.11

Papaver orientale, 4.11

Papaver somniferum, 4.10

Phyllanthus amaracus, 4.50

Phyllanthus fraternus, 4.50

Phyllanthus niruri, 4.50

Picrorrhiza curroa, 3.28

Piper longum, 4.48

Psoralea corylifolium, 3.3

Pterocarpus marsupium, 5.22

Quircus infectoria, 5.27

Rauwolfia serpentina, 4.4

Rubia cordifolia 3.33

Saraca-indica, 5.8

Solanum xanthacarpum, 4.36

Strychnous nux blanda, 4.3

Strychnous nux-vomica, 4.1

Strychnous potatorum, 4.3

Swertia chirata, 3.9

Symplocos racemosa, 3.30

Terminalia arjuna, 5.5

Terminalia belerica, 5.11

Terminalia checula, 5.19

Thea sinensis, 4.27

Tinospora cordifolla, 3.21

Tinospora malbarice, 3.23

Tribulus terrestris, 3.16

Trigonella foenum graecum, 3.36

Tylophora asthmatica, 4.34

Tylophora indica, 4.34

Uncaria gambier, 5.17

Wedella chinensis, 4.40

Withania somnifera, 4.29

Writghtia tinctora, 4.34

Writghtia tomentosa, 4.34

2. SYNONYM INDEX

Adhatoda, 4.38
Adulsa, 4.38
Aghada, 3.1
Amrita, 3.21
Antamul, 4.34
Asgandha, 4.29
Berberis, 4.8
Bhui-nimb, 3.24
Camella thea, 4.27
Cassia senna, 3.48
Chinese Ginger, 3.43
Chirayata, 3.9
Chitra, 4.8
Crow fig., 4.1
Darvi, 4.8
Deadly night shade leaf, 4.17
Durgraha, 3.1
Durlabha, 3.11
Dusparshi, 3.11
Eclipta, 4.40
Fenugreek, 3.36
Galanga, 3.43
Giloe, 3.21
Glycyrrhiza, 3.38
Gota kola, 3.32
Gudmar bootee, 3.18
Guduchi, 3.21
Harmal, 3.45
Hastil odhra, 3.30
Henbane, 4.20
Himalayan yew, 3.51
Hog weed, 4.43

Holarrhena, 4.32
India ipecacuntha, 4.34
Indian berbery, 4.8
Indian gentian, 3.28
Indian Maddar, 3.33
Jesuit's bark, 4.22
Jirna patra, 3.30
Karayat, 3.24
Krishnabheda, 3.28
Krishnaphata, 3.3
Kurchi bark, 4.32
Kushtaghni, 3.3
Lesser glanage, 3.43
Liquorice, 3.38
Madhu nashini, 3.18
Maka, 4.40
Malbar nut, 4.38
Manduki, 3.32
Markat pippali, 3.1
Markati, 3.3
Merasingi, 3.18
Methika, 3.36
Narayani, 3.46
Nerium, 3.25
Nidradi, 3.9
Ninjin, 3.14
Oleander, 3.25
Orkid tree, 4.42
Panax, 3.14
Pannag, 3.14
Peruvian bark, 4.22
Phyllanthus, 4.48

Pipla roots, 4.47
Psoralea, 3.3
Rakta Punarnava, 4.43
Rakta pushpi, 3.33
Rakta samanga, 3.33
Raswanti, 4.8
Sankh vel, 4.46
Saraswati, 3.5
Sarvadanshtra, 3.45
Satap, 3.45
Semen strychni, 4.1
Shankhini, 4.46
Shatimuti, 3.46
Shatkumbha, 3.25

Shatpadi, 3.46
Shatparne, 3.28
Somwalli, 3.5
Sonai, 3.48
Takla, 3.7
Tarwal, 3.7
Taxus, 3.51
Tinnevelli senna, 3.48
Tinospora, 3.21
Triparna, 3.41
Vyagri, 4.36
Wilhania, 4.29
Winter cherry, 4.29
Yew, 3.51

3. CHEMICAL INDEX

Acacatechin, 5.15
Achiranthin, 3.2
Adhatocline, 4.40
Adhatodic acid, 4.40
Ajmalicine, 4.6
Ajmaline, 4.6
Alizarine, 3.34
Alkaloids, 2.1
Aloe-emodine, 3.8
Amorogentin, 3.9
Anaferine, 4.30
Anaferine, 4.30
Andrographolide, 3.25
Arjanofone, 5.7
Arjunetin, 5.7
Arjungenin, 5.7
Arjunic acid, 5.7
Asiatic acid, 3.33
Asiaticoside I 3.33
Atropine, 4.18, 4.21
Bacoside A,
 Bacoside B,
Barbamine, 4.9
Bellndonnine, 4.18
Berberine, 4.9
Betain, 3.2, 4.39
Betulic acid, 3.5, 3.27
Brahmin, 3.5
Brahmoside, 3.33
Brucine, 4.2
b-sitosterol, 3.13, 3.5, 3.27, 5.24, 5.7
Butrine, 3.41

Caffeine, 4.28
Carpesterol, 4.37
Catechin, 5.5, 5.18
Catechu tannic acid, 5.15,
Caumarin, 3.45
Chebulinic acid, 5.20
Chiratin, 3.9
Chlorogenic acid, 4.2
Choline, 3.37, 4.30
Cinchonidine, 4.24
Cinchonine, 4.24
Cineole, 3.44
Codeine, 4.13
Colloturine, 3.31
Connecine, 4.33
Connessimine, 4.33
Cuscohygrine, 4.30
Echinocystic acid, 5.25
Ellagic acid, 5.7, 5.13, 5.20
Fagogenin, 3.13
Galangin, 3.44
Galangol, 3.44
Gallic acid, 5.13, 5.20
Gensinoxide, 3.15
Gentianine, 3.9
Glycine, 3.41, 5.5
Glycosides anthraquinone, 2.7
Glycosides cardiac, 2.6
Glycosides phenolic, 2.8
Glycosides, 2.4
Glycyrrhizin, 3.40
Glycyrrhizinic acid, 3.40

Gymnemic acid, 3.19
Harmine, 3.13, 3.17
Hecogenine A,
Hecogenine B
Hematoxyline, 5.10
Heroin, 4.13
Herpestine, 3.5
Hollarrhidine, 4.33
Hollarrhimine, 4.33
Hydroquinine, 4.25
Hyoscine, 4.19, 4.21
Hyoscyamine, 4.18, 4.21
Indole alkaloids, 4.2, 4.5
Indolenine alkaloids, 4.6
Indoline allcoloids, 4.8
Isobutrine, 3.41
Jetrorrhizine, 4.9
Kalmeghin, 3.25
Kampterol, 4.35
Kinic acid, 5.5
Kinoin, 5.22
Kinotannic acid, 5.20
Kutcoside, 3.29
Kutkin, 3.29
Kutkiol, 3.29
Lencopelargonidin, 5.10
Leucocynidin, 5.10
Loutrine, 3.31
Madecassic acid, 3.33
Mangiferin, 5.5
Manjistia, 3.34
Meconic acid, 4.13
Mericyl alcohol, 3.50
Methyl cinnamate, 3.41

Monnierin, 3.5
Morphine, 4.13
Narcene, 4.13
Narcotin, 4.13
Nascopine, 4.13
Neriodorin, 3.27
Norconnecine, 4.33
Oleanolic acid, 3.2, 3.13, 3.15, 3.27, 5.25
Oxy indol alkaloids, 4.6
Oxyberberine, 4.9
Palmatine, 4.9
Panaxadiole, 3.15
Panaxoside, 3.15
Panaxotrial, 3.15
Papavarine, 4.13
Pectin, 5.2
Pentriacontane, 3.19
Picroside, I, 3.29
Picroside, II, 3.29
Pseudostrychnine, 4.2
Psoralen, 3.4
Psoralidin, 3.4
Purpurine, 3.34
Quercitol, 3.19
Quercitrin, 5.15, 5.19
Quinidine, 4.24
Quinine, 4.24
Quirectin, 5.15, 5.18, 4.35
Reserpine, 4.6
Reserpinine, 4.6
Rubiondin, 3.35
Rutin, 3.45
Salasodine, 4.37
Sennoside A, 3.50

Sennoside B, 3.50
Septicine, 4.35
Shatavarin, 3.48
Solasonine, 4.37
Somnirol, 4.31
Somnitol, 4.31
Stigmesterol, 3.13, 3.19
Strychnicine, 4.2
Strychnine, 4.2
Tannic acid, 5.26, 5.13
Tannins, 2.10
Taxol, 3.52
Thease, 4.28
Thebaine, 4.13
Theobromine, 4.28
Theophylline, 4.26

Tinosporaside, 3.22
Tinosporic acid, 3.22
Tinosporine, 3.22
Tinosporoside, 3.22
Trigoneline, 3.37
Tylophoridine, 4.35
Tylophorine, 4.35
Vasakine, 4.39
Vasicine, 4.39
Vasicinone, 4.39
Vit. C, 5.02,
Vomicine, 4.2
Wilhananine, 4.30
Withaferine, 4.30
Withanolides, 4.30
Yohimbine, 4.6

4. SUBJECT INDEX

Organoleptic standardisation, 1.1
Microscopic standardisation, 1.2
Physical standardisation, 1.5
Viscosity, 1.5
Melting point, 1.5
Palisade ratio, 1.3
Vein islet number, 1.3
Stomatal indes, 1.2
Stomatal number, 1.2
Optical rotaion, 1.6
Refractive index, 1.6
Ash content, 1.7
Acid insoluble ash, 1.7
Water soluble extractives, 1.7
Alcohol soluble extractives, 1.8
Volatile oil content, 1.9
Foreign organic matter, 1.9
Chemical standardisation, 1.10
Biological standardisation, 1.10
Pseudotannins, 2.12
Alkaloids, 2.1
Alkaloids, 2.1
Alkaloids identification by colourlest, 2.2
Alkaloids identification by ppt test, 2.2
Alkaloids function of 2.3
Alkaloids physical properties,
Alkaloids chemical properties,
Alkaloids classification
Role of alkaloids, 2.3
Occurance and distribution on alkaloids, 2.3
Alkaloids pharmacological classified, 2.5
Alkaloids Taxonomic classified, 2.6

Alkaloids Biosynthetic classified, 2.6
Alkaloids Chemical classified, 2.6
Glycosides, 2.6
Glycosides classification, 2.8
Glycosides cyanophoric, 2.8
Glycosides cardic, 2.8
Glycosides saponi, 2.8
Glycosides Isothiocynate, 2.8
Glycosides Phenolic, 2.8
Glycosides Chemical tests for 2.9
Chemical tests for cyanphonic glycosides, 2.10
Chemical tests andhraquinone cyanephonic Glycoside, 2.10
Glycoside classification, 2.8
Glycoside cyanophoric, 2.8
Glycoside cardic, 2.8
Glycoside saponi, 2.8
Glycoside isothiocynate, 2.8
Glycoside phenolic, 2.8
Glycoside chemical tests for 2.9
Chemical tests for cyanophoric glycoside, 2.10
Chemical tests for anthraquinone, cyanophoric glycoside, 2.10
Chemical tests for cardio cyanophoric glycoside, 2.10
Tannins, 2.10
Tannins Condensed, 2.10
Tannins Hydrolysable, 2.11
Tannins Chemical tests, 2.11
Tannins Properties, 2.11
Tannins Isolation, 2.11

HERBALS USED IN COSMECEUTICALS

ALOE PLANTATION

AMLA TWIG

CALENDULA FLOWER

CINNAMON HERB

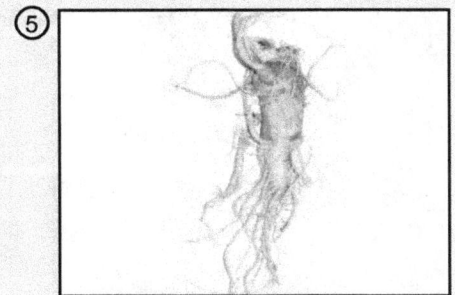
GINSENG ROOT

HENNA TWIG

JATAMANASI HERB

LEMON BRANCH

HERBALS USED IN COSMECEUTICALS

LIQUORICE HERB

NEEM

OAT HERB

ORANGE HERB

ROSE FLOWER

TEATREE HERB

TULSI

TURMERIC

www.ingramcontent.com/pod-product-compliance
Lightning Source LLC
Chambersburg PA
CBHW081919170426
43200CB00014B/2770